We Don't Know How

William and Elizabeth Paddock

We Don't Know How

AN INDEPENDENT AUDIT OF WHAT THEY CALL
SUCCESS IN FOREIGN ASSISTANCE

Iowa State University Press / Ames

1973

ABOUT THE AUTHORS

WILLIAM PADDOCK is a consultant in tropical agricultural development, working primarily with private industry, with time set aside for lecturing on the world food and population problem. A graduate of Iowa State University, he received the Ph.D. degree from Cornell University. He has been a professor of plant pathology at Pennsylvania State and Iowa State universities and head of Latin American Affairs for the National Academy of Sciences in Washington, D.C. For ten years he worked in Latin America as head of Guatemala's corn improvement program with the U.S. aid mission and at an Iowa State University experiment station. In addition he served as director of an agricultural college in Honduras which served students from fourteen Latin American countries.

With his brother Paul he is coauthor of HUNGRY NATIONS and FAMINE —1975! He has written extensively for a variety of publications, both popular (*Saturday Evening Post*) and scientific (*BioScience, Annual Review of Phytopathology*).

ELIZABETH PADDOCK received the B.S. degree from Iowa State University. She has been an instructor of home economics at Cornell University and Pennsylvania State University. In addition to rearing two children and running a household which often served as laboratory and social center for the institution her husband directed, she did social work in a Guatemalan slum and distributed food in rural Honduras as a CARE volunteer.

WILLIAM AND ELIZABETH PADDOCK have traveled extensively in developing nations, researching development programs. Their recent life in Washington, D.C., has provided them with an excellent vantage point to observe government officialdom's belief in the effectiveness of foreign aid.

Composed and printed by
The Iowa State University Press

First edition, 1973

Paddock, William.
    We don't know how.

    Includes bibliographical references.
    1. Economic assistance, American. 2. Technical assistance, American.
I. Paddock, Elizabeth, 1922—joint author. II. Title.
HC60.P22   309.22′33′73   72–14165
ISBN 0–8138–1750–1
ISBN 0–8138–1755–2 (pbk)

CONTENTS

$$\left[\text{P A R T } 3\right]$$

ENVIRONMENT CONTROLS DEVELOPMENT

$$\left[\text{P A R T } 4\right]$$

SCIENCE IS OUR LEADER

$$\left[\text{P A R T } 5\right]$$

CHANGING OVER TO THE INTERNATIONAL ROUTE

The Old Trolley Barn in Georgetown

IN THE 1940s the American people began a long journey
that was to take them to the hungry nations of Asia,
Africa, and Latin America. It became an emotional
crusade involving the government, national foundations,
church groups, universities, and scientists. Other
"developed" countries one by one joined us in this
crusade. The United Nations took up the cause, declaring
the 1960s to be the "Decade of Development." The
total cost to the American people to the beginning of
1971 was 100 billion tax dollars[1] plus the money and
energies of the many nongovernment organizations.

This enormous expenditure has been justified for
many reasons but the dominating motive has been
the conviction that we "cannot live as an island of affluence
in a sea of poverty," that if the world is to have peace
it must be stable, and for the poor nations to achieve
stability they must be "developed."

In the last few years enthusiasm for the crusade
has flagged as the development of the poor nations seems,
somehow, always to recede no matter how much money
is spent, no matter how many new ideas are put into
operation. In fact, by now, the only persons who remain
enthusiastic seem to be those of the receiving countries
(provided they get to spend the money themselves
without strings), and the staffs of the massive (and firmly
entrenched) development bureaucracies inside and

outside the government. As for the stability of the world, seldom has it seemed more elusive. Fighting for it with the sword of development has come to seem rather futile and out of date.

The authors, firm believers in the doctrines of development and long involved in the struggle, believed now was the psychological time for a book about foreign aid which would be not only optimistic but useful as a guide showing how a variety of development projects had indeed succeeded. We were thinking of a book which would be more than a glorification of all those thousands of people who have given up the amenities of their homes and gone out to strike development sparks in the suffering areas of the world's hungry nations. We wanted it to be an account of a dozen or more effective development programs in the hope that the lessons learned from them could be applied elsewhere.

With nothing more definite than this in mind we set out to find the most promising region (not a single country) in the world to study. We began by talking to government officials, businessmen, diplomats, foundation officers, directors of international agencies, missionary groups, and the like. We asked, "What area in the whole world of development can we visit in order to see the most optimistic case for foreign assistance, an optimistic case based on valid accomplishments already achieved, not on blueprints or future hopes?"

The almost universal consensus, at the end of 1967, was that we should go to the region of Mexico and Central America. This was the area with the most promising growth statistics, they said, and the cause for this was largely due to the aid derived from a number of different development organizations. Their answer made us all the more eager to carry forward our project because we had once lived in Guatemala and Honduras for a total of ten delightfully stimulating years and had traveled throughout the region many times. Thus we already had a firm background for the study and many contacts, and we spoke Spanish.

We asked key officials with both private and government development organizations to recommend to us their most effective programs in Mexico and Central America. We asked that they name programs that were at least three years old so we could see the progress already accomplished, rather than progress hoped for. We wanted to visit and examine those specific programs which the administrators of development organizations themselves assured us were especially effective. It was important that the praise for the projects come from the men responsible for the planning and financing of the projects, rather than from the press or the people carrying out the work in the field.

We organized a list of "effective development projects" and traveled some 25,000 miles to inspect them. We not only held more than 200 prearranged interviews but talked with everybody in sight— government officials, scientists, merchants, peasants, laborers, doctors, lawyers, Indian chiefs. Upon arrival at a project, our usual procedure was to be briefed by the officials in charge who then would arrange our tour and go with us or send an aide to answer our questions in the field. Whenever possible, we would later return alone to visit the project so we could study it without official guidance. We would talk to laborers, to farmers, to local people, and to officials who were only peripherally related with its management. For we wanted our study to be a genuinely independent audit.

The oddest thing came out of this research.

When we examined these projects in the field, we found they were not at all as described by the high officials back home (Peace Corps, AID, Inter-American Development Bank, and the rest). The projects were not necessarily ineffective, they were just different, sometimes unrecognizably so.

We do not question the sincerity of the officials who gave the recommendations, but certainly we now question the accuracy of the information fed back to them from the field. Always it is biased in favor of their programs. Always the reports are favorable. Journalists who may write a derogatory article about a project are brushed aside as "unqualified." Qualified professors, however, somehow never seem to write critical records of specific projects; perhaps it is because their studies are so often made on grants from the organizations being studied—or else they are hoping for grants for future studies. For the record, we financed this research trip ourselves, and thus were beholden to no organization. Nonetheless, while ours was an independent audit, we too are fallible and will welcome corrections of any errors in our observations.

Of the approximately fifty projects we visited in Mexico and Central America, we here describe only half, those most representative. We have grouped them into five sections, each with a chapter giving our conclusions.

Inevitably our report is spread thin because of the number of organizations we cover. Inevitably we make a particular project or case study include our reactions from other similar projects visited. For instance, we describe the work of only one Peace Corpsman and then present our conclusions. Officials of the Corps quite rightly will feel this is an unfair, superficial approach. The same, presumably, will be the reaction of the men at the Inter-American Development Bank, AID, Rockefeller Foundation, and the others. Our reply is that our intent was not to give a description of all activities of an organization; we wanted to report only on its *best* projects, the best as judged by the high officials of that organization themselves. The few which we include not thus recommended we so indicate.

Each of the organizations we discuss could obviously be the subject of an entire book. For most of them books have, in fact, already been written, and we refer the reader to them if he wishes accounts of their administrative structure, their methods of granting foreign assistance, their budget planning, and their philosophy in aid giving.

In a book such as this, the background of the authors, husband and wife, is pertinent. Both have been members of U.S. university faculties and have worked in Central America for ten years. One is a plant pathologist—a consultant in tropical agriculture—and was once in charge of an agricultural college in Honduras. The other is a home economist with experience working in a Guatemalan ghetto and a Honduran rural village. It is less awkward to write under the umbrella of "I" than to keep us editorially separated. Accordingly . . .

I traveled in Mexico and Central America on research for this book for over a year, almost entirely out in the field away from the capital cities. An unexpected transmutation occurred in my reaction to the news reaching me from the United States, one that I did not know had happened until my return home. Without realizing it, the press stories reaching me lost importance and pertinence; they just did not sink in; they did not penetrate to my intellectual awareness. As I spent my days looking at wards full of sick Guatemalan Indians, housing in Salvadoran ghettos, and the struggling farmers on newly cleared jungle land, the problems of the United States became distant and meaningless and out of focus.

I was not alone in this unconcern. The officials and technicians with whom I was talking at the development projects also were living in a vacuum of unawareness. I heard none of them express any depth of feeling or worry about the new level of turmoil at home and the new concern for social ills and for the need to protect the American environment. These staffs out in the field assumed, if in fact they thought about it at all, that their sources of support in the United States would continue indefinitely to backstop them. They believed it to be their due to receive even more money from the United States to enable them to do a better job. The startling change taking place in the attitudes of most Americans about the crisis in their nation's domestic problems just did not get through to them just as it did not to me.

I returned from my year of field research in Mexico and Central America when the Black Panther leader, Bobby Seale, was being sentenced in Chicago. I arrived at my house in Washington, D.C., after negotiating traffic snarled by a massive "march against death" of 46,000 people filing past the White House. Within forty-eight hours another group of my countrymen (this time a quarter of a million) descended on the city for a peace march.

The divisive passions of these protests, built up during my absence, caught me off guard.

Unnerving, also, was the zooming crime rate at my own doorstep. A neighbor cautioned me that it had become dangerous to walk to the corner mailbox after dark, although I live across the street from the postmaster general's house.

While pondering the implication of these kaleidoscopic changes, I learned about something else going on a few blocks away. A cavernous old trolley barn on a splendid Georgetown site overlooking the Potomac River had been converted into an international police training academy. There, as part of our foreign aid program—indeed, under the direct aegis of the U.S. Agency for International Development (AID)—my government was using my tax money to school foreign police in how to maintain law and order in their countries. It was diverting its attention away from the unsolved crime problem in its own capital and training thousands of police officers for foreign nations, even sending some of its best qualified men to staff police training programs around the globe.

. . . While Rome burned, her legions marched to battles they could not win.

U.S. Foreign Aid:
After Thirty Years of Hard Work

A psychologist says it is natural for people to be happy and self-satisfied after they have done a good piece of work . . . That may account for much of the misery and gloom we find in the world.

Our Fortress Embassy in Guatemala

"WHY IS IT CLOSED? *What holiday is this?"* I asked, *as my taxi pulled up to the curb in front of the U.S. embassy in downtown Guatemala City.*

The building looked closed. All of the heavy-duty, steel shutters were fastened down tightly over the windows. Five Guatemalan soldiers in German-style helmets, burp guns slung over their shoulders, stood guard at the entrance.

"No, it's open," the taxi driver replied, annoyed by a question he had been asked so many times. "Go on in."

Inside, security was as stringent as on the outside. Plainclothes operatives were lounging about. Uniformed U.S. Marines and soldiers were posted throughout the building.

The major reason for the precautions was the assassination of John Mein, our ambassador to Guatemala, a few months earlier. Also, eight months prior to my visit, two U.S. military attachés at the embassy had been machine-gunned and killed in their car while driving home to lunch.

Such incidents (later our labor attaché was kidnapped) have converted the handling of our diplomatic business in Guatemala, and, indeed, else-

where in Latin America, into a high-risk occupation. To safeguard the lives of embassy personnel battlefield tactics must be employed. The embassy maintains voice contact with the homes and automobiles of high-level officials. The radio call sign that day for the ambassador's home was "Bravo One," for his car, "Bravo One Alpha."

While I was waiting downstairs for permission to pass through the electronically controlled gate to the elevator, I thought back to the five-year period when I lived in Guatemala—part of the time as a member of the foreign aid staff—and when I had frequently been in this same embassy building. The Guatemalan political situation was troubled then—in fact, just about as tense as it is now. Even so I always had the feeling that this, my home away from home, stood above and beyond the local violence.

On this recent visit to the embassy, however, there were few reminders of those earlier, more relaxed days. In the waiting room, a faded old picture of Mount Vernon, captioned "Casa de Jorge Washington," hung in the same place as it had ten years ago. But upstairs I found the ambassador a virtual prisoner.

Three of four windows in his office were shuttered and closed with thick draperies on the inside. The fourth window, which faces no other building, was only partly covered, so the ambassador at least knew the sun was shining. What a pity! It was another beautiful day in the usually smog-free capital of this Land of Eternal Spring, and yet our ambassador dared not stand in front of his own window to enjoy it.

Fortunately Ambassador Nathaniel Davis, a long-time foreign service officer, was an able, calm person. His professionalism and competence were indispensable assets in the difficult new job he had filled for about a month at the time of my visit. When I asked him about our foreign aid program, he was most pleasant but bucked my request for detailed information to his number two man, Max Krebs, deputy chief of mission.

Krebs, whose office was similarly sealed up, requested that our interview be off the record. This was not much of a loss because, just as we were getting into our discussion, the sound of a terrific crash came from the street. This was followed by popping noises like small arms fire. Excited voices drifted up to us. The lights in Krebs' office began to blink and then went out altogether, leaving the office quite dark.

Krebs stood up, crossed the room, and cautiously closed tight the venetian blinds. He stole a quick peek from the edge of the window. Reassured, he flattened out the angle of the blinds to have a better look. Then he raised the blind about a foot. Finally he opened the window and stuck his head out for a look around.

I personally thought Krebs was a pretty brave man! Given the fortress-like atmosphere of the embassy, I had spent those anxious moments mapping out the fastest way to get under the sofa.

As it turned out, a truck had run into a lamppost and knocked it over and had also pulled down the wires which carry electricity into the embassy.

The reasons for Guatemala's present turbu-

lence are complex and many. But at least it is now obvious that U.S. aid money has not itself generated political stability. The U.S. aid to Guatemala ($314.4 million in economic aid plus $16.6 million in military aid from 1946 to 1969)[1] has not prevented the turmoil which now forces our embassy to function as if under seige.

Reinventing the Wheel

AN AGRICULTURAL EXPERIMENT STATION operated by the Guatemalan government is located at a town on the Pacific Coast called Chocolá. This station was once the focus of a major U.S. effort to assist agriculture throughout this coastal area of Central America, and a lot of U.S. money went into it.

I had last visited Chocolá in 1958 with Louis Franke, then head of the U.S. program for agriculture in Guatemala. He was about to be transferred to Argentina and was anxious to show me what he had accomplished before leaving Guatemala. "This is my major contribution," Franke said. He was rightly proud, for it was a beautiful experiment station.

Unlike most foreign aid administrators, Franke had brought to his job a good technical background and a lively interest in tropical farming. He knew that Guatemala's future depends on agriculture and he was able to convert this knowledge into action by getting the United States to put money into this station at Chocolá and another at Bárcenas.

At Chocolá a laboratory was built first, followed by classrooms, dormitories, offices, a cafeteria, and so on—all with U.S. funds. Guest houses were constructed, and the station soon became a favorite spot for U.S. government personnel to visit.

As I toured the station with Franke, the new, all-stainless steel cafeteria was being installed and kitchen equipment uncrated. Chocolá was designed to become a major agricultural research center, concentrating on the problems of major tropical commercial crops like coffee. It was also to be a training center offering short, practical courses to farmers and agricultural extension agents from all of Central America, so they could carry home with them updated knowledge of improved farming practices.

This preface will help explain why I was so pleased when

Covey Oliver, assistant secretary for Inter-American Affairs in the Department of State, told me that one of the projects I should visit was an experiment station established with AID support at Los Brillantes, located near Chocolá. I was doubly pleased because back in 1956 I had had a small hand in selecting Los Brillantes, from several possible sites, for a substation to augment the work at Chocolá. Thus by visiting Los Brillantes, a project which Oliver indicated already shows "evidence of success or which [is] sufficiently well established so that a significant effect on development can be confidently predicted," I could also stop by and see Chocolá.

Now, on this revisit to Guatemala's south coast, I could see at once a definite increase in cattle production. This seemed to jibe with a current policy in economic planning, namely, encouraging the developing countries to diversify their agriculture in order to alleviate dependence on a single crop, as, in the case of Guatemala, coffee. The planners say that such dependence makes a nation highly vulnerable to the vagaries of the international market and most governments have long tried to encourage the production of more kinds of crops.

But how to effect the diversification? That was the specific task assigned to Los Brillantes—a difficult one because theory and practice unfortunately are at odds.

Assistant Secretary Oliver had urged me to visit the experiment station at Los Brillantes precisely because it was effectively solving this difficult, complex problem, that is, it was finding crops into which Guatemalan farmers could diversify and still make money. With half of Guatemala's export earnings coming from one crop, he said, AID is keenly interested in helping Guatemala break the shackles of coffee dependency.

Oliver told me a great deal of progress had been made at Los Brillantes through the introduction of rubber and citrus as new crops. The station was supplying seedlings and advice on how to plant them, and AID was providing the loans needed to support this diversification. In addition, he said, research was moving ahead on other crops, such as black pepper, vanilla, cashews, allspice, mangos, tea, and achiote.

At Los Brillantes (before reaching Chocolá which was farther along the road) the first person I met was Raymond Stadelman, a man whose writings I have admired for so long I thought he must be dead. His *Maize Cultivation in Northwestern Guatemala* still remains the classic background study on the agriculture of the highland Indians of Guatemala.[1] Stadelman was now working here on rubber and AID, according to Oliver, was greatly pleased with his progress.

Earlier, I knew, Los Brillantes had been kept busy for at least five years supplying rubber seedlings to Guatemalan farmers who had planted some 27,000 acres to rubber. Now, to my amazement, the place seemed dead. The reason, Stadelman explained, was that Guatemalan farmers were interested in planting rubber only as long as AID provided money on easy terms (such as a seven-year grace period before repayment begins).

When the loan money was used up (some loans were sizable: one farmer received $884,000) the station, once a beehive of projects, fell into the doldrums. At the time of my visit there was little evidence of activity. However, with prices as they were, neither rubber nor citrus was sufficiently attractive as a money-maker that Guatemalan farmers would plant them without the easy loan money.

Now Stadelman was working alone. Current support from AID to the research station had been reduced solely to providing his salary. No one could have been less optimistic about the future of rubber cultivation in Guatemala than Stadelman himself, the man running what was left of the program. He was even less optimistic about the possibility of receiving the additional support needed to change the direction of this work or to revive it. I commiserated with him and left as he was preparing for a visit by Congressman Clarence Long of Maryland and Nathaniel Davis, the new U.S. ambassador to Guatemala. They would be arriving the next day for the same reason I had come—American officialdom had told them it considered this to be a good and thriving development project. Inasmuch as the high-ranking visitors had presumably never before seen black pepper, vanilla, cashews, allspice, mangos, tea, or achiote cultivated, I am sure they found the station interesting, but not, I assume, stimulating enough to champion its resurgence.

Also, why were the embassy and Washington continuing to send such visitors to see the "successful" AID program at Los Brillantes? Was it that they had not yet heard that the program had dried up?

From Los Brillantes I drove, for old times sake, thirty minutes down the road to the station at Chocolá. Superficially, it looked much as it had in 1958 except that the beautiful buildings were empty.

A second glance showed it to be a disaster area. Its staff consisted of a single agronomist, a Guatemalan, Efraín Humberto Reyna, who had the equivalent of a high school education in agriculture. With the help of only two field hands he was trying desperately to manage this huge station. Never have I seen a harder working, more dedicated, or more lost soul. Poor fellow, he had literally nothing with which to work—no equipment, no help, and, obviously, only hand-to-mouth money. He acted as if I were the first visitor in ten years. He was puppy-dog happy to see me. The whole station is presently funded, all from the Guatemalan government, the equivalent of $3,500 per year! Occasionally, Reyna is able to scrounge a little fertilizer from manufacturers. And that is his support.

And yet at the time of my visit, this was the one and only coffee research station in operation in all of Guatemala, a nation that still relies on coffee to pay for 36 percent of all its imports. The total effort of government research to find more economical ways to produce this crop, to combat diseases and pests, to solve harvest and processing problems rested on the shoulders of this one man.

The dormitories, which U.S. tax money had built, had last been used six months earlier when they housed eight students for six days. The last course, prior to that, had been held nine years ago.

It is painful to go on. The Chocolá station is today a graveyard where the forgotten bones of this carefully planned, major aid program have been left to rot. The chairs, typewriters, desks, furniture—even the microscopes and pH meters—are still there, stenciled with the letters S.C.I.D.A., the long forgotten alphabet soup designation for the cooperative program that operated for a few years as a joint venture of the U.S. International Cooperation Administration (ICA) (AID's predecessor) and the Guatemalan Ministry of Agriculture.

Incredibly, I found there was no cooperation, nor had there been for years, between Chocolá and Los Brillantes a few miles away. These two agricultural stations were separated as if by the Great Wall of China. The reason for this, I learned, was that there had been some jurisdictional scuffling between the Guatemalan minister of agriculture and U.S. AID. The result: neither worked with the other.

Chocolá is an illustration of one tragic aspect of our development work: *AID has no memory.*

AID programs constantly are scrapped, abandoned, or started anew—or forgotten. Budgets are cut and then, as an alibi, Washington primly says it is time for the local government to "take over." The local government, however, usually has neither the money nor the talent (nor, sometimes, the interest) to take over. Thus another orphan program joins the graveyard.

New foreign aid directors arrive in the capital and sweep the decks clean and begin anew. Back home a president is elected and his new foreign aid administrator also sweeps clean. No one takes the time to learn. What preceded? Did it fail? Did it succeed? Why?

A long-time AID friend says, "Every morning we wake up and laboriously reinvent the wheel."

WHEREVER the United States has a foreign aid program it has a staff that supervises the spending of its money, plans its use, and cajoles the local government into actions intended to make the money effective. The staff is called a "mission" and the man in charge is the "mission director."

Deane Hinton, U.S. AID mission director in Guatemala, was fresh from the National War College and recently decorated with a Superior Honor Award. Undoubtedly Hinton, whom I found to be a likable man about forty-five years old, was highly regarded as an administrator at AID's Washington headquarters.

Like AID mission directors around the globe, Hinton was filling an important post within the embassy structure. The AID director is generally the principal economic counselor to the ambassador. In Guatemala, as in most other countries I know, the AID director runs an establishment which is so big it cannot fit into the embassy building, and is therefore located in a separate, impressive office building.

Although this was Hinton's first assignment in Latin America, he had served at several embassies in Europe and elsewhere, mainly as a political affairs officer. As is true of nearly all other AID mission directors, he had had no experience as a technician. Thus I was not surprised to learn that he knew little about agriculture even though this is the major economic business in Guatemala. But I was startled by the way he expressed it, although it was refreshingly honest.

"I don't know a cow from a bunny rabbit," he told me. "I'm a political economist."

Today's Agency for International Development (AID) is the result, depending on the benchmark used, of twenty-one or thirty years of U.S. effort in the area of foreign assistance. It long ago became as bureaucratized an agency as any within the government. This account of an interview with one of AID's administrators could have taken place with any of several other highly regarded AID mission directors whom I have known.

PADDOCK: What is the most effective AID program in Guatemala?

HINTON: The agricultural school at Bárcenas. We were able to convince the minister of agriculture that this agricultural school is important. The United States is putting $100,000 a year into the school, plus a couple of technicians.

PADDOCK: The director of the school told me yesterday that AID has provided one technician and about $60,000 in equipment and supplies. Why the conflict in the figures?

HINTON: The balance of the funding is in the pipeline.

PADDOCK: The director said he was having a problem placing some of the graduates. Of the twenty-six new graduates in forestry, not one of them has a job in sight.

HINTON: I don't know about that.

PADDOCK: I understand Bárcenas includes the forestry school the U.S. government helped establish ten years ago and later helped merge with the agricultural school there.

HINTON: I don't know anything about that. You must remember that I have only been here fifteen months. There is a lot about previous programs I don't know.

PADDOCK: Is any money going into the experiment station at Bárcenas?

HINTON: What experiment station? There is no experiment station there in the sense any of us would think of one. It's a work farm for the Bárcenas students. The farm is terribly run down, stupidly managed, and the United States has never helped it with funds.

PADDOCK: I don't mean the school's farm, I mean the experiment station. When I worked here in the 1950s this and the station at Chocolá formed a major U.S. government effort. The Bárcenas station consisted of several buildings intentionally built on the main highway so they would have high visibility. One of the two entrances into the Bárcenas Agricultural School was through the experiment station.

HINTON: I know nothing about it. I'm still learning. I have my hands full trying to keep track of what is going on today. I don't have the time to go through all the past records.

PADDOCK *(changing the subject):* What do you feel are some of the best ways in which the United States should spend its aid money here in Guatemala?

HINTON: Remember, we have only two and a half million dollars in grant money. The rest is for loans. I have twenty-five staff members and another twenty-five men on contract. This isn't enough to do much with, really.

PADDOCK: But what are some of the things that already have worked out well?

HINTON *(after a long pause):* Well, I think the money the United States has put into highways has been good. However, one might ask what this money might have done if it had been put into other things. Roads have been built at a high cost to the U.S. taxpayer. One project close to my heart was the in-service training for civil servants. We put money into this, and it was working very well. It kept sailing along even without U.S. money. Then one day someone over there in the ministry said, "Here's where we can save some money," and it was cut out of the Guatemalan budget completely. *(I interpolate:* The previous day I had been told by a high U.S. embassy official this was a most successful project; apparently news of its demise had not yet reached the embassy walls.)

PADDOCK: What about the mobile school program which I have heard so much about?

HINTON *(after admitting he is a skeptic):* What will happen when we pull out? The mobile schools are very expensive for the results they give. A project, to be successful, has got to be able to fly by itself. I'm not as starry-eyed as some people.

PADDOCK: What U.S.-supported project are Guatemala's officials most enthusiastic about?

HINTON: None. There is probably no one in the Guatemalan government who would be sorry about our leaving or even notice if we left tomorrow. I'm talking about projects. Loans are another matter. Everybody wants loans.

PADDOCK: I'm interested to know why you chose the Los Brillantes coastal experiment station and the nearby agricultural school at Bárcenas as projects for the new ambassador to see on his first trip into the country last week, and also why you considered them worthy of inspection by Congressman Clarence Long who went with him.

HINTON: The trip was planned for the congressman and he didn't want any briefings. He wanted to get out into the country and these fit his two-day itinerary nicely.

PADDOCK: Did he see anything other than Los Brillantes that had been functioning long enough for him to judge whether it could be considered a success over the long term?

HINTON: He did see some nice self-help programs of the type generated by the Peace Corps—but to answer your question, no.

PADDOCK: What is the most important thing AID can do in Guatemala?

HINTON: Be smart enough to operate as a catalyst for change. We should emphasize the training of people and the need for changes in their fundamental attitudes. In addition to giving them new technical skills, we should expose them to new ideas.

PADDOCK: How would you do this?

HINTON: We are doing it in a training program in social sciences at the local university.

PADDOCK: How did you happen to choose social sciences?

HINTON: We had a study made of the university, and the study showed this was the area of greatest need.

PADDOCK: Who made the study?

HINTON: Gene Martin.

PADDOCK: What is his specialty?

HINTON: He is a social scientist.

This is an old story. In 1963 AID hired the Center of International Studies at the Massachusetts Institute of Technology to find an answer to the agricultural dilemma of the world's hungry nations. The center assembled a group of experts who set about interviewing agriculturalists and scientists from such other fields as anthropology, sociology, and psychology. The $100,000 study, published in book form,[2] showed that each specialist finds solutions in terms of his own discipline. If you hire a social scientist to study the university, you end up with a solution that involves social science.

I myself am no different. Being a former corn breeder, I lose few oportunities to emphasize that corn is of major importance in Central America and Mexico. That I know this about myself makes me wary of the same bias in others.

PADDOCK: What do you consider to be Guatemala's most serious problem?

HINTON *(after a discussion of some political dilemmas):* Agriculture. And for the first time we are going to take a serious look at the Guatemalan farm picture.

He went on to explain that through his efforts, a contract had been arranged with Iowa State University to send a team of agricultural economists to Guatemala to make an analysis of the role of agriculture in the development of the Guatemalan economy. "I hope to be able to use this study," Hinton confided, "as leverage to get the Guatemalan government and AID to spend more on agriculture here."

Inasmuch as the Guatemalan minister of agriculture had told me a few days earlier that he was allotted only 3 percent of the national budget, I could see the sense in what Hinton said.

PADDOCK: Why are you using Iowa State University?

HINTON: Because it's a good agricultural school.

PADDOCK: Are you familiar with the Iowa State-Guatemala Tropical Research Center, operated here by Iowa State from 1945 to 1955? That was the program which brought me to Guatemala originally.

HINTON: I've never heard of it.

PADDOCK: That program emphasized agriculture. It was then taken over by the International Cooperation Administration which, as you know, was the predecessor agency of your own AID. At one time the annual U.S. budget for Guatemalan agriculture was nearly one million dollars. That certainly represented a major interest in those days.

HINTON: I've been here too short a time to know the details of previous programs. However, I know Iowa State is a good university and they have good men.

Of the four authors of the study for which Hinton had contracted Iowa State, only one was then in Guatemala. He was a young graduate student named Eric Graber, and I sensed he was doing most of the field work for the study. Our conversation went like this:

PADDOCK: Are you familiar with an earlier Iowa State agricultural program in Guatemala?

GRABER: I have heard there was some kind of program but that's all I know about it.

PADDOCK: Have you been briefed on the past history of U.S. support in this country?

GRABER: AID used to have a different name than it does now— I don't know what it was. I believe the United States helped with a colonization project but I don't know in what way. I guess that's the extent of the back history I'm aware of.

PADDOCK: I am interested in what you think has been the most effective U.S. effort in Guatemala.

GRABER: The Peace Corps. Of course I'm prejudiced because I was once with the Peace Corps.

PADDOCK: What do you consider to be the most effective AID program in Guatemala?

GRABER: I haven't found one.

PADDOCK: What will your current study indicate?

GRABER: We would like to determine the priorities for investment in agriculture. There is no global plan for Guatemala's development; there are hundreds of feasibility studies but there are no studies to pull them together, to tie the ideas together. AID has no library system for finding these studies and when you do run them down you find there is no continuity in the thinking that inspired them.

PADDOCK: Do you know what use will be made of the report for which you are collecting data?

GRABER: I really have no idea.

In April 1969, Iowa State University published the report, a full two inches thick, titled: *Agricultural Development and Policy in Guatemala*. When I read that its purpose was to review the extent "to which the agricultural sector has changed since 1950," I realized it covered part of the 1945–55 period when Iowa State had operated its own agricultural experiment station in Guatemala. Writing Graber, I asked if his group had consulted any of the reports published during the course of that earlier program. He replied: "I don't remember those specific reports." Thus, like AID, Iowa State too has no memory.

I wrote to Hinton some nine months after the report had been released, asking two questions: How has the report been used? Which of its recommendations have been acted upon? He replied that the report had been circulated widely but had "encountered a fairly general lack of interest."

Not surprising! The report (published by the Department of Economics at Iowa State University) begins with these deadly naive and patronizing sentences about a nation which, it would seem, no one at Iowa State had ever heard of before (in fact, they might have been written in 1852 by John L. Stephens, the first U.S. envoy to Guatemala): "Guatemala lies just south of the Yucatan peninsula in Central America. It is bounded on the north and west by Mexico, on the east by Belice, to the south and east by Honduras and El Salvador, and on the southwest by the Pacific Coast. Although Guatemala contains only 108,889 square kilometers, approximately the size of the state of Louisiana, it has a very wide geographical diversity."[3] This study, remember, was intended primarily for Guatemalan officials and Americans stationed there. I wonder how many read through this two-inch rehash of all the appallingly familiar data which had been kicking around the back offices for years? Fifty officials? Twenty? Five? No one?

In his letter, Hinton commented that it was "still too early" to say which of the Iowa State recommendations would actually be put into practice, but "I am happy to tell you . . . the Government of Guatemala seems to have accepted . . . one of the recommendations, the idea of placing more emphasis on basic grain cereals, particularly corn."

Hinton's letter was postmarked Santiago, Chile. He had been transferred there to head up another program where, in the deeply entrenched tradition of AID, doubtless he was again starting from scratch.

When I wrote to the new U.S. mission director in Guatemala, his assistant answered, "I can assure you that the report has had a major impact . . ."[4] The result: another U.S. loan to Guatemala, this time for $23 million.

I did not have the heart to write to Hinton that the corn seed stock from the old Iowa State College-Guatemala Tropical Research Center is sitting in a storeroom at the experiment station at Bárcenas. It was put in storage ten years ago when ICA stopped funding the program. A faithful Guatemalan there is keeping the seed collection in what he believes is good order, just in case someday someone wants to use it.

2

Development Succumbs to Politics

In 1966 the area along the Motagua River in Guatemala between Zacapa and Puerto Barrios was the scene of a great deal of pro-Communist guerilla activity. Fighting the guerillas proved difficult because they had the support of the local *campesinos*.

Eventually the Guatemalan government mounted a full-scale military drive to wipe out the insurgents, as they were affecting the communications between the capital and the chief port. The United States provided considerable assistance in the form of military aid, including Green Beret advisors, arms, and helicopters—and economic aid.

In mounting the economic aid part of the package, it was considered fortunate a U.S. foreign aid program had been active before in the troubled region.

Back in 1954, just after Guatemala's left-leaning President Jacobo Arbenz was ousted, AID's predecessor agency (ICA) had stepped in to provide the new, pro-American president, Colonel Carlos Castillo Armas, with massive assistance. One area singled out for special attention was this same Motagua Valley where the guerillas now were active. Among other projects, the United States had set up an agricultural experiment station, provided expensive well-drilling equipment to help offset the chronic lack of rainfall (the chief factor causing continued impoverishment of most of the local farmers), and begun construction on an irrigation system. Unfortunately, owing to the high salt content of subsurface water much of the irrigation system was later abandoned.

Now with this new Communist threat, AID took another look at the area. The United States wanted to assist the Guatemalan government's efforts to pacify the populace who were supporting the guerillas. So AID decided to help solve the problems of a local rice cooperative which was beset with red ink. By putting the cooperative into the black and by boosting rice production, the

United States would be improving the local food situation and would thus demonstrate to local farmers that it and the Guatemalan government were concerned about their welfare.

It approached this challenge in four ways:

1. A mobile school was set up to teach improved farming methods. No one with whom I talked was satisfied with the school's effectiveness.

2. The United States dispatched four Peace Corps volunteers, some of them with business backgrounds, to straighten out the finances of the rice cooperative. As it turned out, this was beyond their capabilities, or anyone's.

3. Through the cooperative, loan money was made available to the farmers for seed, fertilizer, and pesticides. Although April is the month for planting rice, the money did not arrive until June. Nor was Mother Nature of much help that first year. The rains were unusually heavy. The rice fields were flooded at the time of harvest. This resulted in the loss of nearly one-third of the crop, which meant that most farmers could not wait for the slow-moving cooperative to pay for their rice. They had to sell at a slightly lower price for immediate cash. The result was that only 900 tons were sold to the cooperative as against the 3,500 tons that had been anticipated. The cooperative went into the red that year to the extent of $120,000, that is, to the amount of the loans extended for fertilizer, pesticides, etc., which were not paid back. I heard (though I did not see the books) that by 1969 the bedeviled coop had a bank account of $6.47 plus a total debt of $238,000. An AID official told me credit had been provided too loosely and too fast because the basic idea was "let's calm the people down and then reform them."

4. Technical guidance was provided to install a rice drying and storage plant at Champona. This was AID's big contribution in the antiguerilla campaign. (Wherever rice is grown in any quantity storage must be provided, and to be stored it first must be dried.)

The erection of such a plant should have been a simple promise to fulfill. The operation is largely mechanical, requiring almost no modifications for local conditions. Thousands of such facilities have been put up in the United States. Basically the whole rice plant is put together as with a kit, consisting essentially of weighing scales, a rice cleaner, a heater for drying the rice, and storage bins. During the operation of the plant, the rice is moved from weighing to cleaning to storage via augers which are powered by a diesel generator.

In addition, making the task of building the plant even easier,

AID should have had a backlog of detailed information on the area because of the technical assistance program it had had in the Motagua Valley ten years earlier. Building that rice plant should have been as easy as falling off a log.

Instead . . .

An agricultural engineer from Iowa was brought in to design the plant. The engineer soon finished his specifications and went back home. The shipments of U.S. equipment for the plant were late in arriving and no one was around to supervise its installation. Eventually the rice plant was put together but too late to be used for that year's crop.

The test came the following year, 1968.

Chaos! The plant was unworkable.

A rush call went out for a U.S. technician. This time a wheat farmer from Wyoming was sent. His experience consisted of having built a small wheat storage facility on his own farm. But he at least knew about the functioning of augers and of storage and drying facilities.

First he set about repairing the augers which had rusted because the overhang on the roof was not wide enough to protect them from rainwater. Next he figured out a way to minimize the inconvenience caused by trucks being unable to unload rice directly onto the weighing scales. He managed to overcome the failure of the builders to follow the blueprint specifications—failures that left some of the stored rice exposed to the elements. There was also the detail that the motors were only one-third as large as they should have been to power the plant. He partly repaired the equipment which had been improperly lubricated because all the instructions for doing so were in English. He replaced many of the air filters in the diesel engine, a difficult matter because those needed were not available in Guatemala.

He was a true do-it-yourself man in the best tradition of American frontier inventor/handyman.

Some things he could not do—such as relocating the cleaning and weighing equipment to a more functional site or relocating the plant itself to a higher spot (it had been built in the one place which became flooded whenever there was a heavy rain) or replacing the drying facility which some felt was of the wrong type.

One cannot point the finger of blame at either of the technicians. The potpourri of mistakes resulted mainly from the rush-rush nature of the whole project, with its vague goal of pacifying local *campesinos* and winning them over to the side of their new government.

Having decided on the project, no one took the time to study the problems involved in building the rice plant at Champona. And Murphy's Law took over: If anything can possibly go wrong, it will.

All the foregoing defects and miscalculations notwithstanding, I was told by a highly placed official in our embassy in Guatemala City that the rice mill at Champona was a fine, effective AID project, one that I should visit.

It turned out to be, at the risk of a pun, a run-of-the-mill AID story. At headquarters the official account of the project was completely at variance with what existed in the field.

I must ask the obvious question: If the United States, after twenty-odd years of so-called "experience," cannot bring off this puny job of putting together a simple rice plant, why should it let itself get involved in more complicated assignments?

Some will argue that the plant itself is not the point at issue. No matter that it was jerry-built and is still thoroughly inefficient. Maybe it did play some sort of psychological role. The area where it stands is presently considered cleared of Communist guerillas.

Surely, however, it is farfetched to give AID any points for having deterred Communism with this rice mill. To the contrary—the community is now saddled with a shoddy, tacky mill and the cooperative, overwhelmed with a large debt, has dissolved itself.

Indeed, how effective is AID as an instrument of pacification? Nowhere have I heard of the AID hierarchy having the flexibility and wisdom needed to meet an emergency with a quick and successful impact program. Yet, by its very definition, pacification calls for an effort which adapts to a highly volatile, rapidly changing situation. (For years Vietnam has received the lion's share of all AID money. When Vietnam's history is written it will be interesting to note to what extent AID's pacification program was successful, both economically and politically.)

In any case, I was reliably informed in Guatemala City that the real contribution of the United States to deterring Communism in the Motagua Valley was military assistance, not AID projects.

THE MAJOR DEVELOPMENT PROJECTS around the world are government financed and supported. Inherent to their existence is the ability of their sponsors to appeal successfully to the political power currently in office.

The survival of smaller projects, those financed by foundations, universities, religious and other nonprofit groups, must similarly depend upon the political winds within their home offices.

The curse of all this is that politics seldom operate rationally. Therefore the initiation and then the survival of a development project is, more often than not, the result of irrational decisions.

To illustrate this I could point to several huge operations, but I prefer to use a small corn improvement program in Guatemala.

In 1945 Iowa State College established an agricultural experiment station in Guatemala. It was to be a purely research operation designed for the benefit of Iowa farmers. Its purpose was to study corn in the place of the corn plant's origin, in the spot where the first man wrenched the first ear off the first stalk—namely Guatemala. There the greatest genetic variability still exists in corn. Thus it was hoped that corns possessing unique and valuable characteristics would be found which could be crossed with and improve the corn sown in Iowa.

This Guatemalan station was proposed by the late Dr. I. E. Melhus, a marvelously dedicated plant scientist who in turn acknowledged a large debt of gratitude to the inspiration of Nicolai Ivanovich Vavilov, a great Russian plant scientist. Vavilov, a contemporary of Melhus, had made a comprehensive study of the origins of cultivated plants. He concluded that today's domesticated plants originated in only a half-dozen places, one of them the area of southern Mexico and Guatemala. He further concluded that the United States, by not taking advantage of the research possibilities of the plant materials at its own doorstep, was being blind to a rich opportunity for improving its own agriculture.

Melhus could see the sense in this and he tried to interest his college in taking up Vavilov's challenge, but without success. (Lest one might think my comments on the deadweight of politics are limited to the Western world, I add: In 1940 Vavilov was the victim when the politically agile, quack agriculturist, T. S. Lysenko, won Stalin's favor. After two years in jail Nicolai Ivanovich Vavilov died in Siberia.)

However, Melhus was able to convince Earl May, an Iowa businessman who had made a fortune in plant nurseries, to test out the Russian's idea. May made a grant of money to Iowa State to found the Iowa State College-Guatemala Tropical Research Center. Over the next ten years the research station in Guatemala flourished under Melhus's direction. Various discoveries were made, such as corns possessing heavy root systems and disease resistance, and these were incorporated into some Iowa corn-breeding programs. Thus the United States benefited.

Melhus, on the side so to speak, also developed a corn which soon became Guatemala's number one variety. It still is, in most of the nation's lowlands. Thus Guatemala benefited.

Melhus took this corn variety to Southeast Asia in 1952 where it eventually was one of several factors resulting in Thailand becoming the world's fourth largest corn-exporting nation. Thus the developing world benefited.

In all, it was a record of which to be proud.

But Iowa State was always halfhearted in its support of the program. Many on the campus resented the end run Melhus had made by finding an outside benefactor after the university had turned down the idea. Earl May died and financial support began to dry up.

However, the U.S. government, by now committed to foreign aid in Guatemala, was willing to consider a grant to the university to keep the station operating. Campus politics intervened. To have continued the station would have been to admit that Melhus, who was now retired (I had become his replacement in charge of the program in Guatemala), had been right all along. So the university withdrew entirely from the station's support in 1955. The whole operation was turned over to the U.S. aid mission in Guatemala City and incorporated into its bureaucracy.

Concurrently the United States undertook a crash support program for a newly installed government which had just won a revolution. Suddenly Washington had a seemingly endless amount of money for agriculture in Guatemala. The heretofore withered Iowa State program took on new life. Technicians were hired; equipment was purchased. Money for the program, now that there was an urgent political excuse for it, was plentiful.

By 1959 the United States was spending $800,000 annually to support a broadly based agricultural program. The U.S. agricultural aid mission in Guatemala now had five Ph.D.'s on its staff and a half-dozen others with graduate or bachelor's degrees in agriculture. Optimism reigned—a true impact at last would be made in behalf of Guatemala's farmers.

The walls soon came tumbling down—plus the roof. The man responsible, according to the U.S. embassy, was Clemente Marroquín Rojas, a newspaper editor who had been named minister of agriculture by the Guatemalan president. (He said he made the appointment to pay off a political debt.) No sooner was Marroquín Rojas in office than he set about making vicious attacks against the U.S. aid program. Thin-skinned U.S. officials, angered, retaliated by canceling the agricultural part of it. Most of the agricultural staff were transferred out of the country.

That put the kibosh to my corn research program which, in spite of the change in sponsorship, had been in operation for fourteen continuous years.

For the record, Marroquín Rojas himself was booted out of office a few months later due to local political reasons, not because of the American action. The U.S. government resumed its support for agriculture, but at a much reduced level of funding. Instead of reviving the old programs, the brand new personnel, typically, started their own new projects.

Though I may be accused of bias, because I was in charge of that corn-breeding program (for the U.S. mission as well as for Iowa State), I firmly believe that any program aimed at helping the economy of Guatemala must include a strong emphasis on corn because it represents 60 percent of the diet of 60 percent of the people.

That may explain why I was so disheartened, while researching this book, by an interview I had with Ing. Alejandro Fuentes, director of agricultural research in Guatemala's Ministry of Agriculture. I have known Fuentes for a long time, ever since he worked for me in that same corn program, but never did I know him to be so discouraged.

He was deeply concerned over his country's future. "We must work out a system to intensify agriculture," he said. "As farmers divide their land among their children, we must come up with a way for the children to produce at least as much on smaller plots as their fathers did on the larger pieces of land." Fuentes emphasized that corn must be the place to begin because of its economic importance to the country.

While no one was really arguing against this, neither was anyone doing very much about it. At the time of my visit, the Guatemalan government was spending only $33,000 annually on corn research and development. This pittance (typical of the level of money hungry nations can afford) had to cover salaries, gas, automobiles, and so on.

Others confirmed what Fuentes had said. Ing. Luis Manlio Castillo, a commercial seed producer, lamented that the government's corn seed program was dead, that the much publicized Rockefeller Foundation corn for the tropics was not suitable for Guatemala because it blows down too easily, and that private firms were doing almost nothing in the way of research to compensate for the lack of interest by the government.

Against that background I called on Marroquín Rojas. He was still editor of his old newspaper, *La Hora,* a sort of second-rate tabloid. However, through the unfathomable vagaries of politics he was now vice-president.

His office was in a small building swarming with uniforms representing the colonels who presently run Guatemala. Other than the presence of the military, there was little to suggest that Marroquín Rojas, at seventy-two years of age, was a man of high position. The walls of his office were plastered with an odd assortment of photos; most of them looked as if they had been clipped from old issues of *Life* magazine. One picture which caught my attention showed merely the back of a man climbing a flight of stairs. Such was the decor of the office of this official who has held important posts under the most diverse of Guatemalan presidents: minister of economy (under socialist-populist Juan José Arévalo), minister of agriculture (under right-wing conservative Miguel Ydígoras Fuentes), and vice-president (under the moderate, middle-of-the-road Julio César Méndez Montenegro).

Though vice-president, he told me he had not spoken to the president for over a year!

I asked my first question, "What is your opinion about U.S. foreign aid today?"

The government's number two man visibly bristled. "Guatemala had a deficit of $60 million in 1967," he said. "This is a big deficit for a country our size. So far, we have been able to borrow money to compensate for the deficit, but a country that sells little and buys a lot must in the end go broke. . . . That's what the economists haven't learned yet."

He placed the blame for this financial bind on the United States and its too-great generosity, its constant pressuring on the Guatemalan government to assume additional debt burden. When U.S. officials talk about diversification of industry and agriculture, he said, they are "talking of hopes." Nothing will come of it, nothing to pay for the debt burden which AID has placed on this country's shoulders.

The vice-president went on to claim that through foreign aid the U.S. government was actually conspiring with the U.S. automobile and oil industries to make Guatemala use more cars and gasoline. He said Guatemala could "never get money for a dam to irrigate land, but it could always get money for a road."

The end result, he said, is "100,000 engines of exploitation" (his synonym for automobiles) and $150 million in outlays for gasoline and roads.

In this he was in accord with Manuel Ayau, a Guatemalan business leader. In a radio broadcast Ayau said much the same thing. He concluded that U.S. foreign aid can have an adverse effect on a poor nation's economy, "because it channels money into the consumption of goods without first providing the capital necessary to produce those goods for which there is increased demand."[1]

Nor is Ayau alone in this opinion. Dr. Gabriel Valdés, Chile's foreign minister before the Allende government said, "We have reached the point where Latin America is contributing to the development of the United States, not the other way around."[2]

Marroquín Rojas suddenly shifted gears and began to talk about agriculture.

"You are helping to destroy our culture," he said. "Consider tortillas and *ají* (hot peppers), for example. Add a little meat and beans and you have a good diet that makes a man strong. But you people are changing all that." Marroquín Rojas complained that the United States was encouraging the production of sheep and cotton instead of basic foods. "But the worst disservice to humanity possible is that of CARE (the privately funded U.S. philanthropic food agency). It is changing our food habits by giving away your surplus farm products (wheat, dehydrated milk, etc.). It gets our people accustomed to charity and to new kinds of foods they cannot afford to buy and cannot produce."

I nodded my head in agreement. In fact, I had stressed the same point in an earlier book. I was becoming favorably impressed with Marroquín Rojas. Why had I found his judgment irrational when he was minister of agriculture?

"I have asked every U.S. ambassador to stop giving us loans and CARE food," he continued, "and to concentrate instead on helping us to increase our quotas for exports. Let us earn our way so that we can work and avoid becoming a nation of beggars."

I asked him what he thought about Guatemala's future prospects.

"Very cloudy," he replied, and complained about the way Africa was capturing Guatemala's coffee markets overseas. Then, erratically it seemed, he queried, "How many children do you have?"

I answered, "Two."

"Good," he said. "Our own population is growing terribly fast, but yours is moving slowly."

In a nutshell he had contrasted the future of the developed

and developing worlds more succinctly than any other official I interviewed.

Then he put another question to me: "Tell me, how can we have a future when all our presidential candidates are army officers?"

I became self-conscious. Just outside the door was a military officer. Marroquín Rojas is a little deaf and we were both talking in loud voices. Our conversation was clearly audible on the other side of the thin door. Fortunately he took me off the hook by answering his own question: "The future will force upon us a social revolution that will push us either toward Communism and a dictator of the Fidel Castro or Ché Guevara type or toward a dictatorship of the proletariat."

I now ventured to ask the question that had brought me here in the first place. "What about the need to improve corn production in Guatemala?"

"We must improve our corn production," he replied. "If I were president I would make the big coffee growers produce some corn and beans on their lands in addition to coffee." He explained that the coffee growers were some of the country's best farmers; they would be able to make the investment to increase production markedly. "The rich, as well as the poor, must have a hand in producing our nation's food," he said, to emphasize his point.

"Another thing," he said, "these scientists should not try to give our Indians hybrid corn. It does not fit into their way of life, because the Indian just isn't accustomed to buying new seed every year."

He was saying something that took many years for both Melhus here in Guatemala and the Rockefeller Foundation in Mexico to discover: that hybrids do not fit an Indian culture.

"And all this fuss about chemical fertilizer is wrong too," the vice-president said. "It costs the Indian too much to make its use economical. We should be teaching him about organic fertilizers, how to save his refuse . . . But we can get this done without experiment stations dreamed up by North Americans. Our corn varieties are good and we don't need any corn improvement program.

"Because Central American corn is already special. It was brought here before the time of Christ by the Lost Tribe of Israel."

Suddenly he had lost me. He was once again the irrational minister of agriculture.

Later I told a Guatemalan friend about the interview. The

friend commented, "I am reminded of a job I had while earning my way through medical school. I worked evenings in a mental hospital. The people there seemed very nice, very normal, up to a certain point. Then wham! For example, there was this gentle inmate who said he wanted to give me a little something for my many kindnesses—it turned out to be a carefully drawn check for one million dollars."

As I think back on my interview with Marroquín Rojas and remember the soldiers outside, I wonder: were they guards or keepers?

I SHOULD NOT CONDEMN Marroquín Rojas just because he believes the Lost Tribe of Israel introduced corn to Guatemala. Everyone has a peculiarity. The British ambassador in Afghanistan when my brother served there was a very capable and intelligent man; yet he believed the future of Afghanistan could be foretold by the measurements of the great pyramid of Egypt.

When U.S. officials closed down their agricultural program in 1959, they blamed the attacks by Marroquín Rojas. Yet he was not the one at fault. Rather the blame should be placed on the impetuousness of some U.S. official in the hierarchy who failed to recognize that the authority of the raucous Marroquín Rojas was a passing thing. Any knowledgeable observer could have foretold he would soon be out of office. Thus our snap reaction to his attacks was the death of a fourteen-year-old corn program vitally needed by Guatemala.

POLITICS HAS BEEN defined as the art of getting along with people. It applies to the man who gets along with his electorate and is elected. It applies to the man who gets along with his boss and is promoted. It also, unfortunately, applies to a foreign aid program because it must appeal to those who authorize its money.

To bring foreign aid programs to a successful fruition they should somehow be given immunity from the political whims and peculiarities of officialdom. For those who advocate more foreign aid, I caution: Most development efforts are doomed to failure if they cannot be removed from the irrationality of politics. Yet how can this be done? I do not know.

3

Supervision by
a Jack-of-All-Trades

"WITHOUT QUESTION, our most effective development project here is the supervised credit program." The U.S. ambassador to Mexico said this categorically. "Let me suggest you visit two Mexicans who have received loans under this program. They are both living near Toluca and I have talked with them personally."

The first man, the ambassador said, wanted money for a well with which to irrigate his land. But the technician from the local bank who gave out the loans found that surface water was available a half-mile away. Thus it would cost the farmer less to dig an irrigation ditch to this source of water than to drill a well on his own property. The ambassador scarcely needed to point up the moral: First-class loan supervision allows the supply of lending money to go further.

The second farmer, he told me, is a dairyman who previously had twenty old, Heinz 57-variety cows and wanted to buy ten more. The bank's supervisor advised him to sell off all the old cows and buy ten new, high-producing Holsteins. Within six months the dairyman had doubled his income. Within two years he was able to double his herd, this time buying ten additional Holsteins with hard cash. Second moral: Proper advice on how to use borrowed money makes it possible for the borrower to increase his income (in this case, four to five times) and to pay back the loan.

"This supervised credit program has gone extremely well," the ambassador said. "The money for it came from a $25 million U.S. AID loan made to Mexico about 1962–1963 under very favorable terms: a forty-year loan with a ten-year grace period, and, thereafter, an interest rate of ¾ of 1 percent. The program has gone so well we have made a second loan." This was for $20 million with a five-year grace period, and, thereafter, a 3.5 percent interest rate for a period of thirty years. This money was funneled to the National Bank of Mexico which, in turn, loaned it to private banks which loaned it to individuals.

"It involves transactions between private banks and small farmers for the first time," the ambassador emphasized, "like the two men at Toluca. The borrowers pay 6 percent interest, a rate much lower than that available elsewhere in the Mexican banking system. The interest is just enough to cover the bank's administrative costs in handling the money, plus a modest profit." The reason the United States arranged the two loans to Mexico, he explained, was "to focus attention on the small landowner." The average loan amounts to about $2,000. The project was designed to put farmers, who previously had not been able to borrow from a bank, into the credit system. Some 20,000 farmers have participated.

"No loans," the ambassador said, "are ever made without inspection and subsequent supervision. All loans are for capital improvement, with only one restriction: that it will not result in competition with a U.S. agricultural surplus. The repayment record is nearly 100 percent."

I thanked the ambassador. This seemed to be an excellent project to inspect since it had functioned for more than three years (a requirement to which I tried to adhere strictly for all the projects I investigated). In addition, with Mexico as the proving ground, this program could be extended to other developing countries. And an added bonus was the names, handed to me on an ambassadorial platter, of two farmers who had profited by their loans and whom the ambassador himself had interviewed.

Off to Toluca I went, a bank official along as a guide.

I found the first farmer, Severiano Arias, repairing a tractor which he had bought as a result of the loan he had received. Arias was about thirty-five years old, a quick, aggressive person. He had farmed all his life. His farm consisted of over 300 acres, with a house, a long shed, a garage, three tractors, a hammer mill, a silage chopper, plus a television set, a truck, an automobile, and maybe a bit more. He was the farmer whom, the ambassador said, the bank supervisor had prevailed upon to dig a half-mile ditch to obtain water rather than a well.

In 1966 he received his first loan (from this supervised credit program) of $21,000. The loan was made at 6 percent interest with four years to pay. Arias said he spent $12,000 of the loan to sink a well and buy an electric pump, $2,400 to install the pump, another $2,400 to buy a secondhand tractor, and $5,600 for fourteen cows and a bull. I know these figures do not add up to $21,000 but that is how he gave them to me.

The irrigation ditch was the first item on my list of questions. No, he had not dug one; instead he had gone ahead and dug the well, no matter what the bank supervisor had advised. In discussing the advantages of the loan, Arias at once mentioned the low interest rate. He said he had previously been getting loans from other banks at 12 percent interest, but sometimes, even at that higher rate, money was tight. Arias had doubled his income from milk production. He said it was partly because of the loan and partly because dairy prices were 30 percent higher than when he had received the loan. However, the land he had been able to irrigate due to the expenditure on the well and pump had increased his income last year but not this year. The reason: poor corn yields, due to frost, he said. He was having trouble meeting the loan payments and had asked the bank for an extension. Thus the money spent on the well and pump had so far not increased his income as projected.

J. Dolores Sánchez, the second borrower whom the ambassador had mentioned, was a typical Spanish-type countryman—short and heavy set—and the owner of sixty-one acres of land, a diesel engine, a tractor, etc. He employed two hired hands. Sánchez is the farmer whom, the ambassador said, the bank supervisor had advised to sell his old dairy herd and buy Holsteins and who had thereby increased his income.

Sánchez had indeed borrowed $8,450 at 6 percent interest from the bank's supervised credit program. He said he had bought "some new Holsteins" with the loan money, but he also said he had not sold off the old cows when he bought the new ones. His faithful old bull of nondescript lineage continues to breed the same old mixed-up lines with the new Holsteins. He had used $1,600 of the loan to bring in electricity to his farm. This source of power was not being used for the dairy business. He did, however, now have a television set.

He told me he was an old-time borrower at the Banco Agricola (The Farmer's Bank) before he applied for the low interest loan under the supervised credit program. Previous rates, he claimed, had run as high as 18 percent.

I was interested that the bank official with me was encouraging Sánchez to take out another loan. It would have been truer to the concept of the AID project for the bank to have placed the additional loan with another farmer in order to bring someone new into the credit system.

I was not able to put together what Sánchez's income was, although he answered my questions readily enough. He did say the herd's milk production was up quite a bit.

I am afraid my mind wandered. I found myself concentrating more on the population problem than on agricultural economics. While talking to the first farmer, Arias, I had learned four families were living off his 300 acres of land. These included his own family, those of two uncles, and his mother. He himself had four children, one of his uncles had five, another uncle had six. This meant, including spouses, a total of twenty-four people.

Now, talking with Sánchez, I realized he faced a similar situation on his much smaller piece of land. With two sons plus their wives and eleven grandchildren, there were, in all, sixteen people, not to mention the two hired cowboys and, presumably, their families also.

A comment of the ambassador haunted me. "We can't convince the Mexican government that a population problem exists; as long as agricultural production is growing as fast as the population, they don't think there is anything to be concerned about."

It is unimportant, I finally decided, that the ambassador's account of the two Toluca farmers was quite at variance with the facts as I found them. For in the long run it would not make much difference. In the coming forty years the Mexican government's need to repay the two loans totaling $45 million would be overshadowed by the far greater crisis of physical survival. In forty years Mexico's population, growing at its current rate, will jump from 50 million people to 200 million.

Nevertheless, the garbled "facts," so sincerely told by the ambassador, rankled. I felt I had been led down a garden path. How could this have happened?

Dean Acheson, former secretary of state, used this same phrase under much the same circumstances when referring to a highly optimistic White House briefing about Vietnam by the Joint Chiefs of Staff. He was reported as saying President Johnson was "led down a garden path . . ." Actually, Acheson is more exactly reported to have said, "With all due respect, Mr. President, the Joint Chiefs of Staff don't know what they're talking about."[1] He claimed that field reports written near the scene of combat in Vietnam were rewritten as they passed through each higher echelon. With each rewriting the reports reflected less and less the pessimism at the front and more and more the optimism that prevailed in the Pentagon.

The same reporting situation occurs with development projects in the "third world," and with the same result. Gunnar Myrdal, writing about South Asia, said, "Optimism, and therefore approaches that make optimism seem more realistic, is itself a natural urge for intellectuals . . . All [economic] planning . . . tends to err on the side of optimism . . ."[2] This Myrdal-reported syndrome from Asia can similarly be found in Latin America and, I am sure, in Africa as well. (In virtually every interview for this book which involved an unfavorable view of a development project, I was told, "Don't quote me." But no one ever said that when their remarks were favorable. Thus the syndrome feeds upon itself.)

The most easily understood examples of this are the numerous congressional fact-finding missions where congressmen travel abroad to evaluate foreign aid projects. The congressman arrives at the foreign capital; he is met by the ambassador and the AID mission director. Off they all go to see the mission's best project, and at its best appearance. You remember, like Sunday dinner for the preacher or parents' day at school. Who shows the failures? Who would be so naive as to suggest showing them? Who even wants to see them?

Vietnam provides an example. Two congressmen, on an inspection trip, startled Washington with news of a previously unknown example of bad treatment of prisoners by the South Vietnamese. The *Washington Post* editorialized that the experience tells "something about the perils and pitfalls of official fact-finding tours, for what happened there is almost without precedent: the fact-finders uncovered a fact. They saw something that was not on the program, something they were not supposed to see. This may not sound like much until you consider the record. With the notable exception of Mr. George Romney, who discovered that he had been 'brainwashed' and had the singular courage to admit it publicly, most VIP visitors do not even know they are getting the treatment; most of them come back burbling about progress . . ."[3]

This does not mean anyone is being purposely dishonest or consciously devious. Rather, everyone is nicely, normally, noxiously human.

Nonetheless, my conversation with this ambassador in Mexico about the absolute effectiveness of the U.S. money put into our supervised loan program still rankled. He had praised it unstintingly; yet I had found almost all his facts to be in error. I knew this ambassador to be one of the United States' best and most experienced officials. Also I liked him personally and instinctively accepted him as a straightforward person.

No, the problem was not with the man.

The problem is with the system.

Gone forever are the days of the diplomat's diplomat, the old-time ambassador whose job was primarily to keep relations between the two countries from becoming unglued, a job requiring tact, good reporting, and the wisdom to suggest policies which would add sizing to the glue.

Today's communications have bypassed him as a policy maker and turned him into an intermediary to deliver and explain directives formulated in Washington and, hopefully, to persuade their acceptance by the local government. In fact Zbigniew Brzezinski, director of Columbia University's Research Institute on Communist Affairs, says, "Modern communications establish a degree of proximity which makes much of diplomatic reporting superfluous and wasteful. In most cases, one can get a better sense of local developments by reading good foreign newspapers than by perusing the cables from embassies and consulates."[4]

Today the work of an embassy has become a messy maze of administrative and emotional problems unimagined by the old-timers. To succeed, the ambassador must cope, for example, with the complex interests of huge, internationalized American corporations versus the local, weak, developing businesses; with nationalisms that are often irrational; and with the mass movement of American travelers, congressmen, and do-gooders of every stripe. He must be able to work with his perversely independent attachés from agriculture, commerce, the Pentagon, and other Washington bureaucracies. (Too often these are inexperienced in coping with foreign living and foreign officials and they are as naive and wayward as children.) In the Mexico City embassy, for example, he must ride herd over an embassy staff of 140 Americans plus 83 additional staff in consulates in seventeen other cities. He must accomplish all this with a staff which has either just arrived or is about to leave under the now firmly established, too-short rotation system that grew up after World War II—a handicap from which he also suffers.

Instead of being a diplomat the ambassador is a jack-of-all-trades.

I should not have been disturbed by the ambassador's misinformation on the AID loans. I should have understood that AID is only a small part of his Mexican involvement. The total amount of American investment in Mexico is $1.5 billion. The $45 million of this one AID effort is a mere fraction. It commands, as it should, but a fraction of the ambassador's time.

He is fed information which he cannot personally evaluate. I hypothesize that his knowledge of the supervised loan project was no more profound than the quick briefing he presumably received as he was driven to Toluca with his wife and a photographer, perhaps, as a guess, to publicize the signing of the second AID loan.

ANOTHER jack-of-all-trades: During the year when the second supervized credit loan was granted, Congress voted on a budget of $160 billion, of which the $2 billion for foreign aid was but a small fraction. Can Congress do any better, relatively speaking, than the ambassador in overseeing AID?

[4]

Mobile Health Clinics
Become a Shell Game

PRESIDENT JOHN F. KENNEDY had been in the White House only a few months when he proposed the Alliance for Progress as a massive U.S. aid plan for Latin America. What was going to distinguish the Alliance from the efforts that had gone before, the administration claimed, was the new concept that programs would now be designed by the beneficiaries—the Latin Americans themselves. This made for good rhetoric; but there was never much doubt from where most of the ideas and money were to come.

In June 1962 President Kennedy called in three key advisers: Fowler Hamilton, administrator of the Agency for International Development (AID); Teodoro Moscoso, U.S. coordinator for the Alliance for Progress; and Edward R. Murrow, director of the United States Information Agency (USIA). The president already was looking ahead to the first anniversary of the Alliance and, like officials anywhere, wanted some ammunition with which to praise his program.

The president reportedly told the group, "We must have some kind of fast impact program to show that the Alliance is really moving. Give me ideas for five such programs that can be supported from funds you already have. I don't want to go to Congress for more money."

Hamilton and Moscoso, the two officials most directly involved, called in their aides. Although it was never clear whether the president meant five different kinds of projects or projects in five different countries, within a week Hamilton and Moscoso returned to the president with a plan for putting mobile health units into operation in Latin America's rural areas. The program would begin in the five nations of Central America (it was later expanded to Panama), and would be called PUMAR (Programa de Unidades

36

Móviles para Areas Rurales). (A program known as "Operation Niños" was also proposed to President Kennedy at this time.)

Credit for thinking up PUMAR is generally given to Dr. Edgar F. Berman, a physician with previous experience in an international health program. At the time Berman first formulated his suggestion, however, he was private physician to Senator Hubert H. Humphrey. This is the same Dr. Berman who in 1970 was to attain national attention for saying women were not qualified medically to be president of the United States and thereby called down upon himself the wrath of the American feminist movement.

Berman, an aggressive, confident, and articulate person, described the early history of PUMAR to me in a letter dated June 26, 1969:

> Prior to 1962, I had worked up an idea for a mobile program, which I thought was rational for underdeveloped countries, for the then Senator, Hubert Humphrey. It was geographically feasible, it had visibility, emotional content (life saving), was inexpensive and was a means of initiating community development.
>
> When it was begun, it was set up for 10 mobile units for each Central American republic and was supposed to continue expanding into the rest of South America. However, in 1963 the budgets were cut and soon funds were no longer available. Most of the Central American nations thought the idea valuable enough (one President told me that it helped reelect him) to continue their own financing.
>
> However, the mobile health unit as an idea was only a foot in the door to Community Development. For each patient was charged and the fund went to an elected committee in the village which decided once a year on its use. In 1963 we added credit unions, agricultural extension agents, a seed and small animal program, increased our health education and later (in some nations) initiated population control. The moneys gathered by the community were frequently used for teachers, building schools through self help or even acquiring a dentist.

As so often happens with such programs, Berman, who helped organize it, soon left it. (As told in his letter, alliance coordinator Moscoso had called upon him late in 1963 "to organize the population control division for the State Department in Latin America.") In retrospect, Berman noted ruefully, "If the program would have gone as I saw it, there would be at least one unit . . . visiting twelve villages a week, catering to approximately a two hundred thousand population in each Latin American nation."

Even though his grand vision for the program was scaled down, Berman could still write, "I think effectiveness of the health programs for the most common diseases (which are the greatest producers of mortality and morbidity) is excellent and I think we were treating somewhere around one million patients a year. However, my real goal was the utilization of this program in initiating community organization, community self-help and involvement, and the development of the Democratic process."

The original blueprint of PUMAR was impressively simple. A doctor and a nurse were to make regular circuits in a rural area by jeep, spending one day every fortnight at each of twelve towns on their run. At each town a small medical center, stockpiled with basic medicines, was to be supervised by a local resident called a "sanitation inspector." Among other duties, he would make sure the patients were ready when the medical team arrived.

Each patient would pay approximately twenty-eight cents for treatment. This money would go into a fund to be spent locally on community development projects. The sanitation inspector would encourage the local people to organize a village committee by an election. The committee would vote on how the accumulated funds were to be spent, presumably on such projects as road building, construction of a health center, digging of a well, purchase of a pump, and so on. The doctor would meet with the village committee members on his visits and offer professional, mature guidance on community projects.

In all, effectively simple.

Equally important, even the nonprofessional in development could grasp at once the impact such a program could have as a device for introducing new ideas to backward, isolated villages and thereby help lead them to a better life.

Before undertaking field research on PUMAR's mobile units, at the suggestion of Assistant Secretary of State Covey Oliver, I interviewed the pertinent officials in Washington and their counterparts in Central America. I read reports. I was briefed. The gist of this background material was summarized by Frederick J. Vintinner, AID's chief public health advisor in Central America, in an article he wrote for a public health journal in 1968, five years after the program was inaugurated.

[PUMAR] provides basic medical care and preventive medicine and services for two million people living in the rural areas of Costa Rica, El Salvador, Guatemala, Honduras, Nicaragua, and Panama . . . Self-help is a cardinal factor and through cooperative community actions basic health facilities have been constructed, health programs implemented, environmental sanitation improved, and roads, bridges, schools, athletic fields, and other community facilities built or established. Foundations have been laid for permanent responsible local groups who can take leadership in community health and development activities and there is a growing change of attitude toward civic responsibility and pride in local organizations and achievements. With improved health and a feeling of new hope for a better life in the spirit of the Alliance for Progress, the people in the rural areas of the five countries in Central America and Panama will become an important component in the total economic and social progress of the region.[1]

Vintinner included a catalog of PUMAR-inspired, self-help community development projects in Central America and Panama:

Health clinics established	443
New buildings constructed	74
Communities employing full-time nurse aides	209
Community centers established	64
New buildings constructed	38
Piped water systems installed	203
Community wells constructed	480
Community wells reconditioned	204
Latrines installed	7,459
Latrines rehabilitated	2,254
Garbage disposal programs initiated	3,799
Community clean-up programs initiated	202
Animal-penning programs initiated	420
Public barns constructed	154
Public laundries constructed	281
New access roads constructed	65
miles	235
Roads improved	49
miles	350
Bridges built or repaired	60
Schools assisted (construction, renovation, supplies)	163
Home garden programs started	581
Small animal-raising programs started	33
Communal industries started	24
Credit unions and cooperatives assisted	64
Communal parks built or improved	18
Athletic fields constructed or improved	38
Libraries started or assisted	28

For my field research it was necessary, in accordance with my pattern of selecting specific development projects, to determine which Central American nation had the most effective PUMAR program. It did not take long to establish that in Washington the Nicaraguan program was reputed, by all odds, to be the best. The late Aaron Brown, who had just retired as U.S. ambassador to Nicaragua, confirmed this conclusion, stressing that the PUMAR program there was "excellent because it includes a community development program." James P. Lockard, development officer on the Central American desk of AID, informed me that plans were afoot to provide the Nicaraguan government with a loan to increase the number of mobile units from eleven to twenty. Since Nicaragua was the only country slated for such an expansion, this seemed to be additional evidence that its PUMAR program had special merit.

When I arrived in Managua, I was particularly impressed by Louis Gardella, AID's articulate public health advisor assigned as liaison with PUMAR.[2]

Gardella had a direct, open personality, and he did not beat about the bush when discussing anything. Besides being a breath of fresh air in the hierarchy of officialdom, he was experienced in AID, having spent six years in Nicaragua and had worked previously in Libya, Paraguay, and Costa Rica. Gardella was considered an expert concerning the health problems of the hungry nations. Actually I hazard that his enthusiasm and his effectiveness as an advocate for the PUMAR program are the underlying reasons the Nicaraguan program is held in such high esteem in Washington and elsewhere.

"We have been too successful in public health here," he told me, referring to the dramatic decline in the local death rate. "We have failed to realize the effect of our success on population growth until recently. We should have started family planning when we began our public health programs here twenty years ago.

"Nicaragua has a lot of good land to expand into," he said. "PUMAR brings medical services to these new areas." (I was surprised to find this able, seasoned official repeating the old, pernicious myth about uninhabited land automatically being good land for farming.)

I asked, "Do these mobile health units offer family planning service?"

"No," he said. "We have too much to do already. When a unit arrives in a town, the doctor has some eighty patients to see that same day. He also has to meet with the local committee to plan community development projects. There is a limit to what one man can do."

Gardella added, "The headaches of just keeping the units on the move tax everyone's ingenuity."

At the time I interviewed him, Nicaragua had eleven mobile units, four of them boats which served communities along rivers near the Atlantic Coast. The boats had been inaugurated by former

President René Schick Gutiérrez as a political gesture to show people he was doing something for the nation's isolated citizens. Gardella said that keeping the boats in operation is a frustrating job because their outboard motors are always breaking down. Since the number of people living in the remote areas is small, the cost of maintaining the waterborne units per person served is high.

But, Gardella emphasized, as had Dr. Berman in his letter, PUMAR's success should not be judged solely by the medical services it provides. He pointed to the importance of the creation of village committees and said they had been an essential factor in teaching people how to operate through the democratic process. "In the past," he said, "there has always been some local czar who ran everything in these villages. We are using the committee system to teach the people they have certain rights." Gardella's enthusiasm was contagious as he spoke of developing democracy this way and of the need to neutralize the "Commies."

I asked how he would evaluate the effectiveness of PUMAR. He said, "It depends, of course, on what criteria you use. Our medical care is only fair and the cost is high. However, our community development aspect is very successful. As far as Washington is concerned, PUMAR's success is measured by the degree the little people in the rural areas gain a knowledge of what the Alliance for Progress means. To them the Alliance is the jeep they see!"

However, I received a diametrically opposed opinion from a young Nicaraguan government official, Dr. José Antonio Cantón, a Johns Hopkins graduate who heads PUMAR for the whole country, and Señora Ortega de Castillo, who is in charge of PUMAR nurses. Both of them said categorically that community development (and, to a lesser extent, the itinerant doctors) is a side issue. The main objective, they emphasized, is to construct a health center in each village.

These differing objectives made my job of evaluating the program difficult. Which to study? The building of health centers? The medical care? The community development? The visibility of AID? The quick impact? I began to feel as confused as an onlooker at a fast-moving shell game.

WHEN I ASKED Gardella to recommend a mobile team for me to visit, he was emphatic in saying I should visit that of Dr. Augustín Brenes Bojorge, who had just been named Nicaragua's "Doctor of the Year." Brenes' unit was the best of the lot, Gardella said.

So I went to Nancimí in the Department of Rivas, a town some seventy miles from Managua. It was a small cluster of houses that belied the 2,000 people said to live in the area. Brenes was late in arriving because his jeep had broken down (that bedevilment of all development activities in rural areas). He was a shortish, stocky fellow wearing a baseball cap and, as I soon discovered, he does not just talk to you, he shouts. The creed of this dynamic, tireless fellow is: "Doing good works in this world will bring you your reward in the next." He wore me out, but the villagers loved him.

About a dozen people were waiting for him when he arrived. By the time he left he had seen twenty-eight people. Dr. Brenes was assisted by a young nurse who seemed disinterested and bored with her job. She handed out medicines with the detachment of a tired drug store clerk.

PUMAR's publicity emphasizes that the sanitation inspector and at least one member of the village committee are present each time the doctor makes his visit. Neither was on hand the day I was at Nancimí. Dr. Brenes indicated this was par for the course. "Quite frankly," he said, "I don't know much about the committee, what it does or who its members are." Brenes estimated that less than 40 percent of the people he treats are interested in the community development part of PUMAR.

Before leaving Managua I had learned five PUMAR projects were listed as completed at Nancimí: a credit cooperative, several wells, the improvement of the road leading to the main highway, a new schoolhouse, and a health center.

Here in the field these "accomplishments" were unrecognizable. I list the projects:

1. A credit cooperative had been started during the first burst of enthusiasm over PUMAR in 1964, functioned for six months, and then died. Of the several loans which the cooperative had made during its brief life span, only two have been repaid.

2. I could not determine exactly how many wells had been built, but I was shown one well dug in 1964. This well was not working because the pump had broken down. Local interest was not sufficient to get the relatively expensive spare parts necessary to repair it. As matters now stood, water technology in Nancimí consisted of a bucket and a rope. A sidelight on the broken pump was provided by Milcíades Chávez, head of PUMAR for the eastern half of Nicaragua. He told me, "Most of the pumps in my villages seem to be broken." The reason, he said, was that AID required the pumps be purchased in the United States and they were never powerful enough.

3. The story of the construction of the road out to the main highway, as told me by local people, bore little resemblance to its description at PUMAR headquarters. PUMAR claimed credit for making it into an all-weather road. "Not at all," said Juan Rodríguez, who was president of the town's road committee. The road had been improved because a total of 300 people had been paid, largely with food, to work on it for one day or more over a period of four months. This work was financed by a special tax levied on Nancimí real estate, not by PUMAR fees.

4. In Managua, PUMAR took the credit for building a six-room schoolhouse, saying it was financed out of Nancimí's 28¢ fees. Armando Ruíz, secretary of the local PUMAR committee, set the record straight. He said the school was built entirely with AID money, the land and some materials were given by the village. The project had nothing to do with the local PUMAR committee.

5. Dr. Cantón, the Nicaraguan head of PUMAR, had told me the program's principal objective was building health care centers. Since Brenes was such an outstanding doctor, I fully expected the town would have at least an adequately effective center. Not so. In 1963 the local PUMAR committee used a borrowed house as a center. This was considered inadequate because of its small size, lack of windows, and dirt floor. So three years later a second committee rented a building with running water and a tile floor for $9.80 per month. At about the same time, in a moment of enthusiasm according to Dr. Brenes, the villagers manufactured 4,000 bricks with which to build a new health center. By 1968 the community had become tired of paying the rent and returned to the original dirt-floored building. Thus after six years, Nancimí's health center project is back where it started except for the 4,000 bricks still piled up, unused.

I recapitulate what I found in Nancimí, served by PUMAR's "most effective mobile unit" and headed by Nicaragua's "Doctor of the Year." The town does have a new surfaced road to the main highway and a new six-room school, neither of which can be attributed to PUMAR. The local village development committee, since the first spurt of energy in 1963, seems to have accomplished nothing at all. The health center is still in the original decrepit building. Whatever community development spark may have once flickered in Nancimí has long since sputtered out.

The pile of bricks covered with dust is PUMAR's monument here. When I said this to Dr. Brenes, he said: "Nothing is perfect, only God."

I visited two more PUMAR villages. The trip to La Orilla—

a wide place in the road for 250 families and more destitute and dusty than Nancimí—proved to be delightful because of the doctor and the nurse. Dr. José Ramón Carvallo, a country-type doctor seventy-two years old, was accompanied by Nurse Sylvia Hurtado, who was as warmly sincere as the doctor. They were both in agreement that health customs had improved in La Orilla since PUMAR began. They mentioned as examples: some seventy-five cement latrines have been built, mothers now cover the nipples of baby bottles to keep them from flies and the danger of typhoid, and fruit is washed before it is eaten.

However, I found the results of community development just as elusive here as in Nancimí. The town did indeed have a health center, a small building with a tile floor. The center had cost $420, a sum which had been paid, I was told, entirely out of the funds accumulated through the 28¢ fees. But the center had developed a leaky roof and it was clearly not the sort of building where a government could locate a permanent staff.

The town's development committee had not met in four months. No committee member was on hand for the doctor's visit, nor was the sanitation inspector there.

Again, the community well, dug with PUMAR earnings, had a broken AID-supplied pump. It had remained unrepaired for three months, due to the lack of money or interest or both. Each family had its own bucket and rope because a bucket and rope left at the well "would be stolen."

Nurse Hurtado railed at the lack of spirit among the villagers: "There is no sense of cooperation here, no community vigor," she said. "Always petty fights between families. They get mad at each other even when a chicken comes over the fence. Here there is no soul. There is nothing."

The doctor attended twenty-eight patients. This was three more than the twenty-five which he said was his average per visit.

The last village visited was Veracruz, population 678. Since it is only some ten miles from the capital, it is scarcely an isolated hamlet. Geographically it is in an ideal position to receive close PUMAR supervision and the town has telephone service.

From PUMAR records at headquarters I had learned that the development committee in Veracruz was considered to be one of the most effective. I drove out to see its accomplishments rather than watch a visiting doctor in action. PUMAR funds, it was officially claimed, had built a ten-kilometer connecting road to the main highway. This road, it turned out, is only six kilometers long and, according to Señora Gregoria de Perea who had been a member of the local committee for almost six years, no PUMAR money went into its construction.

I visited the public well in Veracruz because in Managua PUMAR officials had told me it had been dug with PUMAR savings. But here in Veracruz the people were unaware that PUMAR had been a factor. They told me the central government had dug the well and installed the small electric pump and water tank. The valve had broken three months earlier and had not been repaired or replaced.

One Veracruz accomplishment listed at the Managua PUMAR headquarters was the installation of electricity. However, a former committee member said no PUMAR money had been used. Rather, the government had paid for it, and the local villagers had helped by digging holes for the poles. Twenty-six houses now had electricity.

But, marvelous to see, Veracruz had a beautiful health center, by far the finest building in town. Here PUMAR had indeed accomplished something—or was it a bureaucratic mirage? Just how the construction had been financed was confusing. The village, I learned, had borowed $1,190 from AID to build it. Now everyone locally seemed preoccupied with the $14 which had to be squeezed out monthly to pay off the loan. The PUMAR fees for medical consultations barely covered this sum. Thus there would be nothing left over for any other community project until this long-term loan should run its course—some ten years off. In the meantime, the center itself could become a white elephant since the government now had no plans to staff it permanently.

Maybe I am overly critical. The construction of health centers is, after all, one of the announced goals of PUMAR. Therefore I suppose the center at Veracruz can be tabulated legitimately a success, even though it is used irregularly. For my Veracruz story, none of this is really pertinent. I went there to visit what I had been assured was an effective development committee in action. The town's location, as well as the probability of strong supervisory support from the capital, made me conclude that if a community development committee could work anywhere, Veracruz must be the place. Alas I found the committee had functioned well until it had overextended itself by borrowing that $1,190 from AID. The debt and the obligation to pay it off had been too much. Now there was no committee.

PUMAR, which looked so beautifully simple on paper when it

was set up in 1963, is, in fact, a highly complex organization. Thus it can be publicized in a variety of ways as the need arises or as officials wish to justify their own work while ignoring other parts of the organization. On the one hand, it is a straightforward medical program; on the other, it is a rather amorphous community development program for which the goals have not been clearly defined. There is also, like a halo floating over all, the desire to train backward villagers for "democracy"—itself a vague term.

The main link tying the parts of PUMAR together is not the itinerant doctor, not the officials in Managua, but the sanitation inspectors living in the villages.

Originally it may have seemed these inspectors were to be rather unimportant cogs in the wheel. In retrospect, it is now evident that the failure to create an effective corps of inspectors has had a disastrous effect on PUMAR. The inspector was assigned an enormous and complex job. He was told to develop a democratic institution where none had existed previously, to encourage responsible leaders to come to the fore, and to show them how to run for election and serve on village committees. Yet the inspector is not a local person but one brought in for a two-year assignment from another town, often the capital. In a dull, apathetic, forlorn village (often no more than a few scattered houses), he must show the wisdom of Solomon if he is to bring success to programs, the goals of which even its own officials cannot determine. Meanwhile, of course, he must avoid the petty jealousies of these alien people among whom he has been cast.

The next step, assuming this Solomon has indeed succeeded in guiding the local people through the embryo stage of democracy, calls for him to fade gently into the background as the new local leaders take over all phases of the operation. Yet he is expected to retain enough influence to make sure the funds generated by PUMAR will be voted by the local committee into useful projects. Although these are important responsibilities, one can quickly see that only a few hours a month of actual work are thus involved. In addition he has the job, once every two weeks, of making sure the patients are lined up ready for the doctor's visit. Also he must be able to give injections himself, as he is the only "medical" person living in the village. The real curse of this job must be the deadly boredom.

In all my experience anywhere, I have seldom encountered any paragons able to bring off such an assignment. Little wonder the hastily conscripted sanitation inspectors were not up to it. In fact any person smart enough to handle the inspector's complex role and temperamentally and emotionally dedicated to his work would already have found a fine, worthwhile job elsewhere.

In Managua PUMAR officials admitted that village committees rather frequently spent their development savings on such uneconomic projects as repairing the local church or building a wall around the cemetery. Although clearly this was what the villagers themselves wanted, excuses had to be found for such "mistakes." Often the Nicaraguan officials put the blame on AID. They said AID had changed the rules in midstream. As long as AID *gave* extra money to the villages to supplement the funds derived from the patients' 28¢ fees (an AID contribution not mentioned to me in Washington), the village committees did, in fact, push genuine development projects. But shortly before my visit AID had changed its policy to one of *lending* the money. The result, the Nicaraguan officials self-righteously alleged, was that the villagers lost interest in PUMAR-inspired democracy as soon as they had to assess increased taxes to repay the loans.

WHAT IS the present status of PUMAR in Nicaragua? Señora Ortega de Castillo, head of the nurses, stated that the number of patients treated by PUMAR has fallen every year since 1966.

Milcíades Chávez, head of PUMAR for the eastern half of Nicaragua, attributed the decrease simply to the fact that people are getting healthier—an idea not substantiated by anyone else with whom I talked.

In the end I decided the decrease in the number of patients treated was due to declining efficiency. In part, this was caused because the jeeps and launches were continually breaking down. But most significant of all, PUMAR is on the wane because local enthusiasm and support for the program are fading.

Perhaps this is so because of the collapse of the concept of PUMAR as a channel for community development. But what is community development? The term is bandied about as if we all knew. Yet everyone seems to have his own meaning. For instance, the electricity brought into the village of Veracruz is used for such things as television, radios, and refrigerators. In my opinion, this electricity is a useless luxury rather than an example of community development because it does not further any form of economic endeavor. Yet the advocates of electrification, whose number is legion in the development profession, will sincerely claim the Veracruz electricity is a valid and successful example of community development.

Others say any simple agreement on a single program by a village is development. They would thus consider the following true story to be an example of community development at its best.

A friend of mine has a vacation home in a small, somewhat isolated village in southeast Mexico. The town has little water and the people have few opportunities to bathe; during church services the air becomes rank. Thus my church-going friend decided to help the community. He told the mayor he would pay to build a bathhouse if the village would donate the land. The mayor thanked him for the offer but said he could not accept without first discussing it with his community committee. He explained, "I am a democratic mayor. Please give us ten days to talk it over."

In ten days the mayor reported, "The town is very grateful for your generosity. It is true we have been without a bathhouse for generations. But in reviewing all our village's needs we cannot ignore our reputation in the valley. During holidays we have to hire a band from a neighboring town for our fiestas. It is bad to have the reputation of being so poor we have no band. And so," the mayor concluded, "we would like to ask that instead of building us a bathhouse, would you please buy the instruments for a brass band?"

WHEN RAGNAR ARNESON, AID mission director in Nicaragua, told me PUMAR has "stimulated a sense of hope in the communities," my reaction was that mere stimulation, after six years' effort, would be a strong condemnation of this project of community development.

In Washington and Nicaragua I was told new AID money was going into PUMAR because it was an ideal vehicle on which to piggyback a population control program—the sort of effort Congress is now insisting AID must support. Therefore officials have quickly claimed the $2 million loan for Nicaragua's PUMAR was being made primarily because of the need to support local family planning efforts.

This concept sounds meretricious. Where could the money be better spent than in Nicaragua? The population growth is a frightening 1 percent higher annually than food production. How could AID money be better spent than in family planning? Half of Managua's hospital beds are occupied by women suffering complications from illegal abortions. Roberto Castillo Quant, Nicaragua's vice-minister of public health, told me there are two to three abortions for every live birth.

I discussed the implications of these figures with Dr. Carlos H. Canales, Nicaragua's director general of public health, who is charged with the supervision and planning of PUMAR. Hanging on his office walls were maps identifying the placement of new mobile units and health centers to be funded by the new AID loan.

PADDOCK: What will the centers be used for?

CANALES: They will offer maternity and infant care; family planning; instruction in nutrition, personal hygiene, sanitation, other types of health education, and in prevention of polio and parasite infections; treatment of epidemic tuberculosis, typhoid, and measles; malaria control; convalescent care; and general medical attention.

PADDOCK: And the new mobile health units will offer more or less the same thing?

CANALES: That's right.

PADDOCK: What percentage of time will these new health centers and mobile units give to family planning?

CANALES *(Puzzled look).*

PADDOCK *(Rephrasing question):* Would you say 25 percent of time and money will go into family planning?

CANALES: No, it would be much less than that.

PADDOCK: 10 percent?

CANALES: I would say it would be less.

PADDOCK: Would you say 5 percent?

CANALES: No, it would be somewhat less.

PADDOCK: Would you say about 2 percent of the funds would be spent on family planning?

CANALES: Yes, I think that is about right.

But I would say that even 2 percent is a bit high. The reason for my skepticism is that Gardella, the U.S. public health advisor on the scene, told me bluntly that doctors working with the mobile health units do not have time to become involved with family planning.

In this, as in other ways, I regard PUMAR as a classic story of bureaucracy. The reality out there, in the field, is so completely at odds with the representation here, at the home office. PUMAR began merely as a president's desire to have a fast impact program showing something that would back up his perhaps too-fast rhetoric. It was conceived and set up within a couple of weeks as a health program, then, apparently as an afterthought, combined with the job of stimulating democracy through community development, and then with the building of health centers. Now, so it is announced, PUMAR takes on another job—family planning—for no reason other than it is the presently fashionable catch phrase needed to persuade Congress to expand the program with another $2 million loan.

It makes AID sound like a sort of shell game.

Mysteriously the pea rolls from under one shell, representing one publicized development goal, to another which catches public attention, and then to another and another. The eyes of the onlooker become confused.

Where is AID? Where is development? Under which shell?

Maybe it is not under any of them.

[5]

Conclusions: A "Miracle Drug"

PUMAR, EXPERIMENT STATIONS, supervised credit, and the others are small parts of a gigantic U.S. foreign aid program. Up to this writing, the program, excluding military aid, has cost approximately $150 billion.[1]

Why and how did the United States get into foreign aid in the first place? What was it meant to accomplish? How did it evolve into such a huge, worldwide operation?

Like most mammoth bureaucratic institutions, its origins were humble. How very humble only a few realize. It began with $80,000 and six U.S. technicians back in 1941 on the eve of Pearl Harbor. The U.S. government had suddenly realized the need to cement relations solidly with Latin America where sympathies were often strong for the German Nazis. Also the United States, threatened by Japan in Southeast Asia, looked to Latin America as the only easy alternate source for cinchona (for malaria), rubber and abaca (for naval rope), and other essentials such as tin. To protect these interests Nelson Rockefeller, then coordinator of Inter-American Affairs in the State Department, proposed (with Secretary Cordell Hull's support) an appropriation of $80,000 to pay the salaries and expenses of a half-dozen or so American experts to assist Latin American countries in health, agriculture, and other projects. When Congressman Thomas McMillan, chairman of the State, Commerce and Labor subcommittee, saw the request he instructed Jack McFall (whose story I am repeating here)[2] to inform Secretary Hull the item had not the slightest chance of passage. In 1941 the idea of paying experts to work for the benefit of foreign countries with U.S. government funds was too revolutionary for McMillan to swallow.

When McFall reported this to Hull, the secretary asked him whether he personally thought anything could be done to change

McMillan's mind. Hull's question was awkward because McFall was then the Appropriation Committee's executive secretary and was actually working for McMillan at that time. After some hesitation McFall replied—off the top of his head—"I have no authority to make any suggestions, but you might try to persuade the congressman and his subcommittee to visit Latin America to look into the matter."

Hull acted promptly. The novel suggestion was approved. McFall accompanied the group (the first such congressional fact-finding committee, he says, to tour abroad) on a two-week trip to eleven Latin American countries. The committee was convinced, and the first technical assistance appropriation was passed three months before Pearl Harbor. Foreign aid had begun.

It is important to remember the motivation for this $80,000 precedent: to protect the nation's rear on the eve of its entry into a war. Altruism was not a factor.

After the war the concept of foreign aid was escalated by President Truman. Roosevelt had died and Truman found himself heir to an exploding crisis with Russia. In Eastern Europe Russia was whisking nation after nation behind its Iron Curtain (as it was soon to be called).

When the British announced they could no longer afford to supply military assistance to Greece and Turkey—nations which Russia was eyeing covetously in a renewed thrust to acquire control over warm water ports in the Mediterranean—the United States acted. Under his Truman Doctrine, announced in March 1947, the president asked Congress to appropriate $400 million in economic and military aid to strengthen the two beleaguered nations.

Thus foreign aid was regarded as a sort of new "miracle drug" prescribed by the U.S. government for these two nations to strengthen their resistance to the Russian danger. The label on our foreign aid bottle stated unequivocally: "This remedy is to be used for fighting Communism."

Only three months later, in June 1947, Secretary of State George C. Marshall enlarged the scope of foreign aid by proposing a program to rebuild war-torn Europe. The Russians were quick to call the Marshall Plan an "imperialistic maneuver." We, as a nation, gave or loaned $12 billion from 1948 to 1951 to help Europe get on its feet. It created a strong Europe and one friendly to the United States. It preserved the peace for which we had fought so hard by helping halt the expansion of the Russian empire.

In the process, we came to label the miracle drug bottle: "This remedy is to be used for fighting Communism and making our allies strong in the cause of freedom."

Because the effectiveness of the Marshall Plan was soon apparent, Truman, in his 1949 inaugural address, declared as his "fourth point" that the United States would embark on a program to share U.S. technical knowledge with all the "poor and peace-loving" nations of the world.

With the best of intentions, and with few realizing it, our president had committed us to an overwhelming task:

—to support all those nations which needed help in defending themselves against Communism and/or Russia (e.g., Korea, Taiwan, Vietnam)

—to prop up with our money and "know how" all the newly emerging nations which formerly had been colonies (e.g., Africa)

—to maintain the status of the world's nations already in the column of "the free" (e.g., Latin America).

The Cold War provided the ideological justification to use foreign aid for all these purposes. Communism was likened to a disease. People living in unsanitary, undeveloped places were claimed to be especially susceptible to this disease.

We were so successful in popularizing this rationale for the miracle drug, hungry nations around the world began queuing up for it. Like trusting patients, sick from they knew not what, they had faith in their healer. To get the doctor's attention they often were eager to complain of an occasional "Communist" pain.

Now changes began to take place. We as a nation forgot why we had been administering aid in the first place. A new generation of Americans grew up, many of whom only vaguely understood how threatening Russia and Communism were after World War II. The once war-torn economies of Western Europe and Japan had become powerhouses.

As a summary, John Kenneth Galbraith could say in 1970, "It is fair to assume that the Western concern for a non-Communist development was matched [after WW II] by a Soviet anxiety for the opposite. Now, alas, we know that it doesn't matter. We know that the development [of the hungry nations] will be so slow that the question of what ultimately emerges is academic."[3]

Nevertheless American presidents right down the line (Truman, Eisenhower, Kennedy, Johnson) were all convinced that foreign aid was a crucial tool in their conduct of foreign affairs. Congressman Clarence Long of Maryland told me foreign aid "would be killed off tomorrow" if it were not for presidents fighting for it.

As a presidential candidate, Nixon inveighed against the misuse of aid. He told Republican members of Congress if they were opposed to foreign aid they should vote against it.[4] However, once elected, he too, succumbed. But after all these years the label on the bottle needed changing. The miracle drug could no longer be sold as a remedy merely "to fight Communism." Soon he was telling Congress that the usual political reasons given for foreign aid, i.e., to avert violence in the hungry nations and to strengthen our allies militarily (code words for fighting Communism) "do not do justice to our fundamental character and purpose. There is a moral quality in this nation that will not permit us to close our eyes to the want in this world. . . . A great nation must also be a good nation. We are doing what is right to do."[5]

The label on the bottle was getting longer. It now read: "This remedy is to be used for fighting Communism, making our allies strong in the cause of freedom, and bringing happiness to the unhappy."

Nixon was not the first to use altruism as his main argument for foreign aid. But previously altruism often had caused resentment among some foreign aid supporters. Senator George Aiken of Vermont, for one, did not agree that altruism is an argument for keeping on with aid. While the hungry nations may resent having been dominated or colonized in the past or are envious of our wealth, he said, "It does not follow that the United States and other rich countries should pay reparations in the form of foreign aid for the historical impact they have had. Nor does it follow that we should mount a crusade in the name of development in order to impose our ideas of progress on these countries."[6]

Nonetheless, the ailments for which the miracle drug was prescribed continued to broaden. In fact it even came to be sold as something good for Business U.S.A. In 1969 AID boasted that its programs paid for more than $1.1 billion in export sales by American firms. "These exports create several hundred thousand American jobs and build permanent markets for future cash exports." In addition, AID said, in the same year it had paid American shipping lines $95 million in freight charges.[7]

And to make the value of AID clear to voters everywhere, the agency listed what it spends, state by state, for commodities and for technical service contracts. The following four states were shown to have benefited in 1971.

AID-financed commodities in 1971		Technical service contracts in 1971
New York	$178,829,271	$190,009,364
California	80,508,640	49,965,733
Illinois	73,541,642	28,865,769
Texas	54,930,416	15,291,605

President Nixon endorsed this use of the miracle drug as good for Business U.S.A. by establishing the Overseas Private Investment Corporation which removes much of the risk for Americans doing business in the hungry world. It insures private U.S. investment against loss from revolution or expropriation up to $7.5 billion and guarantees loans against a wide array of risks up to $750 million.[8]

Congressman Thomas Steed of Oklahoma has called AID a "WPA for big business." (Works Progress Administration, a program designed to create jobs for the unemployed in the United States in the depression of the 1930s.)

However, not all industry looks upon foreign aid as a national need. In a memorable full page ad in *Forbes* (May 13, 1969) Warner & Swasey, a Cleveland precision machine company, said, "NO WONDER WE'RE BROKE!" and listed by country where the United States has sent $84 billion as a "give-away" in foreign aid. It concluded, "Any sane American—if he can control his temper long enough—can write his own editorial. Or obituary."

Henry Owen of the *Washington Post* has projected the basic quandary of AID: "Is development aid intended to sustain our foreign policy on a day-to-day basis by rewarding and assisting the faithful; or is it intended primarily to advance our long-range interest in a safer and more humane world by promoting economic development? Is it a spigot to be turned on and off as changing political conditions in the receiving countries dictate, or is it a long-range investment in the future, to be provided regardless of the day-to-day political shifts?"[9]

The quandary arises not only in trying to understand the ills for which the miracle drug is to be used, but also in trying to read the prescription itself. A doctor's "hen tracks" are no more baffling than the language used by AID. In *Front Lines* (January 30, 1969, and February 15, 1969) we find, for example, "deobligations," "obligational year budget," and "reobligations," and a "development loan," a "Cooley loan," a "program loan," a "project loan," and a "sector loan"—each with its own peculiar bureaucratic

meaning. To make use of the miracle drug today, one must understand the differences among items listed as military assistance, technical assistance, supporting assistance, project assistance, and program assistance.

All of which adds to the puzzlement of how much the miracle
drug costs. There is confusion in separating appropriations for
economic aid from military aid, food aid from commodity credit
corporation funds, export-import bank funds from allocations to
the development banks, as well as those mysterious sums which are
"coming through the pipeline." It is the rare accountant who can
understand exactly how much foreign aid costs. As the political
reasoning for its variety of activities becomes all encompassing,
the bookkeeping gets even more opaque. The 1970 AID appropriation was $1.7 billion but, according to Senator J. W. Fulbright,
the actual outlay contemplated was "around $5 billion."[10]

AID itself is a massive bureaucratic agency, a diffuse organization which presently provides jobs overseas for 7,000 Americans
on regular payroll, another 2,000 on contract, and some 16,500
foreign nationals.[11] And, of course, its hierarchy in Washington
is huge.

Writing about how AID has become so bloated, Edward A.
O'Neill likened the organization to the camel in the Arab's tent.
"Once these bureaucrats moved in a little, they kept pushing
farther and farther. Also, the perquisites, prestige and power of
serving the United States abroad became very attractive to department after department, agency after agency. And once a bureaucrat is firmly established, it is almost impossible to move him. For
example, in twelve countries where economic assistance programs
have long since been terminated, AID still has a total of 55 persons stationed."[12]

Nevertheless no agency of the government has been so
thoroughly reorganized, investigated or studied as has that in
charge of foreign aid. *This in itself* should indicate that something must be wrong with the label or contents of the foreign aid
bottle. The agency began as the Economic Cooperation Administration (1948), was reorganized and renamed the Mutual Security
Agency (1949), was reorganized and renamed the Foreign Operations Administration (1952), was reorganized and renamed the
International Cooperation Administration (1956), was reorganized
and renamed the Agency for International Development (AID)
(1962), and in 1970 was again reorganized. But nothing really
changes. As the Frenchman Karr said, *"Plus ça change, plus c'est*

la même chose [the more it changes, the more it remains the same]."

Since it began to prescribe the miracle drug for something more than "fighting Communism" this activity of the U.S. government has been under constant scrutiny. In its twenty-one years of formal life, the agency has been the subject of ten presidential committees; fourteen directors have been in charge of administering it—all in the hope that it could be made more effective. But changing a bureaucracy is difficult. When John Hannah, the Nixon-appointed AID administrator, first testified before the House Foreign Affairs Committee, Congressman Paul Findley of Illinois heaved a sigh of despair. "Why shouldn't I be disappointed?" he said. "The only new face I saw was Hannah's. He brought along with him all the people who have been testifying before us for years. And, of course, they said all the same things."

What "they" said in 1969 at the House hearings filled 1,700 pages of published testimony, a figure comparable to those of previous years—all considered relevant to AID's effort to prove that the United States knows how to conduct an effective foreign aid program.

In 1970, for instance, the subject of foreign assistance was once again studied intensively. Three major reviews by three blue-ribbon groups (Pearson, Rockefeller, and Peterson committees) had just released their recommendations.

The Pearson report was written for the World Bank at a time when its sources of funds were beginning to dry up. The eight men in this group consisted of two politicians, two bankers, and four economists. Their Rx: Give more money to the World Bank!

President Nixon had asked Governor Nelson Rockefeller to study how the United States could better help Latin America. With an entourage of thirty-six "distinguished" advisors (five were museum curators) Rockefeller made a highly publicized tour of the area—complete with anti-American demonstrations—and proposed his Rx: Give more money to Latin America!

To advise him how to utilize AID more effectively, Nixon appointed a super blue-ribbon committee. Led by Rudolph Peterson, president of Bank of America, this group of executives (David Rockefeller, Archbishop Terence Cooke, General Robert Wood, etc.) said they would approach the problem of foreign aid "as beginners, not experts."[13] Their Rx: Set up *four* new aid groups, and mush on!

Why is it that three such top level committees, like their so-many predecessors, made the same predictable recommendations?

Unfortunately they all suffer from a common defect. They do not include technicians who can shout the warning: "U.S. technology cannot do the job, no matter how much money is given!" The committees with their bankers and politicians and theoretical economists can assess the financial and political ramifications of aid, but they are incapable of determining if the money is producing any valid results out in the field, down the jungle trail, or ankle deep in the rice paddy.

WHAT HAS the miracle drug really cured in the undeveloped world? Books have been written and thousands of pages of congressional testimony taken to try and answer this question.

James Greenfield of Westinghouse Broadcasting Company has given the best concise summation I have heard with regard to the largest U.S. program, that for India ($8 billion, plus military aid): "If we did a two-hour documentary on American aid to the Indian subcontinent you'd hate it. There's almost nothing left to show for the money."[14]

The research for this book and my earlier experience in the field testify that when it comes to helping an alien nation cure its socioeconomic problems, we don't know how.

Therefore should we continue this ineffectual foreign aid?

Fifty-one percent of the American voters, when polled in 1969, said "no."[15] A year later 66 percent said foreign aid was the place where the federal government should first begin cutting expenses.[16]

Volunteers:
The Irrepressible Urge to Help

My friend says: "The most difficult thing in the world is to serve mankind, knowing you cannot change it."

The Innocents

EACH NEW GROUP *entering any phase of foreign assistance always seems to approach it as though it was the first to discover the subject or, at the very least, it goes at it with a hearty contempt for all that has gone before. The homily—that one should try to learn from experience—has had little place in either government-supported or privately sponsored aid programs.*

I was sitting at a table beside the swimming pool of the Biltmore Hotel in Guatemala City writing up my log of the day's interviews, when I became aware that six men at the next table were discussing development plans for Guatemala.

Of course, I stopped to eavesdrop.

All of them were Americans and had been talking for fifteen minutes, I guess, before I tuned in. When I went over later and introduced myself, I learned that the advisor of the group was the former executive director of a foundation whose effectiveness in providing overseas assistance had been endorsed by presidents Kennedy, Johnson, and Nixon. Two of the men in the group were wealthy businessmen from upstate New York who had generously decided to contribute money and time to set up their own program to help feed the people of at least one hungry nation.

Why they had chosen Guatemala is irrelevant, for any old-time development man will immediately recognize their attitudes, their words, their infectious enthusiasm, and undimmed optimism as typical of "developers"—even at the highest levels in Washington, Paris, the United Nations, a major foundation, or wherever.

The sincerity of the men in the group and their basic Christian goodwill are also typical, and I urge that their conversation not be interpreted as a caricature of naiveté. On the contrary, they were too highly motivated for that.

I give the discussion unedited—as I wrote it down. My pencil could not catch it all, hence the gaps.

. . . What are the crops they raise here?

. . . Don't know, but we can ask AID or the [U.S.] Department of Agriculture.

. . . How about those silos? Let's put them up in four or five places so we can save time. We need a crash program.

. . . Need to wake people up to the problem. If the silos work in one of the five places, they ought to work in the rest of the country.

. . . We need dual financing . . . financing for experimental work.

. . . What's that?

. . . You know, the four or five locations.

. . . Right.

. . . We need financing for selling the project. Who's going to do that?

. . . That's what we've got to talk about now.

. . . World's going to starve to death in 1976, so we don't have much time.

. . . How much time do we have?

. . . Two years.

. . . Let's work on that basis. We ought to have these silos built by then. These local speculators [in corn] have got to be shown what's what.

. . . That means we've got to have a crash program. Sure, we don't need to take all the time these government people take, hell, they don't know how to come in out of the rain.

. . . How about trying these silos out in the U.S. first?

. . . Why not in Oregon first? The *altiplano* region here is just like Oregon. Same conditions.

. . . Right. Great idea.

. . . Can we get some built by August in Oregon to show these people what we can do?

. . . Don't know why not.

. . . We've got to hurry. That's what we've got to remember. Speed!

. . . Hey, maybe Honduras would be a better place to start. They get three crops a year there and only two here.

. . . How do they plant corn? Anyone here ever planted corn? (Silence)

. . . Hell, the Department of Agriculture can tell us that. What we need to know is how to change the system here. It's bound to be lousy.

. . . You mean we don't have a contract to do this yet? How do we get one?

. . . That's what we're talking about now. We've got to get a plan first.

. . . Right. That's what we need, a contract and a plan. The plan, I guess, comes first.

. . . These people [the Guatemalans] don't even know how to use a screwdriver. You can't imagine how easy it would be to double their food production once you get them to accept our ideas.

. . . What ideas do you mean?

. . . You know, modern machinery. That's what they need.

. . . Right. Think what a tractor would do here!

. . . How about strawberries? Hell, they use a lot of strawberries in the states.

. . . That's a great idea!

. . . Strawberries grow ten months of the year, and all you do is plant them and cultivate. Wonder why they don't raise them here.

. . . Personally, I think this coconut idea is worth looking into. Of course, you can't use them all, but how about 15 or 20 million coconuts?

. . . There ought to be a market for that many.

. . . Why not go into the cattle business or raise pigs. We could feed the coconuts to the pigs. We'll get the natives to harvest the coconuts to feed to the pigs.

. . . You know, we ought really to work with the missionaries here. They have contacts, and contacts count with these Indians just as they do in New York.

. . . Maybe there are [agricultural] experts here who know what the problems are. Some of them ought to speak Spanish. We ought to get them working for us.

. . . There are some people who have tremendous clout in this country. We should take advantage of them. Let's use them.

. . . Right. Fantastic idea.

. . . There's this gringo in Nicaragua. You wouldn't believe what he has done, what he's been through. He's been a miner, a cardsharp, a bootlegger. He's dumped a quarter of a million dollars in the shrimp business off of Nicaragua. That guy's really learned what's what around here. He's just had a plane crash, saved his friend by shooting the hinges off the cockpit door so he could get out. Thinking he had bullets left in his carbine to protect himself against the crocodiles, he floated miles down the river until he was rescued. And you know what?

. . . What?

. . . He didn't have any bullets left for the crocs after all!

. . . Now there's a guy we could use.

. . . And he's young, really knowledgeable.

. . . And there are these Cubans we could use, too. Of course, you have to be careful because the Nicaraguan army just bumps off all the Cubans it finds. Saves the problem of a trial. Lot of them are good and we could use them, but we have to find them before the Nicaraguan army finds them.

. . . Right . . .

[6]

A Peace Corps Star Is Born

I WATCHED the growing legend of great deeds performed by the Peace Corps with fascination, continually amazed at the astounding feats attributed to its youngsters, partly because I myself had worked in overseas development when I was young. Another reason was, I suppose, the admiration of one safecracker for the skill of another, at the smooth, easy way the Peace Corps was able to pry money out of Congress.

Particularly, I marveled at the brazenness with which the Corps "got away with" its own boasts of self-proclaimed successes. Without a quiver, the Corps' first director, R. Sargent Shriver (President Kennedy's brother-in-law), could write, "Each day supplies new evidence that Peace Corps volunteers are the best bearers of good will that this nation—perhaps any nation—ever sent beyond its borders."[1] And neither press nor public, swept away with joy that "goodwill" must somehow mean "success in development," asked for proofs. Think of the trouble AID would have had in justifying an extravagant statement like that. Whatever else it may have aimed for, the Peace Corps has been a wildly successful publicity organization. Only after a decade of operation have cracks appeared in the shiny enamel. With skilled public relations operatives on the payroll and a gullible press, the Peace Corps had presidents, congressmen, and leading citizens from all walks of life glorifying the idea of sending idealistic, totally untrained young folk to "live with the natives" and teach them how to modernize their backward country.

A Peace Corps project was thus a logical item for my research itinerary. Despite my bias, already shown, I was hoping to prove myself wrong by describing an example of the Peace Corps at its best.

I began with a long and pleasant interview with Jack Hood

Vaughn, then director of the Peace Corps. Two of his higher officers sat in on our interview, one of them in charge of agricultural programs, the other a former foreign service officer.

I asked my usual question, "Which projects of the Peace Corps in Central America have been most effective?" (The Peace Corps has never been invited to establish a program in Mexico.) I explained further I wanted suggestions on projects that had been in operation for some time, or at least long enough so I could look into their long-range effectiveness.

Vaughn, a soft-spoken executive, said it was hard to define "effective." With disarming frankness he added that the true aim of the Peace Corps is "to promote friendship and international understanding. Any sort of economic progress that comes out of its activities in a developing country is a side issue. The Peace Corps," he emphasized, "is not a junior AID. The Peace Corps is to bring PEACE."

Thus Vaughn differed markedly from his predecessor, Sargent Shriver. As director, Shriver rarely failed to emphasize that the Peace Corps' first goal was "to help the people of developing nations meet their needs for trained manpower."[2]

Summing up what the volunteers had accomplished in their first four years, Shriver had written:

> They taught literally millions of hours of classes. They fed hundreds of thousands of children in school lunch programs. They stimulated self-help programs in thousands of remote villages. They organized programs in the slums of most of the major cities of Latin America. They reformed agricultural practices, built schools, helped modernize hospitals, organized country clinics. They conducted surveys and geological expeditions, codified laws, organized cooperatives, and found markets for the works of craftsmen where none before existed. They even assisted countries at the birth of nation-wide educational television systems.[3]

In contrast Vaughn avoided making such grand claims. Indeed claims of this sort had created one of his own worst problems: an insistent Congress was pressuring him to send even more volunteers overseas, to multiply the impact of such a fantastically successful program and to placate constituents whose sons and daughters wanted to join up. In fact, Vaughn was trying to curtail some of the Corps' activities. A once small program in Colombia with thirty volunteers when it was launched in 1961 had ballooned into a program with close to a thousand volunteers by the time Vaughn became director in 1966. But he was fighting a losing battle in trying to keep the number of volunteers overseas within manageable limits. The program at that time was just too popular with the American press and public.

During our interview Vaughn expressed interest in my research trip and provided a thoughtful review of Peace Corps activities. But when I persisted in asking *where* in Central America I might see an effective program, he hedged, saying that at the moment he could not think of any specific examples. However, he added, with all the assurance of his predecessor, "no doubt there are dozens of them." He advised me to get the specifics from staff members of the Corps when I arrived in Central America.

This was not the definite sort of answer for which I had hoped. So I reminded Vaughn of an example he had stressed at a meeting at the State Department in 1963.[4] Vaughn was then Peace Corps regional director for Latin America and had just returned from a Central American trip with his boss, Shriver. Vaughn singled out for praise a volunteer named James Portman, working in El Salvador, and called him "one of the Peace Corps' finest." I would long since have forgotten his remarks, except he also claimed Portman had "revolutionized the tomato industry" of that nation. I made notes on this at the time because I had just returned from ten years' work in agriculture in Central America and ought to have heard about such an event.

"Ah, yes," Vaughn answered, seemingly pleased I had jogged his memory. "The legend of the man continues to grow. You know, he lost eighty pounds in El Salvador during his assignment, and his success with tomatoes produced a great leap forward."

I questioned how a young man, fresh out of college, could perform such a miracle—revolutionize a whole industry while spending less than a year in a small village. Vaughn reminded me not to forget that Portman came to his job with a bachelor's degree in plant pathology. I countered by noting that AID then had in El Salvador a particularly outstanding Ph.D., a specialist in horticulture, who had worked there for a number of years. "Wouldn't you expect him to make more progress than a young man just out of college?"

At that point one of the other officials present said, "Maybe the AID man did send in four or five reports, but no one at AID headquarters ever pays attention to such reports. They end up in a file drawer. The Peace Corps knows the importance of such things as tomatoes because it works with the little people, something AID doesn't do."

By the end of the interview Vaughn still had made no specific

suggestions on projects to visit. But because he had again emphasized that Portman's success with tomatoes had "produced a great
leap forward" and that "his legend continues to grow," I said
this would be a good Peace Corps site to visit and I would do so.

As a preliminary, I checked the library and found there was no
dearth of published material on Portman.[5] These included books
and articles in which Portman was cited for working in "the poorest
village of all El Salvador," being "extremely religious," and having
"worked something of a development miracle in the village to
which he had been assigned."

The Published Record of What Portman, One Peace Corps Volunteer, Accomplished in Less Than One Year in the Town of Tonacatepeque, El Salvador

1. He organized a 200-boy 4-H Club. He taught the boys the
fundamentals of nutrition. Out of his own pocket he bought 100
ducklings and 300 chicks to teach the boys how to care for, feed,
kill and dress poultry. He assured the town of an abundant supply
of eggs and poultry. He had his boys plant flowers with seed donated by an American firm. The seeds from these were gathered
and sold at two cents a packet.
2. He started tomato, pineapple, watermelon, peanut, and banana
clubs. Their purpose was to stimulate the raising and planting of
seedlings. "For instance, I would give each boy in the banana club
50 banana trees. The boy would plant these trees, and when they
matured, he would have seedlings to plant the next year," Portman
was quoted as saying.
3. He taught two home economics clubs for girls and gave instruction on such subjects as canning pickles. He persuaded a New
York relief agency to send him two sewing machines and 500 yards
of cloth. With these he set up a sewing class for the girls. He
taught them to make braided cloth rugs from scrap cloth. The rugs
had Amish motifs which Portman had learned while working with
the Pennsylvania Dutch when he attended Pennsylvania State University.
4. He developed a town park and was active in directing recreation activities for the village children.
5. He introduced to local farmers the technique of mulching for
moisture conservation. They harvested a bumper vegetable crop.
He himself planted a huge demonstration garden next to the town's

church. Soon there were enough vegetables for the entire village, and even a small surplus which was sold in neighboring towns.

6. Apparently a Catholic, he worked with the local parish priest to bring people back to the church. He rewired the chandelier over the altar. He attended mass every Sunday and stimulated the local townspeople to do likewise. "Because he was so well liked . . . the Church enjoyed a renaissance."

7. Out of his own pocket he purchased expensive aluminum molds to cast religious statues. Proceeds from the sale of these figures supported some of his many projects.

8. He provided medical assistance. "I did some doctoring—giving vaccinations, helping deliver babies, bandaging cut feet."

9. He completed construction on a football field and a swimming pool.

10. He ". . . also gave haircuts as part of a sanitation program, trying to get rid of lice."

11. He taught weight lifting with barbells "he bought for the town's recreation."

12. "Portman converted [the farmers] to contour-planting and terracing, thereby saving crops and adding three and four hundred dollars a year to each farmer's income—a fortune in the poor country."

The above, plus Vaughn's statement of his revolutionizing the nation's tomato industry, summarize the published record of Portman's activities in Tonacatepeque. Not included are additional accomplishments attributed to him while serving elsewhere in El Salvador as well as during his Peace Corps training period.

One U.S. official told me, "Portman could have been elected mayor of Tonacatepeque." Spurred by these recitals, I was eager to have a look at the village where Portman had made such an impression.

Yet on my arrival in El Salvador, Miss B. Hutchinson, director of the Peace Corps program there, had never heard of Portman! Fortunately the name rang a bell with Mrs. Emmy Velis, an American married to a Salvadoran, who has worked in the Peace Corps office in El Salvador almost from its opening. I found her my most valuable source of information on the history of the Peace Corps in that country. If she is still there, I suggest the Corps would do well to send a stenographer to record her memoirs. The El Salvador office would then be the only one in the world, I daresay, to have an adequate record of its own past.

These two women, assisted by a physician, had the impossible job of overseeing 100 corpsmen scattered over the country. They were responsible for receiving them on arrival, briefing them as to local conditions, arranging for their transportation, and a hundred other details.

However, their most important task was to negotiate job slots for the volunteers in various local government agencies and to arrange for new jobs for volunteers dissatisfied with their old ones —all obviously time consuming.

As if that were not enough, the two of them had to cope with the inevitable personal problems of the postadolescent youngsters entrusted to their care. I soon thought of these pleasant, sincere women as overworked summer camp counselors. They, too, were in the counselors' position of not knowing as much about their children as they would have liked when parents (Washington) called.

Other duties notwithstanding (the day I arrived a memorial service had to be organized for a volunteer who had drowned in the ocean), Miss Hutchinson arranged for one of the corpsmen to accompany me on a visit to the village where Portman had served. The young man, Earl Threadgould, was a likable fellow.

It turned out, somewhat to my surprise, that Tonacatepeque is only fifteen miles from the capital, San Salvador. About half the distance is paved and the rest is exceedingly dusty during the dry season—like other such roads in Central America. But the dust and the road presented no particular hazard, even to my low-slung Detroit car.

From past experience in accompanying visiting brass on inspection tours of U.S.-financed foreign projects, I could see that Tonacatepeque would make an ideal "project town." Including inspection time, the trip from the capital and back was a leisurely half day. Thus visiting officials could be back in time for a good lunch at the big hotel or for drinks before dinner. The dustiness of the road would convince the official he had been roughing it out in the bush.

On arrival I could see at once that Tonacatepeque is not "the poorest village in all El Salvador." On the contrary, it is a better-than-typical, rather large town of a kind one sees throughout Central America. It is not particularly prosperous looking because it is outside the nation's principal coffee-growing region. But it has a sizable central plaza with a church on one side and the mayor's office on another; electric, telephone, and telegraph facilities; wide streets; and nicely plastered buildings.

Jim Carpenter, a volunteer then assigned to the town, introduced us to some of the townspeople. He had recently married a Salvadoran girl and had extended his tour of duty. The Carpenters had ingeniously converted their one-room quarters into a rather pleasant home, with such amenities as a refrigerator and a hi-fi.

As a practice the Peace Corps does not normally staff the same town with successive volunteers, the reasoning being that this builds a "sense of dependency" on the part of the village. By not providing replacement volunteers, the Peace Corps claims it encourages the town itself to follow through on projects already started. (One official said the policy allows the United States to show the flag in more places.) Carpenter, most personable, was the second volunteer to serve in Tonacatepeque.

We walked around the plaza, stopping at various business establishments to talk to the owners. We asked if they remembered Portman and what he was like. We talked to the family with whom Portman had lived and to a local druggist who had won in a raffle one of the religious figures Portman had made. We spoke with the mayor and a school teacher.

To make a long story short, there was no evidence that Portman had "revolutionized" the tomato industry of either El Salvador or Tonacatepeque. Local townspeople did recall he had planted some tomatoes in a garden by the church. Some said he also had a second garden and he had taken good care of both of them. But commercial production of tomatoes in Tonacatepeque is as nonexistent today as it always has been. I am still at a loss, even after raising the question later in correspondence with Portman, to explain just how the original myth gained currency to the point of it being repeated by Vaughn in Washington and, presumably, elsewhere.

I was able to track down only one local reference to his activities with tomatoes. A storekeeper told me Portman had used cow dung on a tomato patch to demonstrate the use of fertilizer. "I was growing tomatoes there myself for my family," the merchant said. "I asked him what I should do to get rid of insects that were devouring them on the stem. He replied he did not know anything about tomatoes, only corn."

In checking out whether use of commercial fertilizer had increased as a result of Portman's stay, I ran into a blank wall. The level of fertilizer sales has remained constant. The local government agricultural extension office could not find records showing any activity by Portman in this or in any other regard, though he had presumably been assigned to work with that office. So much for Portman's impact on the nation's tomato industry.

I asked about the sewing project. No one remembered anything at all about the 500 yards of cloth or the sewing machines. Some remembered that he kept a few ducks and chickens at his house, a not uncommon practice among local people. Others recalled that he had planted some trees in the main square.

In fact the only tangible evidence of Portman's stay in Tonacatepeque was the religious figure the druggist still had.

From my visit to Tonacatepeque I concluded Portman does seem to have impressed the local townspeople favorably. They liked him; he had been popular with the girls and also with their mothers. He had been well behaved, and it is clear he did not in any way damage the image of the United States.

Of his own free will he returned to spend Christmas in the town after he had been transferred elsewhere. He brought with him 400 pounds of toys donated by the office staff of the Parke, Davis Drug Company of Detroit. The local townspeople remembered these toys, though some said they had come from wealthy Salvadorans living in the capital, others from Peace Corps volunteers, and others from Portman himself.

Somehow the picture of Portman playing Santa Claus to the townspeople sticks in my mind. When he had first come to live there, think how he must have stood out—the first American most of them had ever talked with. He must have been like a lighthouse and easily to have outshown the local men. His image must have been cast in heroic dimensions. His Peace Corps leader in El Salvador referred to the "elements of saintliness" in his character.[6] And, to repeat, Jack Vaughn in Washington claimed "his legend continues to grow."

Fortunately Portman himself seems to have been aware of such excesses. "Do not believe everything you read about JJP [James J. Portman] and El Salvador," he counseled Carpenter in a letter. "R. Sargent Shriver in the early days was a little too eager as far as public relations were concerned."

By the time I left Tonacatepeque I had the distinct impression that Portman had been liked because he was young and attractive, courteous, good company, and a new face from a strange land, though the townspeople never understood what the blazes he was doing among them.

In this regard, a remark by Carpenter was illuminating. "My first six months here were mighty rough. There were no friends I could develop. I had no way to identify with the people. I didn't feel needed. There was no way to communicate with them. You can sit around all night and drink beer with the people and supposedly develop understanding. But if you don't have something to do as a job they begin to wonder what the devil you are doing in the town."

While this one case study obviously does not constitute evidence with which to evaluate the whole Peace Corps, I have no reason, based on my personal observations of Peace Corps activities throughout Latin America, to believe that the Portman story is an exception. I have talked with administrative officers in the capital cities and with volunteers working in the field. I cannot recall ever having visited any program or having heard about any verifiable program I would call "effective development."

The exceptions to this statement involve the efforts of volunteers working within existing, well-established programs. Here again Portman is a case in point. His Peace Corps file showed that he worked with some modicum of success with a 4-H Club, an organization which has a long history in Latin America. He raised chickens and ducklings supplied to him through the Heifer Program, a well-established farmer-to-farmer program which operates globally. He set up the sewing project with the help of machines donated by Cáritas, a Catholic relief agency.

And there are several other programs in which volunteers have functioned effectively, for example: the school lunch and school construction programs administered under AID.

My criticism is that Peace Corps volunteers cannot, and do not, fulfill the goal publicized by the Peace Corps leadership, the goal for which Congress annually appropriates more than $100 million. To quote again from Shriver, the first director, the primary goal of the Peace Corps is "to help the people of developing nations meet their needs for trained manpower."

This it does not know how to do.

[7]

Good Intentions Are Not Enough

ANYONE WHO THINKS Christianity is dying has not traveled off the beaten track in the developing world. He would then realize that a missionary outpost from some European or American church is at every crossroad, or at least it seems that way.

The work of these outposts goes on and on even though back home, congregations may get restless and lower their support for activities which do not seem as relevant today as when launched on a wave of enthusiasm yesterday. Today one important change can be found in their type of programs: while proselytizing in the name of one's own God is still theoretically the goal, modern missionaries spend the bulk of their time trying to make some of the benefits of twentieth-century science and technology available to the sick, hungry, and ignorant with whom they have chosen to live and work. Today it is the salvation of development they offer.

A major distinction exists between them and government aid personnel. The latter are carrying forward national policies which are influenced by a multitude of political factors. The missionaries eschew all political (and economic) considerations. Therefore as they gradually eliminate (in most cases) active proselytization as a meaningful part of their work, there remains to them only "do-goodism" in its purest essence. The missionary is content simply to do good and he (or his missionary board) is the sole arbiter in deciding what kinds of projects should be initiated within that framework.

It is inevitable that his compatriots must question why this effort and money should be spent in foreign countries with little or no coordination with the home government or even with other missionary groups. Is he abroad merely because he has an urge to go to some exotic foreign corner to do good rather than to stay at home and face up to resolving local, unexotic problems? Certainly whatever tasks the missionaries take unto themselves to do abroad, they could do just as well (and probably a lot more effectively) in the backward areas of their home countries.

Yet one tends to admire the person who goes abroad solely to do good and thereby gives up personal ambition and accustomed comforts.

To illustrate such a spirit I single out Abelardo Morales as one who surely reveals altruism at its best. Technically he is not a missionary, but he works for a church organization. A Mexican-American from California, Morales grew up on a truck farm, studied sociology, and graduated from San José State College. He married his childhood sweetheart and together they volunteered to work for a Quaker-sponsored agricultural program in Mexico. A big, handsome fellow, he has more than an average share of the paragon qualities found in most of the young people working for U.S. government and privately sponsored programs throughout the world.

But I am getting ahead of my story. In Mexico I especially wanted to visit the community development activities of the American Friends Service Committee (AFSC), a Quaker program that has been active in Mexico for some thirty years (a millenium in the world of short-lived aid projects and organizations). As an old, well-established effort, the AFSC enjoys a good reputation among development professionals. Over the years its program in Mexico has attracted well-qualified volunteers from several countries, such as Morales with his practical background in agriculture. Furthermore, AFSC has survived in Mexico—a country which is chary of foreign-sponsored programs—perhaps because it makes extensive use of Mexicans in key administrative posts.

Another reason for wanting to visit the AFSC was that in recent years it has shifted its emphasis to agricultural and population projects. Before, the AFSC had been involved mostly in numerous small-scale village development endeavors. It helped build recreational centers, install local water supply systems, upgrade housing, and the like. Its reputation for success with this type of project helps explain why it was one of the models studied closely by those who set up the Peace Corps.

However, unlike the Peace Corps which has continually expanded its programs and number of volunteers overseas, the AFSC has kept its effort in Mexico manageably small. There is something peculiarly Quaker about this urge to maintain a sense of proportion about things, of scale, even of inconspicuousness about what they do. Whatever the precise reason, any single AFSC program in Mexico does not involve more than a dozen or so young people at one time.

Edwin Duckles was directing the AFSC Mexican program when I was there. With his wife he also was running the Casa de Los Amigos (The Friends' House) in downtown Mexico City—a kind of half-way station for students and social workers involved in AFSC projects.

Duckles is a dedicated man: a full-time salesman for the AFSC and the guiding force behind the Mexican program. He is clearly in charge. He already knew of my personal interest in agriculture and population control prior to our meeting. Consequently in the beginning I was not surprised that he emphasized the AFSC's special concern with raising productivity on Mexican farms and with strengthening local birth control programs. The AFSC, for example, had sponsored meetings on population issues which had attracted the deans from eighteen Mexican medical schools. It had guided the rectors (presidents) of four Mexican universities on a tour of U.S. universities for the purpose of convincing them of the need for family planning courses in their own institutions. This was no mean feat in a country whose newly elected president, Luis Echeverría, had eight children and who had campaigned strongly against the promotion of birth control.

I was equally impressed by what Duckles had to say about the AFSC work in agriculture. The basic thesis is that the bulk of technology needed for increasing agricultural yields is already known; what is lacking is a willingness by the *campesino* to put this technology to his own use. The reason he does not, according to Duckles, is that the *campesino* is fearful of risking what little money he does make, and even of losing his labor investment should he use the new techniques before they have been absolutely proven—in front of his own eyes in his own valley.

Some years ago the AFSC began working with a group of farmers near the village of San Felipe Cuauhtenco in the state of Tlaxcala to see if a way could be found to overcome this fearfulness. First Duckles and his volunteers made a sincere effort to become acquainted with the farmers and a few of their problems. Then AFSC workers set about introducing the local farmers to local bankers so the latter would understand the farmers' needs. In trying to open up a dialogue between banker and farmer, the AFSC was attacking an age-old obstacle to the introduction of new technology in the developing world, namely, a lack of available credit for the small farmer.

Duckles related the following dialogue to illustrate the difficulties involved:

BANKER: Tell me, how much are you able to produce on your land?

FARMER: Well, that depends. It depends on how good our weather is. It depends on whether the rains fall when we want them to. It depends on how much damage the birds do. It depends . . .

BANKER *(interrupting impatiently)*: Don't bother me with details. Just tell me: how much can you make off your land?

The farmer is left speechless by the question. A local storekeeper from the village who sells a little fertilizer and seed to the farmer speaks up, "I can answer that by asking how much does an automobile cost in Mexico City?"

BANKER: Well, that depends on whether it is a new car or a used car and whether it is a big car or a small car.

FARMER *(seeing the light)*: Don't bother me with the details, just tell me how much a car costs!

In spite of semantic problems, Duckles and the AFSC field workers have often managed to bring the banker and the farmer together. To encourage the latter to take a chance on bank loans in order to invest in new technology, the AFSC guarantees the farmer's basic income. Farmers are told that if their yields are lower than the previous year, the AFSC would make up the cash difference. This has proved to be a workable arrangement. With limited funds, the AFSC has demonstrated the feasibility of raising farm production by taking the risk out of trying new ideas.

I visited some villages where the program has been under way for several years. Abelardo Morales was in charge of the one at San Felipe Cuauhtenco. He was assisted by two young American AFSC couples whose education had not been in agriculture. They were encouraging the *campesinos,* pure-blooded Tlaxcalans, to become involved with the cooperative program.

Their advice to the Indian farmer was simplified to two practices: using a fertilizer that includes trace elements, and seeding each acre more densely.

The AFSC claims that use of this rudimentary technology has increased yields by 400 to 800 percent and brought harvests up to 145 bushels per acre.[1] "As a result of the use of these improved methods, the corn production was increased from an *average* [emphasis added] of 800 kilos per hectare up to 4000 kilos per hectare . . ."[2]

I had no way of checking out these figures. As I went over the fields with Morales, the fertilized ones looked better vegetatively than those not fertilized. However, individual ears of corn were small. In fact I had difficulty accepting such statistics. The eye can lie but, nonetheless, 145 bushels per acre is a superior Iowa yield, and my eye said this was not Iowa. The one big reason for my skepticism was that I saw no hybrid corn seed planted and such high yields traditionally come only with hybrid seed. I asked Morales why he did not request a hybrid seed recommendation from the nearby Rockefeller Foundation-sponsored "Plan Puebla" project. He said he had and was told to plant the unimproved local varieties because they do better, even though Rockefeller-financed corn research is carried on only sixty miles away and has been in operation there for twenty-five years. I later checked with the foundation scientists and they confirmed that no improved corn varieties had been developed for the area where the Quakers are working. Also they confirmed that the foundation itself has nothing better to use in its own *campesino* program—the newly initiated Plan Puebla.

The AFSC claims some spectacular increase in farm incomes as a result of the program (on one farm profit rose from $140 to $3,645, on another from $00.00 to $4,029, and on a third farm from $200 to $1,681).[3] "Thus, in just one year this group of formerly subsistence farmers entered the Mexican economy as producers of surpluses which enabled them to add improvements to their houses, purchase more land and farm animals, buy sewing machines for their wives, and most important, look toward the future with hope."[4] But I question the validity of such a statement as well as the exceedingly dramatic income figures, for data on the farm incomes prior to the arrival of the AFSC were sketchy to say the least, certainly little more than guesses. On such shaky data it would be difficult to justify these statistical increases.

On the other hand, there was Morales—the dedicated sort of young man we all like to picture as the American ideal. On our field trip he rushed me across sandy, broken, eroded fields high up on the slopes of Mount Malinche to show me plots which had been fertilized. He assured me this year's harvest would be better than last year's. He husked an ear, compelling me to say it was fuller, heavier, bigger, more bountiful. He pointed out where the plantings were closer together than they had been in the past. He waited while I spoke with a herdsman, and was proud of the man for identifying the greener fields as those where chemicals had been used. Before our hike ended my shoes were filled with dust and pebbles, my balance had been tested as we forded a stream by "monkey bridge," and my lungs were pumped clean in meeting the demands of such exertion at high altitude.

But in addition to the fuller ears of corn, the thicker plantings, the fertilized fields, I also noticed the Indians. Surely they are as poorly off today as they had been at the time of the Conquest. They live in a village completely isolated from twentieth-century Mexico. For many of them the walk from the village to their *milpas* gets longer each year as farming is forced upwards on the mountainsides by the pressures of growing populations.

I talked of this with Morales and his wife back at their house as we refreshed ourselves with a wedge of pie baked for the occasion. Morales spoke of the Indian's hard life. To him the program is justifiable because it is the first break the Indian has had in centuries. He said the Indian could now pay off his loan and even have a little bit left over. That little extra represented hope, he felt. His question to me was, "How can I help more people? How can I do this same thing again and again?"

When I discussed the effectiveness of the AFSC agricultural program with Rockefeller agricultural scientists in Mexico, I encountered mixed reactions. One said the AFSC program is mainly one of "living together" with the Indians and helping them as best one can. Another was critical of the program at every step of the way and said he felt Mexico could make more progress if "all the do-gooders were run out of the country."

POST MORTEM:

Several months after my visit Morales left the AFSC to work near Guadalajara in a larger rural development program, a cooperative farming project backed by an American philanthropist. The agricultural program at Cuauhtenco continued for a while, but its days were numbered. Today it is closed.

His departure illustrates the major weakness of the AFSC-type program: the organization does not know how to maintain continuity. As one Rockefeller scientist put it, "When the AFSC has someone interested in agriculture, then it has an agricultural program. When it has a veterinarian, it has an animal science program. There is no consistency."

Here I take the side of the people being "helped" as they ask, "Why raise my expectations if you cannot stay long enough to show me how to fulfill them? Your good intentions are not enough!"

Indeed, as a gutsy, old-time missionary friend once told me, "As a development tool, good intentions are no substitute for continuity or for genuine know-how. Good intentions are not enough. Monkeys picking fleas have good intentions."

THE MEDICAL MISSIONARY is a man I have always admired. Few books have made a deeper impression on me than *An American Doctor's Odyssey*, by Victor Heiser, published in 1936. The story tells of a Rockefeller Foundation employee who helped bring the benefits of modern medicine to Southeast Asia, and it contributed as much as anything I read in my formative years toward inspiring me to work among the peoples of the hungry nations.

Nonetheless I would never have gone to visit Dr. Stephen Youngberg's Pan American Health Service on Lake Yojoa in Honduras even had it been only one mile out of the way. I had developed an intuitive bias against his program long before this trip, dating, in fact, from the time I had first made his acquaintance.

In retrospect, this seems strange. He had bought a dozen hard-cover copies of my last book, and we met for the first time when he brought them by my home to be autographed—I have few friends as active in my behalf!

My impression of him then was of a slender, humble person who seemed just too much of a do-gooder. But these visual impressions were not what irritated me; rather it was the approach he was using to solicit contributions for his work.

One leaflet he left at my house showed two frightfully gaunt children, the older one holding the bony wrist of the younger. One had a bloated stomach, the other a concave one. Their arms consisted of mere bones with a thin coating of skin. Both had vacuous, subhuman expressions on their faces.

The picture bore the headline: "Could you help my little brother?" Beneath the photo was this caption:

> I'm Rolando. I'm five and weigh 16 pounds. He's Armando. He's hungry. He'll soon be three and weighs 11 pounds. Every day in this world, 4,000 children like us die of starvation. Send your contribution to the Pan American Health Service.

Another brochure described the precise treatment given to eighty-three individual children in the orphanage-hospital run by Dr. Youngberg at Lake Yojoa. The language irritated me for it was a hard sell for money. An eleven-year-old girl named Elvira, for example, was described as "the one who had the long white worms crawl out of her nose when we gave her medicine." A picture of Rufino described him as "in critical condition a month ago, convulsing, vomiting worms. Had to be carried."

This sort of appeal seemed too shrill, too much of an overstatement.

But fate stepped in; I found myself on the road from San Pedro Sula to Tegucigalpa, the capital of Honduras. This trip was soon to become one of the pleasanter motoring experiences on the continent. At this time the new route was not completed, and I had to follow the old road, which had as many potholes as on the day I had first traveled it a dozen years earlier.

Few cars were in evidence that day, but a fairly constant trickle of trucks carrying produce. As I neared the halfway point between the cities I was tired of following ruts in the road and was looking forward to the view of Lake Yojoa—the one lake of note in Honduras. As I swerved around a bend, I saw a large, somewhat dilapidated sign saying PAN AMERICAN HEALTH SERVICE.

My reaction was not to stop. But, oh well, why not? It would provide a respite from the miserable road and a chance to verify the accuracy of my already formed negative impressions.

I found Youngberg busy at work in one of several temporary buildings. He was treating a woman for a scalp infection, while explaining its causes to two of her friends. He looked up, surprised to see a visitor.

Few foreign tourists made the trip between the two cities by road. No one who could afford air fare drove that road unless he had to. The place was extremely well kept and entirely enclosed by a double fence to prevent the children from wandering off. As we moved about, some of the stronger children swarmed around us and nuzzled us like affectionate puppies. Everything was spotlessly clean, even though it was apparent from the poorly constructed, ticky-tack buildings that Youngberg's was a shoestring operation.

It turned out that Youngberg himself was no stranger to a hand-to-mouth existence. His father before him had been a Seventh Day Adventist medical missionary in India and he wanted a career like his father's. As a boy, he had lived aboard a riverboat on the Ganges, a drawing of which hangs in his clinic waiting room. In contrast, Youngberg had acquired two retired St. Louis, Missouri, transit buses. These, parked by the side of the road near Lake Yojoa, had constituted his first Honduran clinic.

Over the years, support for the Youngberg clinic had been a hit-or-miss proposition. His church did not support him, apparently because the church fathers could see no end to the involvement. Nor did it seem to me there would be any way out for this operation which he had set in motion.

Youngberg lamented the difficulty of getting support. The Rockefeller Foundation, he told me, had answered his request for help by saying the type of medical treatment he was providing was a "bottomless pit" which could swallow up all the foundation's medical money.

And I must agree with the foundation.

"But the Lord," Youngberg said, "has been good to me." As evidence, he told me the giant American engineering company, Morrison-Knutson, of Boise, Idaho, had provided him with his present facilities. The company had built a hydroelectric plant for the Honduran government nearby and, when it had finished the job, sold all its temporary buildings to him for $1,000. One of the company's vice-presidents paid $500 of this sum out of his own pocket. Similar help dribbled in sporadically from other sources. The United Fruit Company had allowed some useful items such as old bathtubs and a water tower to "stray" over to his hospital.

Youngberg's wife kept up a steady stream of letters to the United States. She herself had raised some $60,000 annually in recent years. The doctor had earned another $10,000 a year from his medical practice, paid mostly in the form of food or labor.

From all I could determine, he was the only doctor within a radius of twenty-five miles (except for one who took care of the employees at a silver mine fifteen miles away).

Youngberg was a remarkable example of what one dedicated man can do. Somehow he had managed to put together a sizable staff. At the time of my visit, this included a Mexican and his wife who were teaching thirty-five young girls the fundamentals of nursing, a volunteer U.S. doctor who was temporarily assisting Youngberg, and some thirty local Honduran workers who were on hand around the place for various tasks.

As we walked by, some of these workers were puzzling over how to assemble a recently donated mill for processing peanut oil and soy flour. Youngberg hoped the mill could produce some of the protein needed in local diets, and had encouraged its donation. Unhappily neither he nor his associates knew anything about growing peanuts and soybeans, marginal crops at best in his part of Honduras.

But the main activity, the care of the children, was efficiently, thoughtfully, and lovingly organized. This is what won me over and shattered my previous bias. Youngberg and his wife and one daughter lived on the premises and oversaw activities around the clock. Youngberg's mother, visiting from Boston, was busily involved in making bright cardboard birds to hang over the children's cribs, each bird with the child's name on it.

In exchange for room, board, and training in nursing, the thirty-five girls (few of whom will ever become nurses, according to Youngberg) served as substitute mothers for the children. Each girl mothered two or three little waifs, eating with them and living with them as much of the day as possible. "It is crucial for the children to have an adult or semiadult to whom they can relate," Youngberg said. "It helps them survive."

Many parents had given up all hope by the time they had left their children in Youngberg's care. "Here's Gloria," Youngberg said, patting a frail little girl on the head. "Gloria's mother told me, 'Gloria is not going to live,' but we told Gloria, 'Don't give up!' and she didn't. You never know just what can give a child the will to live."

As I toured Youngberg's establishment, I could see that a great deal of imagination and hard work had gone into providing children with this chance to live. Comfortable bassinets had been built from the simplest materials. Ingenious sanitation facilities had been improvised without resort to costly pipe.

The children, the precious children, were all out soaking up the sunshine—the doctor's great ally in bringing them through to health. The nerve ends of some of the recent arrivals were so close to the surface of the skin that the touch of a hand was painful and their loosely hung clothes were abrasive. With the least bodily jar or disturbance, such children would emit a fussy, raspy, scarcely audible mew. They were too weak to wail.

Youngberg's appeals for funds had not been overstated!

I have seen malnourished children before. I have seen hungry and ill-fed villages. But never have I seen anything like this one group of children under Youngberg's care. They were skeletal, yet alive, so weak they could not sit up, close to death. Even with the loving care of this man and his helpers, recovery was painfully slow.

Given the countless number of undernourished children around the world, I asked Youngberg why he had chosen such an isolated place in which to work. "In all of these countries people are flocking to the cities and cutting their ties with the land," he said. "I wanted to give some assistance in a rural area to help stop this migration."

I asked him whether he gave out birth control information. "Yes, but I don't push it," he replied. "I can't do everything," and indeed he cannot.

Emotionally, few visits have had a greater impact on me. My original negative opinion of the operation was erased by the total self-effacement and dedication of Youngberg, his family, and staff. The tragedy of the lives of those youngsters in the orphanage is still painful to remember.

I asked him, "What happens when you leave or get too old to work?" He replied, "I am the only one. I hope my children or brother will take over, but that does not seem likely. I guess it's like flying off in a single-engine plane. When the engine quits, well, that's the end."

THE IRONY is that the development fraternity does not know how to make the efforts of all the thousands of Youngbergs and Morales effective. Nothing is done to coordinate the work of these men nor to plan for the work to continue when they are gone. And the good intentions of volunteers will not compensate for either the resources or the continuity successful development requires.

Yet I doubt whether this is of great importance to Dr. Youngberg himself. He has his own personal commitment to God and is fulfilling his need to assist his brother man. At this he is successful beyond question. He has found his own destiny on the shores of Lake Yojoa.

Financing a Charity

ABOUT FIFTEEN YEARS AGO Carroll Behrhorst, M.D., was practicing medicine in Winfield, Kansas, a small prairie town near the Oklahoma border. As he reached his midthirties, he faced up to the fact that the town had twenty doctors for 10,000 people. "I felt frustrated. I had studied medicine to help people, but no one's life in Winfield depended on my help."

So Behrhorst began looking around for a change. He saw a notice in a Lutheran paper soliciting the services of an American doctor for Guatemala. Within a short time he and his family of six children had settled there.

The Lutheran Church paid him while he studied three years to procure a license to practice medicine in Guatemala. He would then reopen the clinic and hospital which the Lutherans formerly had operated in Antigua but had had to close for the lack of a doctor.

But Behrhorst, once he had his diploma and license, decided against this. As he told it to me, "I found that the Lutheran mission was not interested in helping the Indians, but only in saving souls[1] and sending back reports to the mission board in St. Louis . . . so I left the Lutherans and began working independently." As a result, the Lutheran clinic and hospital in Antigua which had been designed to help the Indian remained closed.

Behrhorst now moved out on his own to open a clinic in Chimaltenango, a large town with good accessibility and visibility for travelers. It is about half an hour from Guatemala City on the paved Pan American Highway north to the Mexican border via Lake Atitlán, the nation's number one tourist attraction. This is also the main route for tourists who go to see the Indian highland culture, located beyond Chimaltenango. Here Behrhorst has spent the last decade. Most of his patients are Indians from the rural areas.

His clinic was on my list of effective development projects I wanted to visit in Mexico and Central America. In this case my interest had been first aroused because of the great number of reports and newspaper articles which had been written about him by traveling American doctors and journalists. In these he was consistently praised; in fact, "adulatory" is the only adjective.

In an official Lutheran publication, Behrhorst was described as a "physician, teacher, dentist, agricultural expert, anthropologist, diplomat and public health expert."[2] But more significant to me: in Guatemala City, AID's public health advisor told me Behrhorst was operating the country's most effective birth control clinic.

Edwin Newman, introducing him on NBC's Today Show, said, "No doctor has a practice which serves more people . . ." (October 7, 1970). He has been compared with the late Dr. Albert Schweitzer, who established a world-famous medical operation in Africa that provided primitive medical facilities for the natives. Behrhorst has been called "The Schweitzer of the Third World"[3] and is said to have "out-Schweitzered Schweitzer." A book about Behrhorst began with this sentence: "To write of a giant who does not exist is easy compared to writing about one who does." He is credited with running an educational program in which village leaders are prepared to become village doctors; with organizing a wide variety of other instructional courses, e.g., family planning; with promoting better farming practices by organizing courses and demonstrations in which "young men learn agricultural basics, including the proper use of insecticides, fertilizers, and treatment of animal diseases." He has taken on the job of selling fertilizer so the Indian can have a source of obtaining this vital product. Organizing cooperatives, he lends chickens and pigs to the Indians, having them pay him later with eggs and part of the litter. Conducting experiments with apple varieties and vegetables, he is bringing new opportunities to the local Indians.[4]

With my long interest in the developing world's agriculture, I was deeply curious to see how the doctor managed such an extremely broad and time-consuming agricultural program in addition to his medical practice.

The drive up out of the Guatemala City valley to the Chimaltenango plateau is one of the most pleasant along the Pan American Highway. Arriving in Chimaltenango, I found the Behrhorst clinic located in an old, typical patio-style house facing the town square. The entrance from the cobblestoned street opened onto an empty room: no chairs, tables, benches, or stools.

The only adornments were two very fleshy photos of bare, healthy Anglo-Saxon babies, cut out of magazines.

A receptionist, sitting in a cubicle behind a temporary wall and in front of some files, was the only sign of life. I asked for the doctor and was motioned toward a door. I stepped into a tiny room crammed with six or seven chairs already occupied by patients. There were two cots, also occupied, and the doctor's desk, behind which the last empty chair stood in lonely splendor. The doctor had not yet arrived and I stood in a vacant space beside the desk. The longer I waited, the more I felt inundated by coughing babies and sick adults.

Finally, he arrived. A stocky, blond man, Behrhorst told me first about himself, his move from the small Kansas town of Winfield to Chimaltenango. "I was shocked to find 200,000[5] natives, the Cakchiquel Indians, with nowhere to turn for medical care." I asked him about the modern looking clinic I had seen on the edge of Chimaltenango. Behrhorst said the Indians are suspicious of the government, that they distrust the "white man's" medical care, that in the past they have been poorly treated by the doctors and nurses, and that this is a traditional fear from the time of the Spanish settlers who took away the Indians' land and enslaved them. The Indians had retreated into the mountain country and they still shun modern science and medicine. "I have tried to overcome their distrust. I keep things simple so the Indians are not suspicious. I offer my help on their terms."

That he adapts his practice to the level of existing Indian mores was apparent when I returned another day to make the rounds of his entire operation. The hospital building was made of plastered adobe brick with a tile roof and brick floor and had a dozen or so rooms. The cots and cot pads were supplied by the hospital, the bedding by the patient himself. Behrhorst said, "The patient pays fifty cents a day for a cot and a visit from the doctor. All his other needs are provided by members of his family. They cook his food over a charcoal fire by his bed or in the caldron out in the patio. They take care of everything else, from back rubs to bedpans. We don't give hotel service."

That day Behrhorst was accompanied on his hopsital rounds by a nurse and five or six of what he called his "medical Indians." After examining one woman for a moment with a stethoscope Behrhorst said, "She has phlegm in her chest." He prescribed penicillin and a decongestant.

We moved on to the next patient who had phlebitis, according to a diagnosis by one of the medical Indians accompanying us. Again Behrhorst used the stethoscope and then confirmed the diagnosis. Behrhorst used the stethoscope on every patient, even if only for a moment.

Later I talked about the stethoscope with Dr. Phillip Stubblefield, a doctor for the Peace Corps volunteers in Guatemala. The Corps had allowed him to come to the Behrhorst clinic as a visiting doctor one day a week, for a year. I said that to a nonmedical person like myself this use of the stethoscope seemed strange. "No," he said, "Dr. Behrhorst emphasizes this is the procedure to use, no matter if it is an ingrown toenail; always use the stethoscope on every patient, even if just for a moment."

I said this still did not seem very professional. In fact, it would have been something like my handing corn seeds to an Indian farmer and telling him to plant them in the dark of the moon, and just as fraught with possible future misunderstanding.

Stubblefield answered, "Well, Behrhorst says the Indians believe the stethoscope has magical qualities of healing. He always gives medication by injections, too, because they feel better afterwards. They like the needle."

I asked Stubblefield about the quality of medicine at the clinic. He said it was "not as good as in the government hospital in Antigua (20 miles away) or in Guatemala City. But there you might have to wait all day, with a dying child in your arms, and even then might not get in. At Behrhorst's you can always get in."

Stubblefield then analyzed Behrhorst's kind of medical practice, characterizing it as "empiric." He added, "In the United States we think of our medicine as being scientific. The doctor waits until all the tests have been run before making his diagnosis and prescribing treatment, and always with a minimum of drugs." In contrast, under the empirical, or Behrhorst, method, "the doctor takes a look at the patient, makes his best guess as to what's wrong and treats the patient with a spectrum of broad-gauge medicines. He can do this because 90 percent of his cases fall into one of three categories: diarrhea, pneumonia, or malnutrition." The doctor can work fast in prescribing for these ailments. Stubblefield said Behrhorst could see as many as 150 to 200 patients in a single day, and often did. He frequently examines two at a time and may see as many as 30 patients in an hour, roughly two minutes per patient.

Behrhorst himself told me of the need for this "country doctor medicine." "Few Indians will make the trip to the government hospitals for the laboratory tests or the X rays which my hospital and clinic do not have. It is too far away for them to go, too long a trip."

I was curious about this line of reasoning. Was Behrhorst's the only medical help available locally? I remembered having seen a new clinic on the way into town. Actually, as I eventually found out, Chimaltenango must be one of the best medically equipped towns of its size in Central America. Several facilities are specifically designed for these same Indians who go to the Behrhorst clinic.

MEDICAL FACILITIES SERVING THE CHIMALTENANGO AREA:

1. Public Health Clinic—one resident physician and three nurses; all four live in Chimaltenango. In addition, the clinic has the services of three pediatricians who come on weekdays from Guatemala City and a dentist who comes three days a week.
2. National Social Security Hospital—one resident surgeon and six male nurses; all seven live in Chimaltenango. Facilities include fifteen beds. However, this is open only to persons covered by the national social security plan.
3. Maternity Hospital—one obstetrician-gynecologist, twelve nurses and four midwives; all seventeen live in Chimaltenango. Facilities include twenty-five beds.
4. Children's Nursery—nurse and three social workers who care for children during the day.
5. National Health Program (PROSA)—six last-year medical students who work out of Guatemala City. This program, primarily aimed at providing medical care for Indians, is supported by the Institute of Nutrition of Central America and Panama (INCAP) and the University of San Carlos (which has a medical school in Guatemala City).
6. PUMAR—one physician and one nurse who supposedly visit villages in the Chimaltenango area on regular schedules with a mobile health clinic. This is aimed primarily at providing medical care for rural Indians and is supported by U.S. government aid funds.
7. Acción Conjunta—one physician and three nurses; all live in Chimaltenango and make the rounds of outlying villages. Acción is aimed primarily at providing medical care for Indians.
8. Doctors in private practice—five physicians; all live in Chimaltenango. Four of them also work at the facilities mentioned above.

Apart from the Behrhorst Clinic, then, ten doctors, according to my count (assuming no duplication), plus nurses and social workers, and the six medical students are available to serve the people of the Chimaltenango area.

This is all quite contrary to what is believed by most of those who have talked with Dr. Behrhorst. Thus Dr. Jessie L. Brodie of the Pathfinder Fund in Boston wrote me, "As you know, Behrhorst has the only clinic and hospital for an area with 400,000 Cakchiquel Indians."[6] Similar statements that the Behrhorst Clinic is the *only* one in Chimaltenango have appeared in other publications.[7]

When the clinic's American and British volunteers were questioned about the other medical facilities in the area, all told me essentially the same, "Oh, but those are for the *ladinos*. Indians won't go to them." When I asked Dr. Emilio Mendizábal, head of the government's public health service for the Chimaltenango area, he said that in the two health centers he runs and thirteen auxiliary clinics (in the Department of Chimaltenango) they treat approximately 500 Indians a day, five days a week. How did the story get started that Indians won't go to the government clinics? Mendizábal, who has headed the Chimaltenango program for eight years, said, "I do not believe Behrhorst has ever visited the Chimaltenango clinic to see what we do or how we do it." (While I was with him, he confirmed this with his head nurse and the head of PROSA, Dr. Gustavo Víchy.)

Then he added, "Nor do I believe any correspondent or writer who has written about the Behrhorst program has visited our government program."

I asked Dr. Stubblefield about the Guatemalan medical efforts designed specifically for the Indians. He said, "PROSA is a great idea. It is a joint effort of INCAP, medical schools, and the government medical services. Behrhorst is beginning to work with them a little. But sometimes Behrhorst acts if these others are in competition with him. There is no reason for him to feel that way. There are centainly enough sick Indians to go around for everyone."

To REACH the Indians who do not come out of the hills, Behrhorst has a program for training Indians to perform medical services in those villages where medical facilities supposedly do not exist. Behrhorst said the object is "to take people who are not educated and make good doctors of them." He added, "Such persons can make a good living this way, too. I believe in the profit motive and in charging a small fee. These medical Indians come here every Tuesday for their course. They make the hospital rounds with me and then they have classes in agriculture. After a year they get their diplomas and can sell medicines back in their villages, and some fertilizer, too. It is a good business for them; some earn from $300 to $500 a month." My reaction: if true, these must be among the most highly remunerated villagers in the country. Certainly it seems to be a large sum to come out of a subsistence level community.

To help explain the work of these medical Indians, Stubblefield gave me a report entitled "Analysis of Rural Empirical Practitioners," by C. Michael Murphy of the University of Kentucky College of Medicine. A third year medical student at the time he conducted his two-month survey of Behrhorst's medical training program in 1966, Murphy reviewed the work of the medical Indians in the communities they were serving, providing sketches of eight of the Indians.

Of these, one was working in a town which had two pharmacies run by former practical nurses, as well as a public health center staffed by one practical, or auxiliary, nurse.

Another was working in a locality where three pharmacies were available and to which two physicians devoted a total of three days a week.

Still another was located in an area served by one pharmacy and a doctor who had a clinic one day a week.

This sampling indicated the possibility that the situation of Chimaltenango, with its several established health facilities, is duplicated to some extent in communities served by Behrhorst-trained Indians. Thus while it is undoubtedly true that a need exists for more medical care in the Indian villages, it is a gross exaggeration to say that only Dr. Behrhorst, his clinic, and his medical Indians serve the villages.

Murphy noted that making money was an important motive for becoming a medical Indian. Of one of these Murphy wrote, "He is in the business strictly for the money and freely uses such tricks as saying not to go to the doctor because he costs so much, treating the disease after it is cured, and treating people without proper indication." Murphy described another of the eight who is similarly motivated and who "goes to the adjacent towns and seeks out the sick, but does not enjoy his practice." Of still another

Murphy said, "Medicine has made him rich enough so that he plans to build a new house of his own."

In part, making money was inculcated during their training when, according to Murphy, two general rules were established "out of a desire to satisfy local expectations of what a 'curer' should do: (1) every patient must receive an injection; if no injection is indicated by the symptoms, an injection of vitamin B complex is given; (2) if a patient has chest or abdominal complaints, a stethoscope must be put to the affected area."

Finally, the medical Indians were admonished during their training that "fees were to be charged to the patients only for medicines given, not for services rendered. Thus if the 'curer' had no drug therapy to offer his patient, no charge was to be made."

I asked Behrhorst how he justifies sending out his hastily trained Indians to compete with local pharmacists and doctors. Behrhorst said, "Well, I know these students are really practicing medicine. It is against the law for them to do it officially. Actually, the head of the public health service here doesn't like me too well." (Dr. Mendizábal later told me, "These men Behrhorst sends out as medical aids, operate without supervision, have no kind of license, and often call themselves 'doctor.' In every respect they operate illegally and outside the Guatemalan law." Incidentally, a government-financed program in the maternity hospitals which no one at the Behrhorst clinic mentioned, trains Indian women to be midwives. The women are tested at the end of their training and issued a license bearing their photograph, which is validated by the Ministry of Health.)

Behrhorst then changed the subject and mentioned that "the agricultural extension work is basically the most important part of the work of these men." But its effectiveness is open to question, according to a second report written by Murphy. He said, ". . . the student has a strong financial motive to do well in his medical work. Unfortunately, there is no such system to reward the student for his knowledge of agricultural science. The financial reward for applying the latest advances in agriculture . . . is of far less magnitude than the possible financial gain to be made from a successful practice of medicine."[8]

Behrhorst invited me to attend the lesson being given for his medical Indians that day in agriculture. Sure enough, the same men from the hospital rounds were in a class—not in agriculture, however, but in human reproduction. It was given bravely by young Mrs. Paul McKay, who, joking about being very pregnant herself, did a first-class job of teaching the men about human reproduction. She explained to me later they had to understand human reproduction before they could understand birth control. Mrs. McKay and her husband (a trained agriculturalist) were not supported by the Behrhorst Clinic but by an organization called "World Neighbors." Although Dr. Behrhorst is credited, by himself and by others as I earlier indicated, with having organized a variety of instructional courses in improved farming practices, establishing cooperatives, and conducting variety trials with apples and vegetables, I found that in fact this effort was originated by and is *entirely* funded, staffed, and operated by World Neighbors, which rents space from the Behrhorst Clinic. It also finances the Behrhorst birth control program, quietly paying him a salary.

I had heard occasionally about World Neighbors before, but no one in my preliminary interviews for this book had recommended one of its projects. Thus I had given its work no heed. Based on my talks with the McKays and later by visiting their Oklahoma City headquarters, I concluded World Neighbors to be a self-effacing, unpretentious, but effective organization. It has, in my opinion, a most sensible and simplified program for the developing world: agricultural improvement and family planning at the village level. No more, no less.

One of my major reasons for visiting the Behrhorst Clinic was the strong recommendation by U.S. AID officials; they said that Guatemala's best birth control effort was "probably that of Dr. Behrhorst" because his clinic had inserted more IUD's [intrauterine device] than any other. I mentioned this to him and he said he did indeed have an active program and estimated he had inserted "probably 1,100 IUD's."[9]

I asked, "What has been the retention rate?" He said two women had become pregnant with the loop in place, and added, "I have had two patients become pregnant by losing the loop without knowing it, another four or five have lost the loop. Thus only six or seven of the total number have been lost. I have also had to remove fifteen to twenty because of bleeding."

In this aspect of his medical practice it would appear his performance is unique. Statistics from IUD programs in other countries show a retention rate of about 70 percent at the end of the first year.[10] This would mean that one should expect somewhat more than 300 not retained (if 1,100 had been inserted) rather than his 25. And where malnutrition is severe, as he says it is with his Indians, the expected loss could be still higher.

I asked Dr. Behrhorst, "How do you finance your operation?"

He said his annual budget was about $76,000. He mentioned contributions to his support from various sources, such as AID, World Neighbors, and a newly organized Behrhorst Clinic Foundation. He said he also collected fees from his clinic patients but "a good many Indians cannot pay the $1.25 fee so I charge them less, which means there is an annual loss in the operation of about $8,000."

Behrhorst said he did not have permanent sponsorship by any philanthropic, humanitarian, or religious organization. He said he had begun his work in Guatemala as a Lutheran medical missionary, but had left because he wanted to work independently, "not with a group directed from outside Guatemala." This was not the reason he had given me in an earlier conversation (as quoted at the beginning of this chapter), nor was it the reason I later heard: he had resigned rather than comply with the medical requirements of the Lutheran Mission Board for its overseas personnel and their families. In the beginning it had cost the Lutheran Church substantially to bring Behrhorst and his family to Guatemala and to support them while he obtained a Guatemalan license to practice medicine. By the time he had had, as he phrased it, "a falling out" with the Lutherans, the church had invested more than $50,000 in him.

Since, however, a general impression remains among officials with whom I spoke in Guatemala that Behrhorst operates under Lutheran sponsorship, I wrote to the Lutheran Church—Missouri Synod. William H. Kohn, executive secretary of the Board for Missions, replied, "Dr. Behrhorst's clinic and foundation is not under the responsibility and direction of our Board for Missions. For that reason we have no jurisdiction in the matter. At the same time, however, it should be noted that individual Lutherans and occasionally Lutheran organizations have provided support for the project."[11]

The letter went on to say that "the Medical Secretary on our Board has not made a formal evaluation of the effectiveness of the clinic."

While in Guatemala I asked U.S. AID officials about their support for the Behrhorst Clinic. They praised his work, but expressed surprise that Behrhorst had said their organization was supporting it.

Dr. F. J. Vintinner, who was in charge of U.S. government assistance for medical projects throughout Central America, said he was not quite sure whether Behrhorst was receiving any U.S. aid money or not. He was under the impression the doctor's support came from the Lutheran Church and from private citizens.

Dr. James King, medical projects officer with U.S. AID in Guatemala, had been in Guatemala for three months when I talked to him. He had just visited Behrhorst to "offer him U.S. support," but Behrhorst had told him he did not need it. King knew of no U.S. foreign aid money going into the Behrhorst clinic.

A couple of days later King phoned me. With some chagrin he explained that his organization had granted Behrhorst $5,000. I asked King if he had ever seen Behrhorst's financial statement. He replied, "Oh, no, we would not ask for that kind of information. His is a nonprofit organization with which we are dealing."

And that was my introduction to the fact that nonprofit organizations have an implied immunity against questions about money. The U.S. government had not investigated the clinic's financial background before making a contribution. Such financing can be sanctified by *association,* i.e., AID "thinks" the Lutherans are funding the operation; therefore, that is a good enough recommendation.

For budget details about his work, Behrhorst referred me, via the New York advertising firm of J. Walter Thompson, to Columbia University's Edwin Barton, who spearheads a fund-raising program for the Behrhorst Clinic Foundation. Barton, author of a book on Behrhorst, *Doctor to the Mayas,* became somewhat annoyed when I asked about finances; but when I assured Barton my question was meant merely to find out the source of the $76,000 annual budget and not the private income of Dr. Behrhorst, he said, "Oh, well, in that case, what the Foundation has raised is insignificant."

From World Neighbors I learned that this organization contributes about $50,000 a year.[12] Thus this would seem to be his major support.

The more I probed the financial structure of Behrhorst's operations, the more confused I became. Word of my inquiries must have filtered back to Chimaltenango. A letter came from Behrhorst, saying, "If you were to write about us adversely, it would be a distinct disservice to many people and organizations. These include the Pan American Development Foundation and its leaders such as Galo Plaza and Sy Rotter; the Agency for International Development and its Mission to Guatemala; World Neighbors; OXFAM; the United States Ambassador to Guatemala, Nathaniel Davis; Assistant Secretary of State for Inter-American Affairs, Charles

Meyer; all of whom are loyal and consistent supporters of our program."[13]

The name game is an indispensable part of charity donations. However, I wager that with the exception of World Neighbors none of these "loyal and consistent supporters" has any idea of the finances of this operation, or knowledge of the effectiveness of the sort of hocus-pocus approach being used with the Indians.

So what is wrong with the Behrhorst Clinic? Dr. Behrhorst is treating Indians and he is providing a service for which facilities will never meet the demand. So what if the doctor wants the world to think he is the only one serving 200,000 (or 400,000) Cakchiquel Indians—his desire for recognition may be no greater than that of the next man's. No, the problems are more fundamental.

For one, Dr. Behrhorst is competing *against,* not working with, the local Guatemalan medical organizations designed by Guatemalans to help Guatemala's Indians. By denying the very existence of this service, he undermines the potential effectiveness of it. Guatemalans are unlikely to turn to him for advice or to accept any potential Behrhorst inputs to their program. In fact, if I were a Guatemalan M.D., I would probably want to run him out of the country for turning loose on the innocent Indians inadequately trained and supervised medical "doctors" that exploit the superstitions of the uneducated.

But this is secondary to the concern an American might have over the apparent lack of guidance churches give their parishioners wishing to donate to overseas programs. Assuming the Lutheran Church—Missouri Synod is typical, we have the situation where on the one hand it emphasizes it has no responsibility for the Behrhorst program and has made no evaluation of its effectiveness, and on the other hand allows its publications to imply that it both supports the Behrhorst program financially and endorses it medically. For instance, the *Lutheran Layman* (Sept. 1970) said Dr. Behrhorst derives support "from many sources, including the Lutheran Church—Missouri Synod . . . [and] by Lutheran youth organization's 'Hikes for Hunger.'" An entire issue of the Lutheran Medical Missions Council's publication was devoted to Dr. Behrhorst.[14]

How then, does the man of goodwill decide to whom to donate his charity dollar?

My feeling is: if you want to give to a worthy cause, choose one near home as there is a better chance to check its background.

And, if your "thing" is helping Indians, pick a reservation in the United States.

P.S. Senator Fred Harris of Oklahoma (a state full of Indian problems and only eighteen miles from Winfield, Kansas) in a Senate floor speech said recently, "Physicians in [U.S.] Indian hospitals frequently have an impossible patient load, and those physicians going to field stations or clinics see as many as 80 patients a day. One physician at an Indian hospital in Oklahoma has a patient load which allows him only 3 minutes per patient per day. The result is long lines and degrading treatment."[15]

Demographic Leverage

ONE OF THE Washington officials I called on in preparation for the field work for this book was Philander P. Claxton, special assistant to the U.S. secretary of state on population matters. His position had been established in 1966 as a result of congressional pressure (the Gruening Committee) and of new, widespread public concern.

Claxton, a bureaucrat since 1939, had had no experience with demographic problems before assuming the post. His lack of experience was typical, he said, of people involved with population programs in government. "We in government," he said, "are beginning from a standing start."

Claxton was the first person I interviewed who waved a yellow flag of caution about the glowing economic data then coming out of Central America. Even though the statistics about the Common Market (discussed in Part 4) looked great, especially those "proving" increased Central American internal trade, Claxton said he personally was not at all that optimistic.

One reason for caution, he pointed out, was the per capita rate of economic growth. It was falling drastically. Look, he said, at Costa Rica:

Per Capita Economic	1950–55	3.5%
Growth	1955–60	1.1%
	1960–65	0.2%

And all of Latin America, he continued, is in the same boat.

Per Capita Economic	1950–55	2.4%
Growth	1955–60	1.9%
	1960–65	1.5%

"Why is the percentage falling?" he asked, and answered his own question, "Because of the area's horrendous population growth!"

As this population problem gets worse, Claxton said, the problem of providing basic facilities, such as education, is becoming ever more severe. Brazil has more illiterates today than its entire population in 1945. Clearly, population growth in Central America and the rest of Latin America is a terrible handicap to economic development.

Yet earlier that same day I had been told in the office of an assistant secretary of state there was "essentially no population problem in Central America nor population pressures on the land, except for El Salvador."

I asked Claxton to clarify this conflict in analysis. "I am afraid the first thing we must do is to educate our own people" was his only comment.

In 1967, he said, AID published a booklet on assistance to population programs in Latin America. A wire service filed a story on the booklet, accurately reporting that six Latin American countries were receiving assistance for birth control programs from the United States. The result, according to Claxton, was that every U.S. ambassador in Latin America complained to the State Department. The gist of the complaints was: "AID was wrecking our relations" and "Latin America has a long way to go before it will accept population control programs." One big need, he stressed, is to find a way to tell the story of overpopulation graphically and to describe, with no holds barred, the consequences of rapid population growth. Only then will family planning assistance be understood and welcomed and not resented or misinterpreted.

Claxton spoke convincingly about the need for birth control. For example, he emphasized that the nonbirth of an unwanted child has the effect of doubling the lifetime income of the born child. Also the average citizen consumes more while growing up in a developing country than he can produce after he is an adult. In other words, a nonbirth in a country with a $100 per capita income is equal to a $200 investment in the economy, or every $5 spent (effectively) on population control is the same as a $100 investment in development.

In February 1966, about the time Claxton assumed his new post at the State Department, President Johnson put this example in global terms, saying that "population growth now consumes about two-thirds of the economic growth in the less developed world." The example of the $5 vs. $100 was repeated. Great offense was taken in Latin America to the president's statement. To many governments there it seemed as though the United States was

about to substitute birth control for aid. I later heard a great
deal of comment about this on my own trip.

I asked Claxton where I should go in Mexico and Central
America to look at an effective population control program. He
answered that there was no program he could recommend, nor
was there even a specific country where such programs were generally accepted by the public.

He did mention a Robert Nathan Associates report on the
"Population Growth Rates and Economic Development in Nicaragua" prepared the preceding year. Claxton said this gives Nicaragua the best demographic study of any Central American country.

I read the report, written under an AID contract, with great
interest. It furnished me with a handy excuse when I was in Nicaragua to bring up the subject of population growth during an
interview with Dr. Roberto Castillo Quant, vice-minister of public
health. Some ten minutes after we began talking his press officer
entered to tape our conversation for a radio transmission later that
day. The result was a more formal interview, but one that surely
set a milestone in Latin America for frankness on this subject.

PADDOCK: A study has been made titled, "Population Growth
Rates and Economic Development in Nicaragua." Based on that
report what would you say is the future outlook for Nicaragua?

CASTILLO: This is an agricultural country. We subsist on our
land. If we don't do something to control our family size there will
be a cycle of social economic problems. . . . The future will see
us having more hunger, more serious problems. The annual population growth rate is 3.5 percent a year. Agricultural production
is growing at only 2.5 percent. In twenty-five or thirty years there
will not be enough food for this country. . . . There are too many
people within each family. It's a miniexplosion, at the family level,
with an average of four children per family. Seventy percent of
the population of Nicaragua lives in rural areas and this is where
the population explosion is worse. These are the hardest people
to reach and to teach . . . Managua is almost as bad. The abortion
rate here is criminal . . . Just the same, I can visualize Managua
having as many as 8 million people in the foreseeable future . . .
Nicaragua could have 15 million people . . . Where do we get the
money to build the houses, the schools, put in the light plants, the
water systems for so many more people? Our economy is agricul-

tural. But prices are down on cotton and coffee—our biggest exports. How do we support all these people?

When I asked Ragnar Arneson, director of the U.S. AID mission in Nicaragua, what he thought about the Robert Nathan Associates report he said, "I do not know anything about it." His deputy, Charles B. Johnson, said, "The report has been out less than a year and Mr. Arneson simply has not had time to read it." Johnson added, "We were not impressed by the report." Louis Gardella, AID's public health advisor, said much the same thing. "We could not understand it and neither could the economists." Yet it was written under an AID contract and paid for by AID.

The developing world's winding road to progress is paved with shelved reports!

It was my good fortune in Central America to meet yet another official with the courage to speak up with a clear voice. The Honduran minister of public health, Dr. J. Antonio Peraza, had made a name for himself at a meeting where a priest sent by the Archbishop of Honduras had announced, "Anyone practicing birth control is a murderer." The minister answered, "Then I am a murderer. And all of you people out there who use contraceptives are murderers too, because this man said so (pointing to the priest). We Hondurans cannot continue to have this growth of population." Later before a large meeting of doctors and public health officials Peraza said, "We know the majority of our people want to practice birth control."

A third such person of courage lives in El Salvador and because of her efforts I found there an effective population control effort. But a bit of history first.

El Salvador has been described as a demographic nightmare. By 1962 the population density of El Salvador had swelled to an average of 2.2 (in contrast with India's 1.3) persons per farmed acre. Today the consequences of excessive cultivation are to be seen everywhere.

One hundred years ago El Salvador was primarily a forested land; now only 10 percent of the land is forested—and this is mainly a scruffy secondary growth. Conservationists find the level of the water table is dropping. Water must be rationed in parts of the country at certain times during the year, times quite unrelated to the dry season. Most of the hydroelectric power comes from the

Cinco de Noviembre Dam built in 1954. But is is "conservatively estimated that the dam will lose 40 percent of its storage capacity within the next two decades because of the rapid siltation induced by accelerated erosion."[1] One result is that El Salvador faces the "probable loss of its major source of electrical power and much of its irrigation potential within a short period of time," according to Professor Howard E. Daugherty.[2]

Soil erosion problems continue. The Salvadoran soils normally resist erosion, but they have been so abused by the excess population, the original potential of the land has been seriously reduced. Salvador also has long been a food deficit nation. Some nineteen species of local mammals (according to Daugherty) have become extinct, including deer, monkeys, and wildcats. Daugherty says overpopulation may be related to the "high degree of psychosocial stress and may contribute significantly to the national homicide rate which is the highest in the world and which is the leading cause of adult death." (Is homicide to be man's psychological way of adjusting to excessive overcrowding?)

El Salvador has had the typical number of pronatal hang ups. As a Catholic nation, the use of artificial contraception is, of course, firmly opposed at all official levels. The large-family syndrome has been encouraged by important newspaper writers who favor a government pronatalist policy. The editor of San Salvador's influential *El Diario de Hoy*, N. Viera Altamirano, has written extensively with what is called "almost a mystical force" that Latin America's destiny lies in its continuing population growth. Viera Altamirano wrote, "To populate America is to civilize America. To oppose population is to oppose civilization."[3]

The Fourteen Families (cliché title for those traditionally labeled as owning, controlling, and governing El Salvador) have been accused of sharing these same views. Their reason for doing so, according to local talk, is that they wish to assure themselves of a plentiful source of cheap labor. Whether or not such an accusation is justified would be difficult to prove, but that it is believed indicates the biased attitudes concerning population back in 1964.

That was the year the local Asociación Demográfica Salvadoreña was founded. "On May 21, 1964, a group of altruistic persons met; they met because of a preoccupation with the increasing population and its effect on the nation's well being," according to the association's own literature. The publications, however, do not mention that the meeting of twenty-one people was due largely to the efforts of one woman, Señora de Francisco de Sola, an American married to a Salvadoran who is one of the Fourteen Families. Here again was someone with the courage to speak out in a loud, clear voice. This oligarch gathered together a group of sister oligarchs and kept them and the new association pulling together.

Their original purpose was merely to demonstrate the nation's need for birth control and to awaken public interest in government support of family planning clinics. This goal, amazingly, was accomplished within only four years. In 1968 the government directed the social security system to make family planning a part of its responsibility. El Salvador was the first country in Central America with such a regulation. This success was all the more astonishing because the Salvadoran government had seemed as conservative and tradition bound on this controversial subject as any in the world.

The equipment and training films for their first small office had been purchased by the de Sola family originally for use in a small village near their farm. This material was given to the clinic and it soon received its first financial support—$1,000 from the Pathfinder Fund of Boston. This initial sum went to pay for a part-time secretary. To show how such a project can balloon, by 1968 the association's income had grown to a quarter of a million dollars annually, coming mostly from U.S. AID and the International Planned Parenthood Foundation of New York City. The Salvadorans' contribution had political clout, enough to save the program from being abolished by an antagonistic government and an all-pervasive church.

Interestingly, the justification the Demographic Association gave in public for its work in this Catholic country which had such strong feelings about the manifest destiny of more and more population, was that education about birth control would reduce the abortion rate. The rate of illegal abortions was increasing rapidly. Many deaths were occurring and a large percentage of the hospital beds were occupied by women who had developed complications from self-induced or illegal abortions.

The association's headquarters, clean and businesslike, are in a former private home. Its activities were directed by Dr. Oscar Beneke and several assistants. A man of about sixty, he is quiet and able; he has about him the aura of a first-class physician. He invited me to visit their family planning clinic next door, which serves as the pattern for the new social security clinics. In the waiting room were about eight patients. While waiting to see the clinic doctor, they listened to a lecture, illustrated with posters and charts, that enumerated all the good reasons for limiting family size, such as the well-being of the family, especially of present children, when there are fewer offspring. I liked the reassuring way the nurse talked with these women. She was quick to congratulate them on their intelligent decision to come to this office for advice, and she invited them to come back the next time with some of their friends.

The building was neat and orderly; the records were well kept; and the whole atmosphere, though one of genteel poverty, nevertheless would give a patient confidence that she was receiving good care.

From this initial clinic, the program has grown to include clinics in a number of other cities throughout El Salvador where similar advice and care are given.

In terms of the number of women treated, however, this program offers little hope to El Salvador. In all the clinics, Dr. Beneke told me, a total of only 28,453 patients had been aided in the preceding three years. On this basis the program was not inexpensive; the average cost per woman was $15. Furthermore most who had come to the clinics already had had four children or more. Either the "Pill" or the IUD was being prescribed for them. Dr. Beneke's staff had kept records on each patient that were precise and accurate. The IUD, in 22.5 percent of the cases had been expelled or removed by the patient, a statistic not unlike that experienced in other clinics throughout the world. Even so, the association's research indicates this is the most effective device, needing little education or motivation in its use. Recently the women have been showing more interest in the Pill, even though this is an expensive contraceptive that requires daily commitment.

So the number of patients treated is insignificant, the cost is high, the women who are patients have already had several children and are not those just starting families, and the techniques available (the Pill and the IUD) need to be replaced by something far more fool-proof and economical. In spite of all these, I still consider their work to be effective.

The reasons are: The association was able to negate the resistance against family planning and to have birth control clinics accepted throughout the country. The association has continued to function in spite of the disapproval of the Catholic Church, in spite of Pope Paul's encyclical letter against "The Regulation of Birth" issued in 1968. The association, through its dedicated efforts, has caused the government to include a family planning program in its social security program.

As the government takes over the responsibility for the clinics, the association plans to continue to do research but not to treat patients. It will concentrate its efforts on a sex education program for young people and on research in those areas where public funds cannot yet be spent.

The Demographic Association, set up to force government response to the needs of Salvadoran citizens by making birth control information available, achieved its goal. It was clearly a step forward.

But what is El Salvador's future?

"What is going to happen here in El Salvador?" was a frequent question of mine. My conversation with the late George Westcott, a U.S. agricultural consultant to the Salvadoran government, took place in his office in the presidential palace. It bears repeating here.

PADDOCK: What is going to happen in Salvador?

WESTCOTT: Salvador is now striving to increase agricultural production by 3 percent. Even if it succeeds, which is doubtful, this is a losing battle because the population growth is probably over 4 percent.

PADDOCK: Yes, but what is going to happen?

WESTCOTT: We must convince the leadership in Salvador to place greater emphasis on agriculture.

PADDOCK: No, don't tell me what we must do. After all, the minister of agriculture is quitting his job in a couple of days, and who knows what the new minister will or will not do. Tell me what is going to happen.

WESTCOTT: We need to put an average of $450 an acre into improving Salvador's agriculture. People say there isn't enough money for this. But they must find it.

PADDOCK: No, that is not my question. Tell me what is going to happen.

WESTCOTT: Well, if you pin me down like that, it is, of course, obvious. There is going to be an explosion.

And there was one—five months later. War between Honduras and El Salvador broke out. The press nicknamed it the Soccer War, but it was, in fact, a demographic war.

Conclusions:
The Invincible American Out to
Remake the World

Americans can do anything! I was thinking that as I sat in the lobby of the Matum Hotel in Santiago de los Caballeros near the center of the Dominican Republic and watched Neil Armstrong take man's first steps on the moon. No matter who you were or where you were, this was the sight of a lifetime. For me, watching it from this isolated Caribbean town made the marvel all the more enjoyable.

Consider the technical feat involved. Armstrong's image was transmitted to Houston via a television camera on the side of the lunar module. From there it was sent to a satellite perched over the Atlantic Ocean, then to a receiving station in Santo Domingo, the capital of the Dominican Republic, and finally across this country to the television set at the Matum Hotel. Instantaneously! Fantastic!

To my nationalistic pride it was resounding confirmation that Americans can do anything.

Three and a half years before the moon landing, in January 1966, I had stayed at this same hotel one week after it had been at the stormy center of a bizarre skirmish between rival factions of the Dominican army in a local civil war. Some thirty people were severely injured during the scuffle, including some Americans, hapless performers in a carnival which had been set up in front of the hotel.

Tanks had prowled the field of battle during the fight and had blown out all the windows in the hotel, punched gaping holes in the walls, smashed up furniture, and so on. The hotel was a mess.

Now three years later the hotel, a solid building constructed during the Trujillo dictatorship, had been repaired. My room had an air conditioner, new furniture, hot water. The broken windows had been replaced, and in the lobby was the television set on which I watched the stirring events on the moon.

Americans deserve much of the credit for the island's present (relative) prosperity. In April 1965, U.S. Marines landed at the capital. It was never entirely clear why they had come—to safeguard American lives or to stave off the threat of Communism. While our troops did not immediately put an end to the civil war in progress, they did eventually provide the law and order necessary to monitor a shaky truce. Since then two more or less peaceful elections have been held. Thus the American action did help provide the basis for a sort of democratic order following the turmoil of the overthrow of the Trujillo regime.

During our intervention and afterwards we provided more than a third of a billion dollars in foreign aid to get things going again—our usual policy to help tidy up things wherever our troops have been in action.

It is unfortunately true the Dominican government also had thereby acquired a debt of over $175 million, a sum about equal to the total annual revenues of the government. Never mind. The influx of so much American money after the civil war had generated mountains of hope among Dominicans. New roads were built, new university buildings erected, an electrical plant put up here, an irrigation ditch dug there.

The impact of this money was evident. Everyone seemed to own a new transistor radio and many also had new television sets. Japanese-made Honda motorcycles scooted around the countryside. A lively business of importing used refrigerators from the United States had sprung up. The demand for electricity was sharply rising. This helped explain why at times electricity was available for only six hours a day in Santiago, and why the hot water heater and new air conditioner functioned only occasionally.

If such changes could be wrought in the chaotic Dominican Republic so quickly, surely it was persuasive evidence to support our boast that Americans can do anything.

But for another, more personal reason I, as an American, felt confident sitting there in the lobby and watching the moonwalk. On this particular trip I had come to write a handbook for Dominican farmers that I hoped would have an important influence on the country's economy. The idea was to compile in one pocket-sized book all the information useful to the government's farm agents as they taught the marginal or subsistence Dominican farmer how to increase his production. To the best of the knowledge of the team I was heading up, no similar handbook had ever before been commissioned for any tropical country. I felt good about the potential impact the handbook might have.

The handbook itself was to be published and made available on a schedule coinciding with the introduction of a small two-wheeled, garden-type tractor. A product of the Ford Motor Company, this motorized tool, called the DNT (Developing Nations Tractor), was the first ever to be designed by a major company with the specific needs of the small-scale farmer of the tropics in mind. The tractor was engineered to sell at a price comparable to the cost of a team of oxen. Its ingenious metal wheels, looking like over-sized gears, were designed to wear forever. With no belts or pulleys, the machine was built to give several thousand hours of more or less trouble-free operation. Nearly tinkerproof, it was planned for use by the mechanically illiterate.

In terminating this good word for the DNT, I stress that Ford had undertaken development of this machine primarily for al-truistic reasons.

As a consultant I had been in at its conception and then worked with its design and development. I had overseen field tests of its prototype in several Latin American countries. The machine held greater potential, in my opinion, for bettering the lives of poor tropical farmers than anything else I had seen. Why deny a degree of confident satisfaction? I do not remember saying it to myself, but I might have: "An American can do anything. By God, we can even shape up the economy of this country!"

But can we? Can the handbook, the tractor, the massive amounts of U.S. foreign aid help to build a viable, twentieth-century nation here in the Dominican Republic?

Consider some of the problems. At present, the country cannot feed itself and must import a percentage of its food; partly because of this there is a trade deficit. The government operates on deficit financing.

Literacy is about 60 percent. Of 600,000 youngsters in primary school, only 60,000 will ever reach the sixth grade, only 3,000 will graduate from high school.

Over half the nation's income is derived from sugar which frequently is produced at a loss. In 1966, for example, it cost 9¢

a pound to produce the sugar for which the Dominican Republic was paid 6¢ a pound under the U.S. quota. (This quota system is one of several forms of indirect U.S. aid which have become economic necessities for many of the developing nations.) The sugar which the United States did not buy was sold on the world market for 2¢ a pound, or at a loss of 7¢ per pound. The main problem here is that the land produces little else that anyone in the world wants, only the sugar—and of this the world produces too much. Yet the land is the Dominican Republic's only true resource. The nation's future, in essence, must be bought by its agricultural land. Some of it is very good, but there is not enough of it.

In the cities a housing shortage exists and everywhere the terrible unemployment problem reflects the annual average per capita income of only $187.

Throughout the entire troubled history of the nation, political stability has been either dictatorial or not quite attainable. Lately, the U.S. foreign aid program has been providing public safety advisors to help the Dominican Republic police "control civil disturbances,"[1] that is, "to keep the lid on things."

Add to these woes yet another, the biggest one of all: a population which will double in less than eighteen years. Right now, today, half this population is fourteen years old *or younger*, the age when children have the fastest growing food needs. Soon they will be child-bearing young adults themselves.

How can any American, including myself, believe he can make even a small dent in the problems of a nation with a mess like that?

A Dominican friend, Tomás Pastoriza, once answered that question: "When a ship is sinking, does the captain say, 'Tonight it will be black tie and dinner at 8:30'? No, he shouts, 'Man the lifeboats!' "

Then Tomás asked, "But where is our lifeboat?"

Surveying the leaky Dominican ship of state, can anyone honestly believe American know-how can be the lifeboat?

So now, after finishing my research trip and seeing the successive failures of development projects, I say to myself, how naive I was to think "my" agricultural handbook could compensate for the shortage of agricultural land. What an innocent I was to think the new Ford tractor[2] in itself could produce what the land cannot. How blindly we contribute to all those private, voluntary, nonprofit organizations involved with foreign assistance around the world— from the giant CARE program down to the small charity clinic (more than 2,000 of these agencies are operating from the United

States).[3] We make the contributions in the altruistic belief that such efforts can solve the problem. As for the Dominican Republic, can even a third of a billion dollars in aid make up for what the country does not have in resources?

Why is it we Americans are so supremely confident we can remake the world? I know of no other nation which believes it can.

I have concluded that this confidence—that we can remake the world all at once—is an admirable (although sometimes irritating) trait that is bred into us. This source of strength (or weakness) springs from the happy union of the American man and the American land.

Thanks to our land, some so extraordinarily fertile that it was farmed intensively without fertilizer for a hundred years, America has been the home of plenty. In this basic respect, America has stood apart from all other nations.

And our good fortune does not end there. The mineral resources, too, are enormous. The United States is the largest producer in the world of such important minerals as barium, cadmium, coal (though there are estimates that the U.S.S.R. now outproduces us), copper, feldspar, natural gas, gypsum, lead, mica, molybdenum, petroleum, salt, silver, titanium, uranium, vanadium, phosphate,[4] as well as a number of ores of lesser importance.

Over the first three centuries of our history, attention was centered on developing the land—a land endowed with everything a nation could ask for. The resulting image of a country flowing with milk and honey made America the envy of the world. Immigrants and native-born Americans alike came to believe that there really, truly, actually, honestly is a special quality that sets the American apart from everyone else on the globe, a quality often called Yankee ingenuity or get-up-and-go. It has been an integral part of the makeup of America's folk heroes from Benjamin Franklin to John Glenn and Neil Armstrong. That quality, wedded to a superior technology, makes it possible, so goes the myth, for an American to do things no one else can do. Through the Peace Corps, through miscellaneous volunteer programs, through a personal semireligious calling, through an uncontrollable urge to help, Americans have gone off to live cheerfully in a lot of God-awful places. They have gone believing their ingenuity, their Yankee uniqueness, could single-handedly and within a fraction of a lifetime improve the lot of the hungry nations. Thus high American officials believed, without questioning it, the rumor that an American kid straight out of college had revolutionized the tomato industry of an entire nation within just a few months. Journalists, television panelists, and doctors themselves accepted as fact that one American doctor out of a Midwest town was making medical services available for 400,000 Indians.

Americans believe such reports because our own country is so full of fantastic success stories. They forget the uniqueness of the American land. They forget that countries where we have gone to bring progress and development are what they are because of a lack of resources. The cultural stagnation there, which we are trying so hard to jog into life, is not the result of any inferiority in the caliber of its citizens. It is due to the harsh fact that those citizens have so little with which to build a modern nation.

They are trying to lift themselves by their bootstraps when they have no boots.

Environment Controls Development

"*If we must force putty through a keyhole, then it should be of excellent quality, warmed carefully, pushed slowly but firmly, and we must be prepared for unexpected developments and be willing to take the blame or to accept the glory from such an unpredictable situation.*"

—MILO L. COX

What's Right Is Right

IF THERE LIVES *one group of persons who has an unusually sharp perception of what will or will not survive in a small tropical nation as a development project or as an investment opportunity I suggest it is the local bush pilots. They have seen the development experts and investors come and go.*

Spend a few days around the office of the local charter plane service and you will see what I mean. A U.S. embassy economist arrives to fly to a neighboring town to check out a report that it is buying a new electric power plant; a salesman charters a plane to fly to a distant coffee plantation that is expanding its processing plant; an American oil company official and his geologist "would like to just fly around for a couple of hours—we'll tell you where when we're airborne"; a veterinarian has a hurry-up call from a rancher with two of the six cows he imported last week dying; a World Bank education specialist wants to estimate by air the number of houses in a zone scheduled for new schools; an exporter has an order for 500 boxes of wild orchids and wants to check his suppliers' source to see if he can complete the order; a construction company has a crate of spare parts for a road grader which has broken down on a remote highway being built with U.S. money, etc., etc., etc.

Recently I reminisced with Tom Keane, a former Iowan and my onetime flying instructor, who runs a charter service in Central America. For twenty years he has flown investors, development experts, and all—hundreds of them—back into the hills on business, on feasibility studies, on errands of mercy. He has listened to them talk. He has sat and waited and waited and waited on remote grass runways as they collected their data, paid their employees, or heard the complaints of their associates.

I asked him, "How's Juan doing on the coast?"

KEANE: *Apparently O.K. He just bought a new plane so he must be making money on his slaughterhouse.*

PADDOCK: *And Armando? How's his coffee plantation?*

KEANE: *Again, everything seems to be going well.*

PADDOCK: *How's Joe?*

KEANE: *Oh, he left years ago.*

PADDOCK: *You mean his plans to raise pepper and coffee for A & P fell through?*

KEANE: *A & P didn't back down. It turned out he just couldn't raise anything on the land he had.*

PADDOCK: *Wasn't that at Ixcan? I just read where a Catholic priest has a new colonization program there.*

KEANE: *Yeah.*

PADDOCK: *Well, I read it was great. Full page story about him in the* Washington Post.

KEANE: *Yeah.*

PADDOCK: *What do you mean, yeah?*

KEANE: *Publicity doesn't make a success.*

PADDOCK: *What are you saying?*

KEANE: *Watching all these schemes get started and then suceeding or failing, I've learned one thing. If a project succeeds, it is because it is right for the place, because the air and the water and the land are* right. *Some know-how may be important, some money may help to get it going more quickly, but no amount of either will make a project right for the wrong spot.*

He added, as an afterthought, "And when things aren't right, publicity can act as a smoke-screen covering up the failure until people forget about the whole scheme."

How to Start a Boom

"To see what Mexicans can do, go to Monterrey. It is the most fabulous development story in all Latin America."

That is what Hugo Margáin, Mexican ambassador to Washington, said in reply to my question on where to see an effective development project in his country. Though I had not thought in terms of cities or regions, if this knowledgeable and enthusiastic Mexican envoy rated Monterrey as a development success then it should fit within the scope of my research.

Since 1932 I had been to Monterrey a half-dozen times. But I had not been there in the 1960s. The appearance of this mighty industrial city today, contrasted with what I had seen in my previous visits, was overwhelming. For one thing, I could see the city's smog from twenty miles away. During the last fifteen years the number of industries in Monterrey has doubled as part of an accompanying 500 percent increase in capital investment.[1]

Then, too, the contrast in the number of people was great; when I first visited Monterrey its population was 137,000. Sixteen years later the population had doubled. In each of the next two decades the population again doubled, so that by 1968 Monterrey had 1.1 million people. Within the next thirty years it is estimated the city will have 5 million inhabitants.

A boom city of extraordinary proportions! *Business Week* (October 25, 1969, p. 70) calls it the "jumpingest place in Mexico . . . a bustling center of industry and widespread business empires."

And yet, according to all the rules, Monterrey should be nothing more than a forlorn, dusty village of adobe huts—like others throughout the dried-out, semidesert interior of northern Mexico. Monterrey has no more resources than they. Its only unique feature is Saddleback Mountain—twin peaks that provide a dramatic scenic backdrop.

Worst of all, Monterrey has a chronic shortage of water. No one is so bold as to predict where the city will get its water ten years from now. My hotel room had a notice asking guests to conserve water. I was told that new wells had to be drilled to an incredible depth of 3,000 feet to reach water. Whenever the "normal Monterrey drought" becomes slightly more severe than usual, it is cause for alarm as the water in the wells becomes dangerously low.

Water or not, according to *Terry's Guide to Mexico* (pp. 183–85), Monterrey "has become the richest and busiest industrial city in Mexico," with, unfortunately, all the familiar dislocations of population explosions around the world: jerry-built housing, widespread slums, an increasingly visible cleavage between the very rich and the very poor. I felt a nostalgia for the quieter, more relaxed life of only a few years ago.

One of the not-so-old residents put it this way: "When I was a boy I knew everyone and everyone knew me. When I came out of my house, I would say, 'Good morning,' and ask, 'How is the weather?' 'Is your cousin getting married next week?' 'I hear your niece is going to have a baby.'

"Today, no one seems to know me. I go to the cinema and to my bank in the morning and to a concert in the evening and I see no one whom I know. It is terrible to live in society and to be alone." He was quiet a moment, then remembering a more golden time, he said, "Twenty-five years ago, the promenade was a precious thing to watch. There is still a promenade, but it doesn't amount to much compared to what it was once."

His words reminded me of the first promenade I had seen in Monterrey. According to custom, the señoritas walked in pairs or groups in one direction around the downtown park, or plaza, on Thursday and Sunday evenings; the young men walked in the other direction. This provided each with the opportunity to flirt with "the one" twice on each circuit. Exciting business. The band played. The old folks sat on benches and gossiped. The youngsters darted here and there playing tag around the bandstand.

Today, in a city of over a million, the promenade can hardly provide the meeting ground it once did. The young people from society families prefer the country clubs. The poor cannot afford the extra bus fare to and from their outlying slums. "Everyone" does not know "everyone" any more in Monterrey.

Nevertheless it remains a charming city and generally makes a good impression on the American who has come south of the border for the first time. If it is his first glimpse of Mexico, or even if he has already visited the truly romantic and lovely cities of central Mexico, those first delightful impressions of Monterrey will stay in his memory.

Income from U.S. tourists in search of something colorful and strange in a convenient foreign country was one of the first hypotheses I tested to explain Monterrey's development. But I soon discovered Monterrey's bustling industries could not remotely have been sparked by tourism alone. Also there is the great range of its industries, matched only by those of Mexico City.

What is paradoxical is that Monterrey, with almost no natural resources nearby, has both heavy industry and, literally, hundreds of kinds of light industries. The latter include firms making cigarettes, pottery, glass, textiles, cement, beer, and plastics in prodigious quantities—solid evidence of industrialization in depth!

Would that every developing nation had a "Milwaukee" like this!

To get to the bottom of the mystery, I asked everyone I met, from cab driver to prominent industrialist, "Why is Monterrey booming? Why has it developed faster than any other Mexican city?"

"Because we're a different kind of people here," said a bellhop. "We work hard and save our money. See that dip between the peaks of Saddleback? The reason it's there is because a Monterrey man was told a penny was buried there and he went up and dug and dug until he found it."

José P. Saldaña, Monterrey's official historian and author of several books on the city's background, gave the bellhop's view a sociological twist: "The character and the quality of the people here are different. When the Spanish first came, the Indians were nomadic, in contrast to the pyramid builders of central and southern Mexico. Only after 300 years of fighting were they eventually driven out to Texas and Chihuahua. Thus the Indians never interbred with the white settlers. All Nuevo León (the state of which Monterrey is the capital) is European. Then, when the French came with Maximillian, they liked the girls of Nuevo León because they were white. We had a large influx of French blood at that time."

Eduardo Hovelman Peña, head of the local Chamber of Commerce, was much less confident of such reasoning: "I don't know what started our boom, but we can go on indefinitely like this. We have only one worry—water."

Andrés M. Sada, manager of the huge Fibras Químico (synthetic fibers) and member of one of Monterrey's most prominent families, answered my question by throwing up his hands and saying, "I don't have the slightest idea. I take part in committees and groups designed to get all Mexico industrialized, but actually we don't know 'Why Monterrey?' We don't know why some areas industrialize and others do not. We just don't know."

Sada went on to make a comparison between Monterrey and Guadalajara, Mexico's other big provincial city. Guadalajara is only now beginning to compete with Monterrey for new industries, Sada said. "The people there are different. It is an easier life in Guadalajara. There they have agriculture just around the corner. But here, what else is there to do but industrialize? We can't farm."

Antonio L. Rodríguez, retired head of one of Mexico's largest insurance companies, also made a comparison with Guadalajara: "They (the people of Guadalajara) have more potential than we do because they have more electrical power, more water, and they are closer to a larger market for their products, which includes Mexico City. But Guadalajara does not have the quality of people found in Monterrey."

Rodríguez also said, "We retain the inherited traits of a frontier people. We had no connections with the rest of Mexico. The Indians around here were nomads and dangerous. We learned to take care of ourselves. And we still do."

John H. Barber, commercial officer of the American consulate general, agreed about the improbable nature of Monterrey's growth: "Frankly, industrialization here does not make sense. The iron ore used at the steel mills comes from Durango and the coke until very recently was imported from the United States. The paper industry here is based on wheat straw brought all the way from Sonora. And there are a dozen other illustrations of the distances involved in manufacturing in Monterrey."

A cab driver had his own definitive answer: "Our Three Families are very aggressive." And indeed everywhere in Monterrey I heard about the Three Families, the richest and most influential in town and owners of the largest businesses. Their names (Muguerza, Sada, and Garza) cropped up in every discussion I had about the growth of Monterrey.

At first I tended to discount this exaggerated emphasis on the Three Families, and most of the other comments seemed to stem from local chauvinism.

Driven by my quandary, I put a leading question to Edward Jamison, the U.S. consul general in Monterrey: "Don't you think the reason Monterrey has developed is due to its proximity to the United States?"

"You might think so at first glance," he said. "But that isn't the case. What has the United States done for Monterrey?" he asked, before lauching into a variant of the cab driver's answer. "Monterrey's present level of industrialization is the direct outgrowth of the economic base created by the early members of the Three Families. Unlike most other such families, the business abilities of their forebears have been transmitted intact through several generations to today's sons and grandsons. Go back and check out how those families got started. This may provide the answer you are looking for."

And so I shifted my attention in that direction.

The Three Families, it turned out, are indeed at the heart of Monterrey's development story. But why these three families? What got them started?

In the beginning it was only one man, José Calderón. In 1830, when Monterrey was still a small settlement lost in the reaches of the arid, virtually unpopulated Mexican Northeast, Calderón, then a young man, had a local "transport company"— a euphemism for what I suppose must have been a few mules.

Calderón's business consisted in carrying supplies between Saltillo and the dusty hamlet of Monterrey. Saltillo, fifty miles southwest of Monterrey, was the area's administrative headquarters and metropolitan commercial center. At that same time, San Antonio, Texas, was still a Mexican town and some Mexican-U.S. trade trickled through it to Saltillo via Monterrey.

Then came the independence of Texas, its annexation by the United States, and the Mexican-American War. When the dust had settled in 1848, the border had been redrawn. San Antonio was now inside U.S. territory and Monterrey, lo and behold, had become the closest Mexican town to the U.S. border.

Virtually all overland trade now passed through Monterrey and Calderón found his business prospering, as did Monterrey itself. Saltillo, not so well located, began to wither on the vine. With the advent of the U.S. Civil War, Calderón prospered even more. He was paid well for organizing a mule transport system to carry cotton out of the South, through Monterrey on its way to the Mexican port of Tampico, and to Europe.

By the close of the war Calderón was rich. In 1874 he hired an assistant by the name of Isaac Garza and then took his brother-in-law, José A. Muguerza, into the business. When Calderón, who apparently had no children, died Muguerza and Garza (who married a Sada) took over the business. The Three Families were born. Their source of wealth came from the backs of Calderón's mules.

In 1882 Calderón's business was further blessed when a railroad was built between the U.S. border and Monterrey. This was the only Mexican rail service to the United States. Again Calderón's fortune swelled as he fanned his mules and oxcarts out from the railhead at Monterrey.

Thus, as Consul General Jamison had suggested, I did find a part of the Monterrey story in the history of the Three Families. However, the answer to the puzzle "Why Monterrey?" was not as Jamison had anticipated. Calderón must have been an excellent muleteer and a businessman with a daring frontier spirit, but he would have died a much poorer man had it not been for Monterrey's strategic location, its timely proximity to the "Colossus of the North." This propinquity was a commercial asset during the Mexican-American War and was further enhanced by the U.S. Civil War.

And therein lies the answer to Jamison's question: "What has the United States done for Monterrey?" It has been next door.

In 1886 Porfirio Díaz, Mexico's longtime ruler, gave Monterrey certain tax incentives to stimulate local industry. The Three Families, with their store of capital, were in a position to take advantage of the tax breaks. Their first major investment was in the Cuauhtémoc Brewery in 1890. This brewery made use of Louis Pasteur's recent research findings. Pasteurization enabled the Families to bottle beer and to ship it long distances, apparently the first such beer in Mexico.

The brewery, which became successful beyond anyone's wildest dreams, is still very much a part of the Mexican scene. It put the Families on the road to real wealth. Soon they formed Compañía Fundidora de Fierro y Acero, the first steel mill in Mexico to produce, among other things, bottle caps for their beer. This was done in partnership with two U.S. metallurgical companies (American Smelting and Refining and American Metal

Climax). To make bottles for the beer, the Families formed a glass company in 1909; it quickly became the largest in Latin America.

Soon another bonus from proximity to the United States came in the form of a gas pipeline which was built in 1915 from Rome, Texas, to Monterrey. Thanks to the pipeline, Monterrey now had the cheapest fuel in all Mexico.

The Families' "empire" continued to grow with the city. By the mid-1930s they had branched out into department stores, banking, textiles, and paper manufacturing. In the 1960s they built the area's largest power plant and a major chemical complex producing such products as petrochemicals and rayon fibers. They also entered the investment banking field. And the expansion still goes on. According to the U.S. consulate in Monterrey, the Three Families were worth an estimated $250 million by 1962.

But to imply that today's industrial boom was solely brought about by the Three Families is obviously an exaggeration. Though they spearheaded the city's industrialization, today hundreds of other successful businesses are contributing to the astounding industrial diversification of Monterrey. Indeed, one feature of diversified growth is that in the right environment it can feed on itself. This, plus the sizable sector of the economy catering to American tourists, adds up to an amazing business activity in Monterrey.

At present, the city is bigger and wealthier and carries more political weight than any other provincial Mexican city. With only 2 percent of the nation's population, the city generates 10 percent of all Mexico's federal revenues.

I FIND the answer to my question, "Why Monterrey?" a sad one. I wanted an answer which could be used to turn development programs that had failed into successes. I wanted an answer which said, for example, that people had to be more ingenious than others, or that they had to possess more know-how than their neighbors, or that they had to work harder than their competitors. Instead I found the Monterrey answer said that to achieve development or prosperity or progress, call it what you may, there must be resources to support it. For Monterrey, its geographic proximity to the United States has been a resource as valuable as oil in the ground, iron in the hills, or agricultural abundance in the surrounding valley.

HONDURAS is a poor and backward country, a statement I must make categorically.

I hasten to add that the Hondurans themselves are a delightful people with a graciousness and a sense of personal dignity worthy of study by the world's proud nations. Hondurans, perhaps more than any other nationality, are proof against that tired argument that a country is poor because its people are innately lazy or unteachable. No, the nation is poor for the same reason I repeat like a litany: It is damned with too few resources.

Topographically Honduras is a beautiful country with vast expanses of rocky, Appalachian-type mountains and enormous quantities of clear, clean air. One day these may well become a merchandizable resource. Until then, Honduras must limp along as best it can.

The nation has no coal—no petroleum—a bit of silver—some pine forests—nothing else. Patches of thin agricultural soils are strewn carelessly about among broken mountains and inaccessible valleys. Though Honduras fronts on two oceans, this does little good. Its Pacific coast is largely a swamp, unapproachable by ship. Until recently its Atlantic coast has been remote and almost unreachable from Tegucigalpa, the capital.

Population growth is another albatross around Honduras's neck. Its 2.7 million citizens are increasing at the rate of 3.4 percent per year, meaning they will double in twenty-one years. Honduras has the same population per arable acre as India did in 1970. How the country will cope with the oncoming cataclysm is anyone's guess. At the moment, Honduras has one doctor for every 9,200 citizens; one nurse for every 17,000. Its annual per capita income is $235, one of the lowest in the Western Hemisphere. To repeat: Honduras is a poor country.

But where is the one genuine boom city in Central America? the fastest growing? the liveliest business hub? the place where a cement mixer churns at every street corner as new offices and stores spring up like weeds?

San Pedro Sula, Honduras—that's where!

San Pedro (no one ever seems to add the Sula) is located in northern Honduras. Its population of 100,000 is growing at the rate of 10 percent per year. The city has already established itself as Central America's principal textile producer. Plastics, cement, and beer are also important industries. The Coca-Cola plant bottles more of that stuff in San Pedro than anywhere else in all Central America.

Why the boom in San Pedro? It is an old, old town, true enough. Its founding dates back to eighty-four years before the Pilgrims stepped ashore at Plymouth Rock, but this is not unusual for Central America. It has had its share of disasters; what town in this part of the world hasn't? Pirates raided San Pedro in 1660, floods washed it out a number of times, and yellow fever nearly wiped it out on several occasions. Why now, suddenly out of the blue, has it become Central America's boom town?

Though I have been in and out of San Pedro several times in the past fifteen years, this was the first time I had gone there specifically to study the mystery of its development explosion. Why, for instance, should San Pedro, which is thirty miles from the sea, have thrived and not nearby Puerto Cortés, the nation's one good port? Why San Pedro and not Tegucigalpa, the capital?

Indeed, the road from San Pedro to the capital is deplorable, although a new one is under construction. As recently as 1930, travelers between San Pedro and the capital had to make part of the trip by horse and another part by boat across a lake. If it was the rainy season, flooded rivers had to be forded.

On this visit I reached San Pedro by a good, new highway along the northwestern boundary from San Salvador, the capital of neighboring El Salvador. The road, an expensive development project financed by the Inter-American Development Bank, was built to provide El Salvador with a means of easy access to the Atlantic port of Puerto Cortés.

I had the highway pretty much to myself. It was a luxurious experience to drive comfortably across the mountainous terrain I had once partially traversed on the back of a rumpspringing horse.

For years I had heard people in Tegucigalpa talk about the great agricultural richness of the region over which I was motoring. I had been skeptical because I had flown over the area several times and had applied a simple test I have devised for estimating the value of such lands from the air when I do not have access to soil samples and surveys. If a bird's-eye view reveals bare soil between the trees I conclude the land cannot be easily farmed because it is obviously deficient in nutrients or water or both.

On those flying trips, the land between San Salvador and San Pedro had definitely failed this test. Now, on the new road, I was able to confirm this finding; agriculture was virtually non-existent for three-quarters of the way, no matter what the optimists in Tegucigalpa said. This does not mean there were not people trying to scratch out a living. There were. But it was not the sort of farming that would support what one calls a livelihood.

The wood frame shacks scattered here and there along the roadside were identical to those in the poor rural areas elsewhere in Honduras. Some of the shacks were made of adobe, but in all cases the floors were of dirt. The windows had no glass. The courtyards were enclosed by fences of spine-covered brambles, with a solitary cow or more often a couple of pigs or goats inside.

My visit coincided with the dry season and dust was every-where. Nothing, absolutely nothing, was being cultivated. The men passed the day lounging around with their neighbors and smoking and waiting for the rains to come—when the land would again give them something to do.

The people seemed thin and hungry. Through open door-ways I could see inside the houses the usual rickety furniture, a couple of home-made beds and a few crude chairs; a kerosene lamp; and, of course, the one luxury—a transistor radio.

Eventually the road reached a narrow valley where tobacco is raised on scattered parcels of land. This "rich tobacco land" (as I had often heard it described) consisted of plots of from one to five acres, though even these were few and far between. An acre of tobacco here can produce what is in Honduras a reasonably good income, $300 or more per year. I noticed the houses now were better built—some had cement floors. More activity was apparent along the road. What a pity the area of this prosperity was not larger!

Obviously these San Pedro backlands have not fueled the city's sudden takeoff. When the road broke out of the hills and into San Pedro's valley, I could see broad expanses of sugar cane, some orange groves, and a lot of bananas. The land was flat and the grazing cattle looked healthy. But in a few minutes this prosperous flatland gave way to a sprinkling of factories and I was in San Pedro.

As with any boom town, the enthusiasm one senses in San Pedro is immediately contagious. Everyone seemed busy and pur-poseful and everyone was full of statistics and gossip about new businesses that were starting up. Cab drivers proved to be wildly loquacious and their semiknowledge impressive.

But when I asked people, "What started this boom in San

Pedro?" they only shook their heads in puzzlement. Only the most reflective of the town's businessmen seemed to have given the matter any thought. The rest appeared to accept the town's flourishing as a sort of miracle of the eighth day of creation.

The man on the street usually replied chauvinistically, "We people here in San Pedro are of better stock than those up there in the capital."

I did find, however, three men who tried carefully to reason out their answers. The first was Gabriel Mejía, president of a local semiofficial development bank which, incidentally, channels some U.S. foreign aid funds into local capital-short businesses in need of loans. He was also manager of the local cement company, formed a few years ago to take advantage of the Central American Common Market and which quickly became an industrial giant by local standards.

While waiting for my appointment, I noticed a sense of confidence and professionalism among the people who came and went in his bustling outer office. They acted as though they could tackle a job and get it done, a marked contrast to the atmosphere of the average office in the capital city of Tegucigalpa.

I was impressed, too, to be greeted in English by the receptionist and truly surprised to hear English spoken interchangeably with Spanish among Mejía's office staff.

Mejía himself seemed to epitomize the aggressive entrepreneur, a man willing to gamble on a new enterprise, an aspect which people in this tropical Honduran city claimed to be typical of their energetic business community. Mejía met me in his shirtsleeves, something that would have seemed unusual in Tegucigalpa.

Personable and lively, he was easy for an American to sit down and talk with. I commented on this attitude of confidence and ability in San Pedro and asked what was the cause.

"Mostly because our salaries are high here on the coast," he replied. "This means our workers are better than anywhere else. We attract good workers."

To illustrate this point, Mejía told me about a World Bank official who had come to Honduras to make a technical study of projected investment opportunities over the following five years. The technician became so exasperated with the delays and lackadaisical methods in Tegucigalpa he was about to leave the country and recommend to the World Bank that it drop the study altogether. Fortunately he came to San Pedro first and found the atmosphere completely different and the businessmen aggressively eager to participate in his study. He stayed on and wrote a fine report—fine at least from the point of view of San Pedro.

Mejía then repeated, as others had, "We are different here. We are tropical. Back in the capital, in the interior, they live in another world. Our spirit is different. We don't have to wear a coat and tie and act formal to impress our associates and our visitors."

Before attempting to answer my question about the reasons for San Pedro's boom, Mejía leaned back and reflected for a moment. "You know, I have tried to understand the background of all this and I have concluded the reason is that we live right next door to the United Fruit Company. The company taught us how to organize ourselves. It taught us that if we work we will live better. It brought us useful technology. It is this, I have decided, that makes us different from people in Tegucigalpa and the rest of Central America, too."

"But where is the money coming from for the new industries in San Pedro?" I asked.

"It's mostly Honduran money," he said. "Some of it is personally owned and some comes from the government via development loans originating with the World Bank and the Inter-American Development Bank. Some loan money also comes from the U.S. government.

"But in the beginning it all started because San Pedro merchants had accumulated some extra capital by trading with United Fruit employees. We Hondurans ourselves began the expansion of our industry. Only later did other private and U.S. government capital come in.

"Once capital began to be generated, the area became a melting pot of peoples: North Americans, Salvadorans, Lebanese, Germans, and others, all busily developing new enterprises in league with the Hondurans."

Later I talked with Luis Fernando Fonseca, assistant manager of the port development program at Puerto Cortés, some thirty miles distant. Fonseca was born and raised in San Pedro, and people at the local development bank said he was the most knowledgeable person about the area and especially about San Pedro's industrial history.

Fonseca gave me the following explanation for his hometown's boom: "The reason for it is that San Pedro has always been the town most easily reached from La Lima, where the United Fruit

Company has its headquarters. Another town, El Progreso, is as close to La Lima but it is on the other side of the river and sometimes, before the bridge was built, you had to wait five or six hours to catch a boat or ferry across. It was always easier to come to San Pedro.

"On every company payday, you could see the effect on San Pedro stores. They were filled with people spending their money and it was this money coming into San Pedro from the company which made the town boom."

I pointed out, "United Fruit has a dozen big plantations throughout Central America. All have towns that have sprung up around them, yet none has boomed like San Pedro. Why?"

"You have to remember this boom did not begin overnight. It was fifty years in the making. The important thing about our location is that we are next to the tropical headquarters of United Fruit and the company has always had its headquarters here."

I could see at once the significance of this fact, for the other banana plantations are comparatively new and are essentially field offices. The towns around them have had less time to accumulate capital. In contrast, San Pedro, with the headquarters of United Fruit next door, has always had more white-collar workers trained for office and managerial jobs by the company; more of their children have been taught English at company-provided schools.

In addition, the company's research laboratories placed a demand on the local community to provide helpers for their technicians, requirements that led to upgrading the region's working force. Thus a technical as well as a monetary spillover resulted from the company's presence in the San Pedro area.

Fonseca continued his explanation of San Pedro's rise. "In 1954 the company was hit with a labor strike, the worst in its history. At that time the company was employing about 25,000 people in the San Pedro area, but the strike reduced the size of its labor force to about 3,000. The town was immediately hit by a terrible depression, for up to then our economy had been pretty steady, thanks to the company.

"Our local businessmen realized they would have to do something—and do it quickly—to stay in business, because it appeared the company's labor trouble would last a long time. Because our store owners and businessmen had saved some money over the years they now had something to invest.

"The first investments were in two shirt factories which were an immediate success. Then a brewery, located originally at La Ceiba, moved to San Pedro—I suppose because a bigger market was here. Our boom had started."

Though various people with whom I talked came up with different ideas as to precisely when the boom began, the consensus was that it started around 1955. This means it followed immediately on the heels of the 1954 strike and it preceded the establishment of the Central American Common Market. The boom also occurred long before the new roads were built that ended San Pedro's previous isolation.

Later, in Tegucigalpa, I met Ing. Humberto León, head of the industrialization section of the National Development Bank (Banco de Fomento)—a Harvard graduate and a true whiz-kid. Although young, he seemed a bit worn out, presumably from the uphill battle to motivate the average Honduran worker to attain the efficiency needed for his country's industries to compete with those of other nations in the Central American Common Market. This was reflected in his first remark to me.

"When you pay good wages," he said, "you attract good workers. In the beginning, United Fruit drew the best workers into their area. Then San Pedro employers had to pay good wages to attract them to their own businesses and to hold them. The result is the most efficient labor force in the country; in fact it is so good San Pedro can compete with the best labor force in Salvador and Guatemala."

León felt it was United Fruit Company wages that had sparked San Pedro's expansion. He pointed out that the average salary in Honduras at the time of my research was $1.40 per day, but the minimum paid by United Fruit was $2.80. Later on, in going over company figures, I learned that the average United Fruit daily wage, including fringe benefits, was actually $4.97.

"The United Fruit wage means two things to the San Pedro area," León said.

"First, the people there have a high purchasing power resulting in a ready, built-in market for any industry on the north coast. They don't need highways or a new transportation system to reach a market. They already have their market. It is there.

"Second, the high wages stimulated by United Fruit led to general improvement in worker training in the San Pedro area. You can't afford to pay high wages to poorly trained employees. Then, too, the company itself trained a lot of workers who were able to command good wages from people who later employed them. A lot of men who were not trained by United Fruit had some of that training rub off on them from those who had been company trained."

So, just as the basic resource for Monterrey's development was proximity to the United States, San Pedro's resource was proximity to the United Fruit Company.

The Plantation Economy
of El Pulpo

BEFORE ARRIVING in San Pedro Sula I had asked many officials and experts to name an effective development effort in the area and to indicate what was responsible for it. No one had mentioned the United Fruit Company as a development success story.

While some might identify the United Fruit Company as a major resource and a key to development success in the Central American low tropics, the fact remains that the vast majority of Latin Americans hate and fear the company.

> **Octopus** . . . most species are . . . usually timid and in-offensive (*Webster's New Collegiate Diction-ary*, 1953)
>
> **Octopus—Pulpo** . . . an organization said to be highly dangerous (*Velazquez Spanish-English Diction-ary*)

Seldom were there two more diametrically opposite definitions for the same word. It is not by chance that in Latin America the United Fruit Company is known far and wide as "El Pulpo." And therein lies a lesson for the development specialist.

SAN PEDRO SULA and Honduras have been fortunate that the hot, humid environment on the Atlantic jungle-like coast is the place where bananas grow best. Found there is the right combination of soil, rain, sun, and temperature—the right ecology for bananas. This was, of course, what originally caused the United Fruit Com-pany—El Pulpo—to set up operations there over seventy years ago. During that time, fact and fiction have built up around the com-pany as insidiously as that around any monster of the deep.

The true beginning of San Pedro's success story goes back, really, to the herculean task initially performed by the company to modify nature so that money could be made from bananas.

Swamps had to be drained, the jungle land cleared and ferti- lized, pipelines laid to carry irrigation water, a spraying system in- stalled for insect and disease control, and dikes built to prevent flooding during the rainy season.

Throughout the company's areas of operation in Central America whole new ports were built from scratch, railroads laid, roads leveled, and laboratories set up with modern equipment—all paid for by United Fruit as normal development expense. Ordi- narily no government funds were received, although the original jungle lands were often given free and customs duties waived on equipment and supplies and tax concessions granted. The invest- ment of money and labor was tremendous. For the company had to provide the total system, an elaborate complex of facilities com- prising whatever was needed to get bananas to grow—to grow big- ger, better, and handsomer so they would catch the eye of the housewife in the stores up in Yankeeland.

The company had to give birth to a gigantic new business organism after a pregnancy fraught with prolonged complications. Only then could the bananas—without a bruise on their tender skins—flow with seeming effortlessness from the plantations to the waiting ship. Only then would the bananas ripen during the voy- age and arrive on time, not too soon, not too late—either way spelling commercial disaster—but on time.

It takes BIG BUSINESS to create and operate big plantations —and it takes money. Today it costs from $1700 to $2500 to turn an acre of jungle into an acre of producing bananas, without re- gard to the other expenses of transportation, overhead, taxes, and the like.

In spite of all that is written today criticizing the plantation system, there remains a major reason why this is the most econom- ically feasible unit (and, generally speaking, the only feasible unit) for cultivating the coastal tropics of Honduras. That reason is the weed problem.

A man with a machete, an axe, and a pair of oxen simply can- not keep ahead of the voracious jungle, no matter how industrious he may be. Through a prodigious effort he can clear the land, even plant the land. But then he will find the jungle has already risen to strangle the crops standing in his fields. Not until the farmer can muster enough capital to buy a tractor, herbicides, and fertilizers can he begin to dominate the inexorable encroachment of weeds. To mount a profitable farming operation in the tropic lowlands, the farmer needs capital and efficiency, plus a good business head.

With this in mind, consider the first United Fruit plantation I ever visited. It was located on the southern coast of Guatemala at Tiquisate and at that time was reputed to be the world's most modern banana operation. For an agriculturalist like myself to see it was an exciting experience.

This one plantation had twenty-eight square miles of uninterrupted banana fields, all irrigated by an overhead sprinkler system. The water was sprayed over this expanse by revolving nozzles mounted on steel towers. At each revolution the nozzle sprayed water over 3.3 acres. A completely separate system of pipes, operated from their own central pumping stations, provided Bordeaux mixture, a standard all-purpose spray of copper sulfate and lime used to control the banana leaf disease called sigatoka which (as is told later) the company struggled to overcome early in its development.

The headquarters compound consisted of several hundred houses. A hundred of these were modern two- and three-bedroom homes for the managerial staff. The others were small and plain and, by comparison, primitive; these were the quarters for the field hands. Nevertheless they were far more modern and better built than comparable housing for the local people outside the company's boundaries.

Included also in the compound were two club houses, a swimming pool, a golf course, a church, schools, a hospital, an airport, and miles and miles of gravel roads. The $25 million involved in setting up this one plantation was large by any capitalist's standard. For officials and citizens in Guatemala City it was scarcely possible to visualize the total figure involved. Yet eighteen years after my visit, the whole banana plantation had been dismantled because transportation costs to the Atlantic port had become prohibitive. The land had been sold to Guatemalan farmers for new uses—cotton plantations and cattle ranches.

I cite this as one illustration of how even big plantation agriculture must remain flexible in order to make money in the tropics. Indeed it is a constant challenge to grow a crop, any crop, in the tropics. Meeting that challenge takes money and a quick mind capable of making fast decisions, such as when and how to gamble a few million dollars.

An example of one such decision was told me by two of the

men directly involved in the incident—Walter Turnbull and Vining Dunlop.

In 1935 a dreadful disease suddenly developed out of nowhere in the company's plantation near San Pedro Sula. The disease did not have a name then, but today it is known as sigatoka. It can turn an entire lush field of bananas into brown and dying plants within a matter of weeks.

Walter Turnbull was head of the company's tropical operations at the time. Headquarters were at La Lima, a few miles from San Pedro. When the first field turned brown no one knew the reason. Turnbull immediately dispatched a radiogram to United Fruit headquarters in Boston saying, in essence, "Help!" He wanted a specialist to advise him on what was happening to his bananas. But Turnbull did not receive satisfaction on this score. He sent a second cable. Still no answer.

Out of desperation he went to Boston (in those days by slow boat) to see the head of the company, the legendary Samuel Zemurray. Zemurray, who never really learned to speak English clearly, was the son of a poor Bessarabian farmer, and at one time owned $31,600,000 in United Fruit stock. Having come out of retirement to rescue the company during the depression years, he was now in the middle of his second career.

"Sam the Banana Man," as he was popularly known, listened politely to Turnbull's story and then said, "Walter, you have been working too hard. Bananas always have problems, and we are always being threatened by something that is going to wipe us out, but it never does. Go take a vacation. I'll charter a boat for you if you'll go off fishing for a weekend. Then go back to La Lima and forget about this problem."

"So," Turnbull told me, "I did what the boss said. I went off on a long relaxing weekend and returned to Honduras."

Two months later he received by radiogram a request from Zemurray to meet him in Miami for a week's fishing. At the end of the first day Zemurray said, "Say, Walter, remember a couple of months ago, you came to Boston in a stew about something that was killing the bananas and we were going to be wiped out?"

TURNBULL: Yes.
ZEMURRAY: What's happened to the problem?
TURNBULL: What I said would happen. We're being wiped out.
ZEMURRAY: What are you doing about it?

TURNBULL: Just what you told me to do. Forgetting it.

ZEMURRAY: What do you want done?

TURNBULL: Have someone come down and tell me what we can do.

Zemurray turned the yacht around and headed full speed for Honduras.

On the evening they arrived a party was given for the boss. United Fruit Company officials have always had a reputation for hard drinking, partly because other entertainment in company towns is so limited. The next morning the hungover Zemurray entourage toured the plantation in a railroad car. In addition to Zemurray and Turnbull the group included company vice-president Arthur Pollan and a young plant pathologist, Dr. Vining Dunlop, whom Turnbull had himself hired out of desperation a few weeks earlier to study this new disease.

When the train reached the first farm, Zemurray could see at once the bananas were blighted and a large number had died. It looked as though a giant blowtorch had scorched the fields. Zemurray was appalled by the sight. After a few more miles, they came to a beautiful blue green patch of bananas which stood out in striking contrast to those in the disaster area.

ZEMURRAY: Why is this so healthy?

DUNLOP *(in awe of Zemurray and suffering from a glorious hangover)*: Well, I sprayed it with Bordeaux mixture.

ZEMURRAY: Why?

DUNLOP: I didn't know what the trouble was. Bordeaux is a standard all-purpose spray. My first reaction when I saw the bananas dying was to get out and spray with Bordeaux. I still don't know what's causing the trouble but Bordeaux seems to have stopped it.

ZEMURRAY: How did you do it?

DUNLOP *(gaining confidence)*: I put a couple of men in there with knapsack sprayers and they have been spraying those two acres every four or five days.

ZEMURRAY: Could you do the same thing with 100 acres?

DUNLOP: Sure, don't know why not. *(In recounting the experience to me Dunlop said if he had not had such a hangover, he would never have been so positive.)*

ZEMURRAY: Could you do it with 1,000 acres?

DUNLOP: I guess so.

ZEMURRAY: How?

DUNLOP *(enjoying the challenge):* I'd get a hundred men out there with knapsack sprayers and just spray the hell out of it. No, I have a better idea. I'd buy a big pump and run pipes through the thousand acres and spray them from a central station. *(Dunlop told me this was a spur-of-the-moment idea that had not occurred to him before.)*

ZEMURRAY: What size pump?

DUNLOP *(ignoring the penalties of a poor guess):* I don't know, just as big a pump as you can get.

ZEMURRAY: Pollan, you heard him. Buy us a batch of pumps and enough pipe to cover the farm.

POLLAN: Right.

ZEMURRAY: Well, what are you waiting for?

POLLAN: I'll do it as soon as we get back to the office.

ZEMURRAY: Office, hell, see the line phone on that pole. Get on it and start buying now!

And that is how the largest plant disease control program the world had ever seen started—from a line phone in the middle of a banana patch. It was an emergency, and Zemurray took the gamble that Dunlop had the right idea. From that phone were initiated orders to buy $6 million of pumps and pipe. United Fruit's outlays for sigatoka control eventually reached a figure of more than $10 million per year.

To make its banana business profitable United Fruit has not only had to work within the limitations of the agricultural environment—disease, drainage, isolation, fertility—but within the limitations of the political environment as well.

The Central American political scene has been one of constant civil warfare. Historians cannot even agree on how many revolutions there have been in the area. Honduras alone has had at least seventy-five, and no elected president in Honduran history has served out his full term. Dictators have seized the numerous opportunities to step in and fill the power vacuum.

As a consequence, until recently, banana companies that had signed agreements with one president frequently found the papers worthless with the next; that is, assuming the company officers were aware of the change in government. Even a few decades ago messages between the banana lands and the highland capitals often had to be carried by horse. Weeks would go by with those on the coast blissfully ignorant as to the composition of the central government. Thus in the early years the company often made its own rules.

Once I tried to buy a coconut from a Carib Indian on the north coast of Honduras. The fellow was paddling a dugout with a pile of coconuts in the bow. I asked him in Spanish, "How much for a coconut?" and he replied, "Un búfalo." It took me a while to figure out that the old U.S. nickel with its buffalo was to him a Honduran coin. At one time the United Fruit Company imported U.S. currency for its local operations.

Generally the company insisted that Central American governments allocate to it huge tracts of virgin jungle lands (in the same way railroad companies did in the United States in the early days, thus obtaining huge western land concessions from the government before laying a single tie). The company also obtained tax concessions comparable to those these same governments are granting today in an effort to lure foreign capital into their Common Market area.

In reviewing the history of the dealings of United Fruit, Stacy May and Galo Plaza, former president of Ecuador and currently secretary general of the Organization of American States (OAS), wrote:

> To the foreign investors, the terms [granted to United Fruit] did not appear to be unreasonably cheap, in view of what they conceived the risks to be—a judgment that has been vindicated by time. Even from the vantage point of hindsight, it is difficult to say whether or not, if the producing countries had set harder terms, the job would have got done. It did, and most of the modern ports of Central America are there because banana pioneers built them. The early contracts made by United Fruit in tropical countries fixed low export taxes on bananas for a period of years and granted certain tax exemptions.[1]

These early company contracts have grated on the nationalism of Latin America for a long time. Not infrequently people blame all the sorry political and developmental history of Central America on El Pulpo. The company, they claim, has sucked dry the economic resources of the area and has pressured against legislation necessary to carry out needed social reforms in order to protect its own economic empire.

As one result of modern communications, the governments of the banana republics have become more centralized and better organized. Political chaos may reign but now the chaos is more "controlled." Thus governments are better able to exert pressures on foreign businesses working within their boundaries. They have made it more difficult for all foreign businesses—of which United

Fruit is only one—to function. And it often is good politics to charge these companies with all sorts of misdeeds. As for El Pulpo, it is always open season.

Today the company's political power is but a shadow of its former self. But distrust of the company and its motives are as intense as ever. By comparison to everything else in most of these nations, the company is so huge! And a huge image is never lovable.

"As United Fruit goes, so goes Honduras." The Honduran government budget is influenced heavily, even dominated, by El Pulpo's profit and loss statement.

In 1963 the Honduran budget was $85 million, of which only $2 million came from company taxes (it was a poor banana year). But in 1967 (a good banana year), the government spent $133 million, of which $14.4 million, or 11 percent, came from company taxes—not to mention the income taxes paid by company employees and the taxes from firms supplying United Fruit.[2]

In Central America the company raises bananas on 75,000 acres and has contracts for bananas raised by independent operators on another 45,000 acres. In addition, the company has 8,500 acres in sugar cane, 33,000 in cacao, 38,000 in oil palm, and 45,000 in pasture supporting sizable cattle operations, plus the areas given over to townsites, roads, and other infrastructure. The company has a fleet of 80 ships, 900 miles of railroads, not to mention the Tropical Radio network, a major communications system.[3]

I am reminded of a long-time friend from the Middle West who has spent many years in Central America. Recently, visiting him for the first time in ten years, I saw he was still operating out of the same old run-down building.

"How's business?" I asked.

"Great."

"If it's so great," I kidded him, "how come you still keep this crummy office and shop?"

"I have learned something in my years here," he replied. "As soon as it looks as if you're making some money, you're in for trouble. The government raises your taxes, or requires new licensing, or holds up on okaying imports. The nationals find a dozen ways to move in so you have to move out. The secret is to *look* as if you're not making money. Keep small and no one will notice."

But El Pulpo cannot duplicate my friend's blissful anonymity. So the erroneous belief continues that El Pulpo is strangling the economy with one tentacle while with another it draws off huge profits from Latin America (a belief not held by Latin American investors, who themselves hold little company stock). Twenty-seven cents of each dollar the U.S. housewife spends for bananas are retained in Latin America. This is approximately the same percentage the American farmer retains for his produce. Yet out of this residual twenty-seven cents are paid the social benefits for company workers, their education, hospital care, and pensions—greater benefits than are provided by any other organization or government I know in the area. Equally important, it includes the taxes which help pay for the social programs of local governments for the rest of the populace. The company's sales of bananas bring in, via taxes, salaries, and purchase of fruit raised by independent operators, 35 percent of all Honduras's foreign exchange. That means 35 percent of all light bulbs, telephone wires, asphalt, aspirin, tractors, structural steel—all of the material things Honduras does not produce itself—a fair share of everything not eaten.[4]

In other words, one-third of Honduras's share of the twentieth century is paid for by company activity.

What if, say forty years ago when the winds of land reform agitation first began to blow, United Fruit had graciously broken up its huge plantations into small plots and turned them over to peasant agriculture? By now El Pulpo would be only a footnote in the area's history, and subsistence farming would prevail throughout the region. And today no one, I hazard, would have heard of San Pedro Sula (or, dare I say, Honduras).

Or what if, say forty years ago, El Pulpo had made the mistake of trying to raise apples instead of bananas? The fatal results would have been the same.

The Honduran low tropics have the right environment for bananas (not apples) and happily the world is willing to buy bananas and happily El Pulpo knows how to raise and sell bananas.

Honduras is a poor country. Think how much poorer it would be without El Pulpo.

Rather, think how much richer Honduras would be if it had a dozen other businesses which were as efficient as El Pulpo and employed as many of its citizens.

Extend this to the tropics of the rest of the hungry world. In each area the size of Honduras put a dozen businesses, no matter whether locally or foreign owned, whose products the world will buy, businesses which are right because the air and the water and the land are right.

An impossible assignment? It must be, considering all the failures of the hundreds and hundreds of development projects already attempted throughout the tropical world.

Land Reform via Integrated Colonization

AMONG DEVELOPMENT EXPERTS no formula for economic progress is more universally embraced than that of land reform. With the possible exception of the need for more education, the hue and cry for reforming the pattern of land holding is the most strident crusade advocated throughout Latin America, Asia, and much of Africa.

Repeatedly one hears from these experts that agricultural production is low because the landed gentry do not take a sufficient interest in their land, that absentee ownership is the curse of rural areas, that the peasant does a poor job of farming because he does not have the stimulus of controlling his own land. They say give the peasant his own piece of land and he will roll up his sleeves and hoe faster, plant more, plow deeper than he ever has in the past, and agricultural production will bloom and the nation will prosper.

No one has a precise idea of how much has been spent to further land reform in the developing world during the past twenty-five years, but the sum, including several billion dollars in foreign aid and government loans, has been enormous.

When President Kennedy's Alliance for Progress came into being in 1961, its charter specified that it was designed "to encourage, in accordance with the characteristics of each country, programs of comprehensive agrarian reform leading to the effective transformation, where required, of unjust structures and systems of land tenure and use, with a view of replacing them."[1]

It has been estimated that to accomplish such an enormous objective, 650,000 to 750,000 rural families "would need to benefit" each year for a decade. A low estimate of the cost for doing this for 400,000 families is $1.5 billion a year. Therefore actually to fulfill the reform goals "would exceed this cost."[2]

I have seen no comparable figure for Asia or Africa, but if one exists, it must be equally large.

Agrarian reform comes in a variety of shapes and sizes. Essentially it boils down to two methods: (1) take the land away from the big landowners, with or without compensation, and divide it among the landless and (2) take an unused piece of land, clear it, and colonize it with settlers.

By now a fairly well-accepted fact is that something more than a mere reparceling of farmland is necessary if land reform is to increase agricultural production. Simply taking farmed areas away from the landholder and giving them to the landless does not do much good, most now agree.

The result of this new enlightenment is the *integrated colonization program.* Today dozens of these can be found throughout the developing world.

With a few variations, the following pattern develops: The government comes into an area; takes possession of unfarmed or undeveloped land; clears and levels it; builds roads, houses, schools, power plants, and agricultural experiment stations. Meanwhile the landless are brought in and settled, and at the same time adequate credit is made available to them. Thus, it is said, the government has physically relocated the peasant but his former problems have been left behind. With this type of integrated colonization program the government is confident it is providing the peasant with the tools he needs for success. It claims it has defused social unrest in the countryside.

Mexico is a good example. After the big push in the "old-fashioned" land redistribution programs of the 1930s and 1940s (and still going on), Mexico embarked on a few land utilization programs in the form of integrated colonization. The most highly publicized such program in all Latin America during the 1950s was begun by President Miguel Alemán at Papaloapan, southwest of Veracruz. Because I had visited this project when it was getting underway, I was delighted when both Mexico's ambassador to the United States, Hugo Margáin, and the nation's minister of agriculture, Gil Preciado, now recommended that I revisit it to see an outstanding example of an effective development program.

PAPALOAPAN

PAPALOAPAN is not isolated, but neither is it on the beaten track. In 1957 I had reached the area by train, traveling in a World

War I-vintage Pullman that went on through to Tapachula on the Guatemalan border. Soon after leaving Veracruz the train chugged through a thorn forest—one of the most ubiquitous forms of tropical vegetation and one that writers never seem to mention. Every conceivable plant was covered with thorns: long ones, stubby ones, skinny ones, fat ones, on branches, on leaves, on everything. Then the rainfall pattern of the area changed; the train left the thorn forest and began passing a few cleared spots with patches of corn. One often thinks the palm tree is the typical tropical American crop. Not so. It is corn. This has been corn country for several millenia. More corn is grown in Mexico and Central America than any other crop. Today most of the cultivation takes place just about the same as it did 5,000 years ago with Indians slashing and burning their land and planting the seed with a stick.

Of course other tropical crops were grown: small groves of mangos, with corn planted between the trees; fields of lemon grass and citronella; a few papaya; occasional plantings of bananas, oranges, pineapples, limes; and some bamboo. But each clearing had its little field of corn. All these crops were isolated from one another, scattered here and there. Nowhere were there vistas of cultivated fields except for some commercial plantations of sugarcane and, to a lesser degree, of cotton.

Within a few hours I arrived at Papaloapan. Throughout Mexico and in development circles great excitement and talk were generated about this region. It was expected to become the world's most productive tropical farmland. I saw giant Caterpillar tractors clearing wide jungle tracts for future colonists. Those already settled there considered themselves pioneers. Though the Mexican government had built a new town (appropriately named Miguel Alemán), most people were living in thatched-roofed *ranchitos* near the freshly bulldozed fields.

On that first visit, I particularly remember meeting a fellow American who ate ice cream continually, although in this rough country I never quite understood where he obtained his constant supply. Somehow he was symbolic of the opportunistic kind of person attracted by the gold-rush atmosphere of this colonization project. Between bites he told me about his line of work, insurance, and how he had established several companies in Texas and Colorado. I asked, "Isn't that rather hard to do, with all sorts of insurance companies these days to compete against?"

"Not at all," he said. "I find the insurance business is just right for an aggressive guy like myself—it takes a staid business like insurance to feel the impact of a new hard-hitting approach."

It turned out, as he admitted later in the conversation, that the way he sold shares in the companies to policy holders had something to do with the secret of his success. After each of his companies had operated for some time, he had moved on to organize a new company in a new town. Insurance commissioners began to look askance at these financial goings on, and he had found it "convenient" to move to Mexico. When I met him he had just returned from Tiajuana where he had discreetly tested the length of memory of those north of the border. The inquiries had resulted in his decision to stay on in Mexico for a while longer. At Papaloapan, in the meantime, he was using his "hard-hitting approach" in a newly organized partnership with a Mexican to raise sugarcane.

PADDOCK: But isn't this land going to be divided into small-sized peasant holdings? You can't raise sugarcane profitably on small plots.

INSURANCE MAN (*gulping more ice cream*): Ah, these Mexicans have a thousand ways from Sunday to get around their laws. We're getting a hunk of that area down the road before the *colonos* arrive. (One of the stimulating things about traveling in these out-of-the-way areas is that most of the foreigners you meet are either abnormal or subnormal; the *normal* folks stay at home—back in Kansas City or Hamburg or Liverpool.)

I tell about this greedy entrepreneur to emphasize that in 1957 Papaloapan was a hustling area—like a hastily thrown together oil town awaiting the first gusher from an untapped field. But I also tell about him because while his vision of what the area was to become was 180 degrees out of phase with the government's announced goals, his was, nevertheless, far more accurate.

Now twelve years later I returned, driving a car over a good road. Even before getting out of the car it was obvious that dry rot had set in. Paved roads had been built, to be sure, and electrical power lines fanned out across the countryside. But the main commercial crop was plantation-grown sugarcane. In fact, I guessed it represented most of the farm production. The small farmers had either banded together to farm their land as a plantation type unit or they had leased it to larger growers—perhaps to men similar to my ice cream-eating acquaintance. Some land, indeed, was in rice, mangos, lemon grass, citronella, papayas, and the ever present small plots of corn. But the *colonos* were living much like those first pioneering settlers I had seen. The hopes of the original program clearly were not yet fulfilled.

Yet I had come here because two high Mexican officials had especially recommended it as an outstanding example of an effective development program.

The core of the Papaloapan colonization scheme is a huge dam on which stands a monument to President Miguel Alemán, complete with the inevitable and beautiful Mexican murals. These depict the area before the dam was built and the artist's prediction of after. In the "before" scene, *peones* are living primitively in dirt-floored *ranchitos* and planting their corn with a stick. In the "after" scene the modern, happy life has arrived—the colonists are living in well-built homes, reading by electric lights, and farming their endless fields of corn with tractors.

The "after" never happened!

The region today looks about like the "before" scene except the Mexicans no longer wear the white pajamas the mural shows, but this change has occurred everywhere in Mexico.

What had gone wrong?

The people who had prospered from the new agriculture were not, apparently, those who were actually farming the land.

NUEVA CONCEPCION

ANOTHER COUNTRY where an intensive integrated colonization program has been launched is Guatemala. Its first "enlightened" program was initiated in 1956 at Nueva Concepción, located on the hot Pacific coast.

Actually I had myself been in on some of the original planning for Nueva Concepción. Thus I wanted to visit it again as I was in the area, although in this case no one had recommended it to me as an effective project.

For one thing, it illustrates what few people realize, that the United States had itself been involved actively in supporting land reform and colonization efforts long before the advent of the Alliance for Progress. Nueva Concepción was an early and major U.S. effort.

Nueva Concepción is situated next door to the old United Fruit Company banana plantation of Tiquisate. During the time of the quasi-Communist regime of Arbenz (1950 to 1954), squatters had come into this area, all of which was then owned by the United Fruit Company. The company was not farming the land, but was holding it in reserve in the event its other banana lands became infested by the soil-borne fungus causing the root disease called

"Panama." At that time the only remedy for the disease was to move off the contaminated lands onto new land. When the Arbenz government fell, the government of Castillo Armas took over. The problem of the squatters who had settled on this land had to be resolved. The United Fruit Company arranged to give to the government 100,000 acres at Nueva Concepción in return for its help in removing squatters from land which the United Fruit Company owned elsewhere in the country.

These 100,000 acres of level friable loam were (and are) good for farming. But when United Fruit made the gift the land was covered by jungle.

The pro-Communist Arbenz government had formulated a land reform program which became law in 1952. Most impartial observers have since agreed it had considerable merit. The most serious criticism against this program was that it had been put into operation with too much speed. It was one more exercise in political expediency rather than a plan to bring financial security and stability to a rural population. Another fault was that the lands given out were in plots too small to produce a decent living. Also the bank which was to have supplied credit for the new land-holders "was badly underfinanced, was poorly, if not dishonestly, managed. The programs for technical assistance, education, medical aid, community development, and the like, had no preconceived plans for operations and did little if anything constructive."[3]

When Castillo Armas overthrew Arbenz it was politically necessary to devise a better program, if for no other reason than to show that this new government could do a better job than the previous, Communist-infiltrated regime.

Against that background, the dust had hardly settled from the revolution of Castillo Armas when the U.S. government opened up its coffers (no other expression is really adequate) to help establish Castillo Armas's regime firmly in control after the several years of Arbenz's turmoil.

A Washington-based consulting firm, International Development Services (IDS), received a contract from the U.S. government to help Guatemala with its colonization programs on the Pacific Coast. Beginning with an allotment of $393,000 the contract grew to $2,336,500 which, however, in no way indicated the eventual total cost of the program; by 1963, the U.S. government had spent at least $4,600,000.[4] I have asked personnel of AID and OAS and also Guatemalan government officials how much money has been invested in the Nueva Concepción colonization program. No one knows, but it must be enormous. The first step to colonizing the area was to build a road into Nueva Concepción costing, as I remember, $300,000. Since then dozens of additional roads have been built, telephones installed, schools and houses constructed, a town laid out, etc., etc.

A common characteristic of all integrated colonization schemes is that they are very, very expensive. The fact that no one knows the total cost of Nueva Concepción is not surprising. An IDS report on the land reform program there describes the political and governmental conditions prevailing in Guatemala at the time, conditions not too dissimilar from those in other hungry nations where similar programs have been attempted:

Because of political unrest and political change the program operations were handicapped by an abnormal amount of indecision and delay. Consequently, results were not in keeping with expectations and I.D.S. technicians were continually subjected to frustration and disappointment in their efforts. A large percentage of government employees under the communist-oriented Arbenz regime were unacceptable to the Castillo Armas government which therefore had to be staffed largely by inexperienced government servants. The most difficult period was in the year following the assassination of Castillo Armas, which was marked by a succession of constitutional governments, a military junta, a presidential election declared unconstitutional by the Supreme Court, a second presidential election, and finally the delay of a program review and extensive re-programming of funds at the request of the new constitutional government.[5]

Nevertheless, progress of a sort had been quickly reported in development circles. By 1960 Nueva Concepción had become a "major center of population on the Pacific Coast"[6] with 8,200 inhabitants. Data released claimed that corn and platano production was up 500 percent with comparable increases in other crops.[7] Fifty percent of the land had been cleared and, supposedly, was being farmed. Optimistic claims flowed in: "A substantial acreage that formerly produced little is now under cultivation."[8]

I was looking forward to visiting this area again. Not only had I known it under the precolonization days of Arbenz, but later, during the days of Castillo Armas, I had planted experimental corn plots on land immediately adjacent to it and knew firsthand the harsh difficulty of growing corn and beans in that region.

Actually I had spend my first night in the tropics since Guadalcanal and World War II at nearby Tiquisate. There had been a typical noisy downpour on the tin roof of the United Fruit Company guesthouse. I thought I would need an ark to get out. In the morning, however, there were only a few puddles, even though six inches of rain had fallen during the night (not an unusual amount during the rainy season). These volcanic soils drain quickly.

Now back again, I found the bananas at Tiquisate were gone. United Fruit had sold its land to well-to-do Guatemalans and there were now only endless fields of cotton and pastures for cattle. How ironical. The Nueva Concepción colonization had been started with a gift of land in order to protect the Tiquisate banana plantation but high freight rates imposed on the government controlled railway had made the company's operations uneconomical.

However, while the new cotton and cattle plantations had prospered at Tiquisate, prosperity had not yet arrived next door at Nueva Concepción. The colonization community was run down; it still consisted of rutted streets and largely temporary buildings— though the years had turned these into permanent ones.

At government headquarters there, I was told that one Benedito Morán Hernández, a "very progressive farmer," could best tell me how well things were going. The officials recommended him to me as one of their most knowledgeable farmers.

I found Morán's house down an even ruttier road than the one I had been on. It was made of wood and built on a cement platform—a typical government-designed colonization house. Next to it was a native-type dwelling, or *champa*, made of branches, with a thatched roof. Part of his large family lived there.

Morán, the first of several farmers in the area with whom I talked, was quite a fellow and most likeable. After being with him an hour, I agreed he was indeed a progressive farmer. He was also the head of a farmers' cooperative with 157 members.

"They elected me president because of my intelligence," the modest fellow said, and described his farming operations. He was a member of a tractor pool with which he contracted to have his land plowed. He also grafted some orange trees which he sold. He bought and sold fertilizer through the cooperative which he ran. He was reasonably pleased with the government that day because, he said, the cooperative had just received $48,000 of credit. It was the very first time this had happened.

I talked to him about land reform. He described it as a "joke" *(broma)*. He said the government promised everything but did nothing. I asked him about a new proposal which OAS was asking U.S. AID to fund to redivide the land in order to compensate for demographic changes (i.e., population explosion) in the colonization area. He quickly said, "It won't work. They can't take away land that is ours. We will fight." But he did agree that only half the land in the area was cultivated even though the population had spiraled upwards (the 8,200 inhabitants in 1960 had grown, by births and immigration, to 45,000 in 1968). However Morán himself seemed oblivious to his own miniexplosion of human mouths to feed—six children plus a nephew with four more, a total of fourteen living off his thirty-seven acres.

Morán had lived there seven years. He had arrived with some capital (how much he did not say) and had bought his land and the improvements from the previous owner who had received it from the government. He felt it was then worth $5,000. Although his living conditions were rather primitive, they were definitely better than most of his neighbors.

When I asked him about the Peace Corps group which was working in the area, Morán said they had promised him a trip to Puerto Rico to study cooperatives, "but it hasn't come through yet," and he was clearly disappointed. "The Peace Corps helps a little but," he smiled, "they are also learning themselves." (Unfortunately I could not talk with any of the Peace Corps volunteers as they were all attending a meeting in the capital.)

Earlier I had talked with an old friend of mine, a cotton farmer, Mario García Salas, whose large farm is a few miles from Nueva Concepción. Buying up land as the United Fruit Company pulled out, he had prospered marvelously by raising cotton on a plantationlike scale. The problem at Nueva Concepción, he said, was that the colonists had no equipment nor were they given the technical knowledge to raise cotton, which was then the region's money maker. Neither did the government nor any other organization help in this respect, at least not in an effective way. "Raising cotton is for the educated farmer," he said. "It takes great skill to control cotton diseases and insects. The risks are enormous."

My general conclusion was that Nueva Concepción is virtually stagnant. A few—a very few—Moráns are able to prosper, apparently because of superior diligence and ability.

Back in Guatemala City, I went to the office of OAS and asked to look at a study they were just completing on Nueva Concepción. This exhaustive, one-year-plus investigation had involved nearly fifty specialists from several nations, including four from Israel. The reason for making the study was that by 1966 it had become evident Nueva Concepción was in serious trouble. The colonization area was suffering from a surfeit of social and political problems, including killings, robbings, and rapes, and these were increasing at an accelerating rate. When Nueva Concepción was started it was to have been a model for all Central America to follow. But the milk had turned sour.

The OAS study showed that in 1967, of the 4,756 Nueva Concepción families, only 1,392 had actually received title to their land. The original settlers were supposed to pay a total of $600 over a ten-year period for their fifty acres (later this was extended to twenty years), but only fifty-two had completed requirements for ownership. Why not more? Because many colonists had abandoned their land and moved on, often to be replaced by squatters. Some were now farming land that had been set aside for roads. Others had settled on what was supposed to remain a forest preserve and had cleared the land. Others could not farm all the land granted to them without machinery to help. Others could not clear their land or drain it.

Ninety percent of the colonists, the study showed, were having a pretty rough go of it, with farm incomes averaging $338 per year. Only 10 percent of the farms were achieving the $1,857 predicted when the program began. All of this indicates that those who advocated the creation of the colonization project at Nueva Concepción in the first place and those who still continue to urge similar programs elsewhere have yet to find out how the small farmer can profitably use the land granted to him, or to find out how governments can be persuaded into backstopping, financially, the small farmer until he learns how to use his new land.

So what is in store for Nueva Concepción?

The OAS now calls for a new plan. These "experts" propose that the area be divided again in order to meet the land hunger of the growing population, that the farms now be cut to half the size originally planned so that one farmer can cultivate all his allotment. And, of course, they propose to spend a lot more money—not, unfortunately, on providing technical assistance to show the farmers how to grow crops profitably, but on the same old things as before: schools, town centers, houses, roads, and the like. The figure recommended this time is $12 million, or about $4,600 for each of the 2,600 families to be assisted.

I asked U.S. AID mission director Dean Hinton what he thought about the OAS recommendations.

"Ridiculous. An extravagant use of money!"

I agree. But I add that the unknown millions of dollars the

United States put into the project in the first place were also ridiculous because they were irresponsibly dumped into a scheme which had had almost no preliminary analysis or preparation.

Now, at last, the United States apparently has washed its hands of this, its first major effort at colonization in the tropics.

And so, for that matter, has the Guatemalan government. I was told by official sources, who asked not to be named, that "Nueva Concepción is a Castillo Armas program. It was his first program and was next door to the town where he was born and grew up. Today's president is not likely to invest money in a program which will merely give glory to one of his predecessors."

Politics! Thou art sand in the wheels!

ON MY RETURN through Mexico I found this same political self-glory expressed about Papaloapan by Carlos Franco Castell, the engineer in charge of Grijalva,[9] a relatively new colonization program located in the state of Chiapas.

"Papaloapan was a one-man project," he told me. "It was President Miguel Alemán's idea and he gave it his stamp of approval. When he left office, support for it died. No president since then has been interested in furthering it because it would only enhance the name of Alemán."

Yet Alemán in Mexico and Castillo Armas in Guatemala remain highly respected and admired presidents both among the populace and in the government hierarchy, and in no sense have they been maligned.

Franco admitted the planning at Papaloapan had been poor. But when solutions to the errors had been found, they could not be put into practice because whoever was the current president would not allocate the money or the manpower. "This is not going to be the case here at Grijalva," he said without batting an eye, "because it has attracted the personal interest and support of two Mexican presidents. Grijalva is considered a national program, not a personal one."

GRIJALVA

THE MEXICAN MINISTERS of foreign affairs and of agriculture, as well as specialists at the National Agricultural University at Chapingo and the Inter-American Development Bank in Washington had urged that I visit Grijalva to see a most effective project. It was to become, they said, the largest development program in all Mexico in terms of area and money. Located on the main road south from Veracruz toward Yucatán, Grijalva lies between La Venta (the archaeological site where the huge, football-helmeted Olmec heads were found in the jungle) and the ruins of Palenque, the most spectacularly located ruins of the Mayan civilization.

It is a truly enormous development effort. It involves clearing and draining more than 700,000 acres and building a huge hydroelectric plant and dam. One local official who had spent fifteen months with the Tennessee Valley Authority quite rightly referred to it as a Mexican TVA. Initial programming had begun in 1957, but it was ten years before the project started to function. How much Grijalva will cost is anyone's guess at this time. (Billboards in the area say that 52.1 percent is being paid by the Mexican government and the rest by a loan from the Inter-American Development Bank.) Several officials have estimated the cost of clearing, draining, and installing irrigation water will be $400 an acre, a figure in line with similar projects throughout the world. So there alone is $280 million, plus the cost of roads, dams, schools, and the like.

After clearing the land and putting in flood control and drainage, the government divided the area, by roads, into units of 10,000 acres. Each unit is to have 260 families. Each family is to have ten acres to cultivate and another twenty-five on which to raise livestock. Community pastureland will also be provided. In addition, each unit is to have a town site located centrally to the fields. Each of these impressively planned towns will be where the farmers live and their children go to school.

The planners have even taken into consideration Mexico's population explosion. Today's average Mexican family consists of 5.6 individuals, and the population is expected to double within twenty years. So planners have arranged to have enough land for the colonists' children (though no one talks about what is going to happen in behalf of their children's children).

As at Papaloapan, power lines from the hydroelectric plants march out to nearby towns and to more distant cities like Villahermosa and Veracruz. This power is expected to spark an industrial revolution; the sale of electricity, I was told, will amortize the cost of the dam within ten years, and it probably will.

Authorities are equally confident that the colonist will be supported effectively. Plans have been drawn up to help him cultivate his land, to bring him modern scientific technology, and to boost yields per acre.

This was not mere talk. Outside the town of Cárdenas the government had already established a beautiful, starkly modern experiment station on some 2,500 acres of level, well-drained land; a subprofessional school in agriculture and buildings for graduate study are also included. The equipment had not arrived at the time of my visit, but I am certain that when it does the agricultural scientists and teachers will have what they need. However, the station and school face one serious drawback: they are located twenty-five miles from Cárdenas where all the technicians live. The planning prospectus failed to show that this will always be a difficult spot to staff and run because of the distance from town.

I had the good fortune to talk with several technicians of the station, as well as with its director, Fidencio Puente, who holds a Ph.D. from the University of North Carolina. He had spent two years planning and setting up the station.

"How's the land for agriculture?" I asked him.

PUENTE: Excellent.

PADDOCK: What are the best crops for the colonists to raise here?

PUENTE: We aren't sure yet. We are still doing research to determine this.

So Mexico City had not learned the lesson taught by all the previous colonization programs. Exactly like all the rest, the bulldozers arrived first, the colonists second. Next, credit was rushed in for seed and fertilizer—all of this before research results were available to show if small plots in this area could be farmed profitably!

In 1964 Stanford University's Thomas Poleman wrote about Papaloapan:

In [no] zone was colonization preceded by a period of preliminary experimenting. True, one of the Commission's two agricultural stations had been set up in 1950 . . . but its personnel had been mainly engaged in plant breeding. No attempt was made to simulate expected operating conditions. The first colonists arrived before anything had been learned about likely yields, methods of maintaining soil fertility, the local suitability of various types of machinery, and similar matters critical to the planning of a sound system of farm management. . . . Instead of being in a position to order combinations of crops and cultural systems whose practicability under local conditions had already been proved, the Commission was forced to operate the colonies essentially as experimental farms and to formulate its instructions around the presumptions of its agricultural and colonizational staffs. Inevitably mistakes and unforeseen complications were numerous.[10]

Nevertheless officials at Grijalva boasted to me that, unlike all other colonization programs, technical assistance in all forms was going to be made available throughout the project. The amount of help they listed was formidable. Each 260-family unit, I was told, already had one university graduate agricultural extension agent plus four assistants; thus every 260 families were to have a total of five technicians guiding their agricultural efforts. However, at the time of my visit, I was also told that of the fifty agriculturalists then scheduled, only twenty-four were on board.

In line with the theme of my research I asked which unit would be the best one for me to visit in order to evaluate the results to date. I was directed to unit #28, which then was two and a half years old.

It was physically impressive to see. Its town had wide streets, a lot of machinery in a community shed (three large self-propelled rice combines, seeders, etc.), a school, new houses, a warehouse, and the surrounding farmland was well cleared. But when I asked where I could find the office of the extension agent, no one knew. Nor did anyone know the whereabouts of his assistants. In fact, no one had even heard of them! They did not exist. But, The Plan, the beautiful plan, claimed five technicians for each 260 families.

Once again, the slip between the cup and the lip, between good intentions and reality, had left the hapless colonists to their own anguished resources.

I ASKED the directors of both the tropical experiment station at Grijalva and that at Cotaxtla (the station near Veracruz which serves the Papaloapan area), "If you yourself won a couple of million pesos in the lottery, how would you invest it? What would you do with it?"

The director of the older station at Cotaxtla, where more data had been accumulated, said, "Actually, to satisfy my loyalty to farming, I suppose I would put some money into agriculture, but agriculture is certainly not a good enough business to put all of my money into it. I would put most of it into industry." At Grijalva, where little data were available and the station was still under construction, the director said, "I would put it all into agriculture. I am convinced there is money to be made here in farming." The replies were themselves good illustrations of the pessimism of the man already experienced in the troubles of a colonization program and of the optimism of the man who has just arrived at a new, highly publicized project.

Rather unfairly, perhaps, I asked both directors whether one could, in Mexico, legally put such a sum into agriculture. Each agreed that Mexico's land tenure laws do, in fact, prohibit large, single land holdings. But they said (not implying they themselves would do so) that people do get around the spirit of the law by registering land in the names of their brothers and sisters and in-laws.

Thus we have come full circle, back to that obnoxious insurance man at Papaloapan who ate ice cream all the time and boasted how he was going to get around the law and create a big farm.

Even though the Mexican government refuses to support, or allow, large-scale plantation agriculture in its colonization projects, this is the kind of farming which today's technology can make economically most successful in the low tropics. We don't know how to make peasant agriculture prosperous in an area such as this.

Hence I forecast: All the millions of dollars the government is spending, and will spend, on roads, dams, schools, and drainage ditches at Grijalva will not make the colonists there any more successful than their predecessors at Papaloapan or Nueva Concepción or at any of the dozens of other similar projects throughout the tropics.

It is the heartbreaking truth.

[14]

Land Reform via Confiscation

WHILE INTEGRATED colonization programs have received the most attention by development experts, it is the other route which many feel will bring the most rapid and radical change in the rural community. That is government confiscation, with or without compensation, of the big holdings and dividing the land among the landless. This has been carried out most spectacularly in three Latin American countries: Mexico, Cuba, and Bolivia.

Mexico, because it was the pioneer, has been the model for other countries to follow. Indeed, the main issue in Mexico's long and bloody revolution from 1910 to 1920 was "land for the landless." Since then, Mexican governments, with varying results but always with great hoopla, have been distributing land parcels to landless families. This process of land distribution is still going on. In 1968, after four years in the presidency, Gustavo Díaz Ordaz had given out more land than any previous president but, ironically, to the smallest number of landless. The land left to be divided is "woodlands and pastures," and the law today requires that such marginal stuff be a minimum size of about fifty acres (in contrast to the five acres, or less, of earlier parcels).

Pictures continue to appear with monotonous frequency in Mexican newspapers of the president personally handing out land certificates to *peones,* their hats in their hands.

I was an observer of this kind of land reform during one of Mexico's most turbulent periods, and was able recently to study the results from the vantage point of the same piece of land. The comparisons were instructive.

The scene was Hacienda San José, one of Mexico's fine old-time establishments, located a few miles beyond the village of Atotonilco el Grande in the state of Hidalgo. In 1933 I lived there for three months.

This was a time of great turmoil due to the agitation for agrarian reform and the resulting wave of formal land distributions. Considerable unrest was present in the region, even a degree of physical danger for those traveling the countryside. Landowners generally found it unsafe to ride alone on horseback around their lands. At a neighboring hacienda, the *agraristas* (land reformers) would occasionally shoot through the windows at night.

Hacienda San José was a somewhat slowed-down operation in the 1930s. It had seen better days, as well as worse, since its *casa grande* had been built in 1725. (The family had received title to the land from Charles V of Spain a hundred years earlier.) The hacienda had at various times entertained the nation's leaders and horses of revolutionaries had been stabled in its *salas*. Built like a fort, its rough exterior walls had turrets with gun slits ready to fight off bandits.

Although it covered 27,000 acres in 1930, most of the land was semiarid and little of it was irrigated. However it did support a considerable variety of cash crops, such as corn, walnuts, cattle, and maguey (for pulque, the Mexican beer). The owner and his family lived in Mexico City, but spent much of their time at the hacienda; management of the farm was in the hands of a cousin, Don Roberto Quesada, who lived there.

Conditions on this hacienda were quiet and we could all ride freely throughout the area. I attributed this peacefulness primarily to the good relations the family had maintained with the *peones* through the years. Members of the family would call on the sick, attend weddings, and sympathetically try to help them through their assorted troubles. Also they maintained a school. Perhaps even more important, they made the town house in Mexico City available as a base of operations for occasional members of workers' families who went there to seek their fortune. All this, of course, was the traditional paternalism all *hacendados* claimed they honored, but in this case, the family worked hard at their duties.

This is not to say the owner did not fight just as firmly to hold onto his acres as the other *hacendados,* but, so far as I know, he did so through the courts and legitimate government channels. Fortunately his lands did not abut on any town. Thus he was spared the pressures of townspeople and local politicians who wanted to get in on the action.

In the end, the *hacendado* lost—or so I thought.

Twenty-six thousand acres were taken away, leaving the

owner with only the great house and some 750 tillable acres, including the site for an irrigation dam. The *peones* who worked the land were given the 26,000 acres and they thought the millenium had arrived.

So much for my earlier visit.

Now, thirty-five years later, I returned to Hacienda San José. What did I find? My old friend Roberto Quesada is still managing it. He is a bit stiff in the joints, no longer the gay bachelor of his earlier days, but a settled man who has nutured well the 750 acres. For the farm has prospered.

Rough-hewed stones still form the walls of the house and the turrets still stand with their gun slits. The new generation of the family still lives in Mexico City where it also has prospered. The *casa grande* has become a pleasant weekend retreat, sleeping a dozen or more guests. It now boasts not only electricity but a sizable swimming pool.

Five hundred acres are irrigated by a new dam. While no one seems willing to admit it, total agricultural production is probably more today than it was thirty-five years ago on all 27,000 acres, due, of course, to the new irrigation.

No longer are there dozens of *peones* lolling around the main gate of the hacienda waiting to see the manager as in the days of old. The place is empty, as the former several hundred farm workers have been reduced to a permanent staff of only eight—two cowboys, two field hands, one truck driver, one gardener, one houseboy, and one bookkeeper. Extra labor can be hired quickly and easily from the area whenever it is needed for planting or harvesting.

By contrast, in wandering about the acres formerly a part of the hacienda and visiting the homes of *peones* working the land they now own, I saw far less change than on the farm operated by Don Roberto. The main change was in the clothes. Previously, the local men had worn the typical white pajamas and serape, the women a bedraggled skirt and shawl (generally with a tiny infant wrapped inside). Now they wear standard-cut pants and ready-made dresses—cheaper, because of Mexico's industrial surge, than those they used to make themselves. The most noteworthy change was on their feet: all of them were wearing shoes in place of the old *huaraches* (leather sandals).

Today the *peones* are called *ejidatarios* for they have become the "owners" of the *ejido*, the name given to the consolidated parcels of land. Superficially the *ejido* looked much the way the land used to when it was part of the hacienda. However an increased number of houses sprinkled the horizon. Indeed, there had developed a great overcrowding of houses in proportion to land use.

I had not noticed in the 1930s how many persons lived in the small houses, perhaps because I had not heard about the population explosion. But on this visit two or three families seemed to be living in each house where I stopped to talk. This included the parents and their sons, each with his own batch of children. Each household also seemed to have several members working in Mexico City and, in most cases, sending money back home to help support parents, brothers, sisters, wives, and children.

A final major difference in life on this arid, beautiful plateau: I found many of the men had been to the United States as *braceros* (migrant farm laborers). They were eager to argue with me about the injustice of the new U.S. policy which restricts migrant labor from crossing over the border to help fill seasonal labor shortages in the United States.

I talked about all these matters with Don Roberto, and he said, "Look out there, at the *ejido.* What strikes you first that is different from 1933?"

He had to tell me and I was chagrined not to have seen it at once. The sun was glistening on the galvanized corrugated roofs of dozens of houses. In the old days, all the roofs were either thatched or of homemade tile. Now they were metal.

"All those roofs were bought by *braceros,*" he said. "Nearly every house with a metal roof has men in it who were able to work in the United States. They brought back some money and part of it went into roofs."

Now that the *bracero* program has been canceled (many people say it is still going on clandestinely), the economy of the area is hurting. No longer is money coming through the pipeline from the United States.

Locally, much dissatisfaction existed because no more land was available for distribution in the valley—nothing to give to the surplus children of the *ejidatarios.* Farm production has not increased as much as had been hoped; in fact, agriculture on the *ejidos* seemed stagnant. I saw no evidence of modern technology, nor could I see that "land reform" per se—the dividing of the land— had made much difference in the standard of living.

Yet change was everywhere on the 750 acres managed by Don Roberto. He now worked irrigated land, thanks to the new dam.

He had three tractors and planted wheat and hybrid corn developed by the Rockefeller Foundation, and he used commercial fertilizers on all his crops. He still complained (an occupational disease with farmers) of government bureaucracy, the inefficiency of modern labor, and the low price of corn and wheat (both of which he was going to stop producing and change to cattle). To hear him tell it, it was easier to farm when he had twenty teams of oxen to plough the fields instead of a tractor. He reasoned: if one team broke down, the work went on with another team, but when the tractor breaks down, planting must be delayed (reducing yields) while he sends to Pachuca or Mexico City for the spare part.

In spite of Don Roberto's grumbling, it was obvious he had carried forward at Hacienda San José an astounding agricultural revolution.

This was not true of the *ejidos* worked by the *ejidatarios* and their exploding families.

In researching some of the reasons for this failure to progress on the *ejidos*, I spent three days in and around the town of Atotonilco el Grande, a few miles from the hacienda. Back in the 1700s, when they had owned the entire valley, the town had been the residential seat of the owners of the hacienda. In 1933 it was a sleepy, dusty town of 3,000, but was becoming the administrative center for the new *ejidos* in the surrounding areas.

Today it continues to be the administrative center and although its population is still essentially the same size, the town is certainly no longer sleepy. I found many significant changes which belied the lack of prosperity on the surrounding *ejidos*. The biggest change of all was the new buildings. Although new houses seemed to be few, government administrative buildings and schools have proliferated. A new municipal building, new market, new communications building, and so on, have been built. Most in evidence are the new schools.

The primary school looked as though additions had been made several times in the past years, resulting in a sizable structure which accommodated several hundred students. People were particularly proud of the new high school. I was pleased to see it named ESCUELA JORGE VIESCA Y PALMA, after my old friend who had been head of the family which owned Hacienda San José and who had died thirteen years ago. Thus the family had retained local respect through the whole turbulent period of agrarian reform.

Four hundred fifty-six students had been graduated in the thirteen years of the high school's existence. Since high schools are rare in rural Latin America, I was interested in learning what impact these graduates had had on the community. First of all, I was told by the heads of both primary and secondary schools that the academic programs were planned by the government in Mexico City and given to them as a package. No freedom at all to tailor the curricula to the needs of the town and the surrounding countryside existed. The most popular courses were designed to train auto mechanics, radio repairmen, metal workers, and typists. Those graduates with the best school records seemed to end up in Mexico City, though the school directors did not like to admit it.

When I asked if any courses in farming were offered, I was told no, that these could not be offered without special permission from Mexico City. Of the 456 high school graduates not one had gone on to study agriculture at a university. Given an area wholly dependent upon agriculture and given an enrollment of which at least 35 percent consisted of students from *ejido* families, it was surprising to learn that the educational system was designed entirely to train students *not* to return to the land.

This seemed strange until I realized that on the *ejidos* there is one, and only one, surplus crop—children. The only function of the schools in Atotonilco is to process that surplus in order to make it marketable in the cities. Once I realized that, the rest fell into place.

The reason for the stability in the population of Atotonilco and its lack of new houses was the large-scale migration of *ejido* children to the state capital of Pachuca, or to Mexico City. Estimates on the rate of migration varied according to the government officials with whom I talked: some said 40 percent of the young folks; others said 90 percent.

Whatever the percentage, this processing of migrants, combined with its new duties as a regional administrative center, has made Atotonilco a busy place, a kind of gateway to opportunity. Back in the 1930s, two buses a day ran to Pachuca; now a bus leaves every twenty minutes, and even a fleet of taxis is stationed at the plaza.

Before, the road in the opposite direction had petered out thirty miles beyond Hacienda San José; now it is possible to drive through to Tampico and the Gulf of Mexico. The valley is still off the beaten track and is visited by few tourists, but before it was the absolute dead end. The sense of isolation is gone, not only because of the extension of the road, but mainly because of all the movement of people.

This movement has created a flow of money back into the town from those who have gone to seek their fortune elsewhere. The incoming money buys the new television sets (from the roof of the seventeenth-century church I counted eighty-three TV aerials). It buys the electricity, now available everywhere in the community, and the bottled gas for cooking, and all the other new amenities of a prosperous town. For those who can afford an education (the time or money or both) Atotonilco's schools have taught them the skills needed to be workers in the city. For those who cannot afford an education, Atotonilco el Grande has helped them on their way to wherever rural workers are needed, whether to the next valley, to a faraway valley, or to Texas. The function of the town is to process the area's surplus crop (people) and package it for delivery.

As far as meeting the agricultural needs of this purely agricultural area, the town is not a mite more useful than it had been in the 1700s when it had served merely as the residential seat of Hacienda San José. It still provides no agricultural education or agricultural industry. Not even an agricultural extension agent is stationed there. Nothing!

Back in Mexico City I asked Mrs. Ana Gómez, statistician at the U.S. embassy, "Just how prosperous are the *ejidatarios?*"

GÓMEZ: That's like asking, "how high is high?" The *ejidatarios* differ too much. If they have good land, they're doing all right, if not, they can be the poorest part of the Mexican economy. Up in the northwest, around Ciudad Obregón where they have fifty acres of irrigated land, you could consider them rich.

PADDOCK: How about the *ejidos* beyond Pachuca where the land is not irrigated?

GÓMEZ: That land was passed out early in the land reform program when no minimum amount was set. Some of those farms are too small to support a family.

PADDOCK: Aren't all the *ejidos* the same size?

GÓMEZ: Far from it! Originally the government said five acres was the minimum and I guess they planned to give out larger amounts. But the minimum came to mean the maximum as well. The minimum was raised to twenty-five acres and then to fifty acres when the poorer land was divided. But it is better to have five good acres than fifty poor acres.

PADDOCK: Why is it some of the farmers are so rich in the northwest?

GÓMEZ: Because the land was passed out before it was irrigated; at that time it was some of the poorest in the country. With irrigation it immediately became some of the best. But then, politically, it was impossible to redivide the land or to take away from the *ejidatarios* what had already been given to them.

Mrs. Gómez went on to say that only about 15 percent of the new owners are considered good enough risks to get a loan from the Banco Ejidatario, the bank set up specifically to make loans to them. And without credit it is almost impossible to create a prosperous farm.

I ALSO FOUND a new attitude has grown up among these farmers. The *ejidatario* now considers himself to be "part of the government's responsibility." An interesting evolutionary process! Before the land reform he sat at the door of the *hacendado* waiting for the paternalistic handout. After land reform he must await the largesse of his government.

Land reform is not a guarantee of either an increase in agricultural production or of an improvement in the national economy. For when a man is given land without also receiving the technology that will permit it to be farmed more efficiently, then land reform contributes only political pizzaz to the nation's development.

Conclusions:
The Practical Priests
of the Ancient Mayas

THE ANCIENT MAYAS, whose civilization once covered southern Mexico and much of Central America, were governed by intelligent and dedicated priests who had worked out, over the centuries, an extremely ingenious calendar, more accurate than the one in use in Europe at the time of the conquest. It was the duty of these priest-rulers to maintain the calendar with continuous astronomical observations and calculations. They also had the duty to utilize the calendar, in the name of religion, as a highly practical instrument for guiding the citizen-farmers of this completely agricultural society.

Some believe the calendar was applied in the following fashion.

After each harvest the Indians made a pilgrimage from their lands to their nearby city, not a city as we think of one today, but a religious center with a concentration of pyramids, temples, and priests. Each Indian family brought with it a portion of its harvest as an offering, a tithe, to support the temples and observatories which the priests used to check the accuracy of the all-important calendar.

Ceremonies and sports events were held, and I suppose the visits to the pyramids were a great social event.

But the most important event, what made the payment of the tithe worthwhile, occurred when the priest, in exchange, gave to each Indian farmer a handful of carefully counted pebbles. Then probably with some kind of ceremony, the priest instructed the farmer how to use the pebbles: take them home; put one pebble on the shrine each day and at the same time clear, burn over, and prepare your land; when all the pebbles have been put on the shrine, plant your seed.

Both the Indians and the priests had learned from experience that knowing when to plant was extremely valuable information. The availability of a precise calendar was essential to mark the seasons which occur with a high degree of regularity in Middle America. There is a clearly defined wet season and a clearly defined dry one. The Indian knew if he did not clear and burn and then plant his land before the rains came, the rains would prevent his doing so. He also knew that were he to plant too soon, the birds and insects would eat up his precious seeds as they waited for the rains to germinate them.

Only by knowing the correct planting date would his harvests be good and furnish the surplus needed to support the Mayan civilization.

No one knows for sure why the Mayan civilization collapsed so suddenly, unlike other great civilizations which slowly declined and faded away or were destroyed by invaders.

Consider Palenque, for example, one of the most magnificent of the Mayan ruins—rows of shining white, elaborately sculptured and adorned buildings covering several square miles and sparkling like diamonds in the lush green setting of the surrounding forests. One year it was there, bustling with activity. The next year (so to speak), the farmers failed to make their annual pilgrimage to the temples and it became a ghost town of fabulous dimensions.

Why did this happen? No one knows.

I personally favor the theory that the Mayan people rose up against their priest-rulers over some grievance. But when they destroyed the priests, they also destroyed the very knowledge on which their great civilization was based: the carefully counted pebble calendar and the knowledge of how to produce an agricultural surplus in the tropics. It was this surplus that had paid for the construction of Palenque, Tikal, Copan, Chichén-Itzá, Uzmal, and the other great Mayan religious centers.

UNFORTUNATELY today's priestly class of government officials, international technocrats, development experts, and foreign aid advisors still have nothing to offer the peasant farmer that will enable him to produce a surplus. For one thing, handing out parcels of land with insufficient accompanying technology is like handing out the handful of pebbles without counting them.

In addition, the modern day priesthood of the development

religion has had its mind diverted and fixed, trancelike, on the dogma of building infrastructure for the rural areas: roads, housing, powerplants.

In fact, the priesthood is only now accepting agriculture as important to its religion's dogma. The change came about through no clairvoyance on its part or through any wisdom evolved in thirty years of development experience. The discovery was forced upon it as a result of the threat of famine in Asia in 1965 and 1966.

One reason it took so long for the priesthood to turn its attention away from infrastructure and industry has been the belief that the hungry world contains vast resources lying just beyond the city limits begging to be exploited by modern man. American know-how, its get-up-and-go, its technology would unlock these resources as soon as roads and industries were ready to exploit the wealth. Nowhere is this view more firmly held than in development planning for the tropics.

I remember a conversation with the governor of the Brazilian Department of Amapá, located at the mouth of the Amazon. He said, "My department is the richest in the world. We have diamonds, copper, nickel, gold, coal, and oil, and we are *hunting* for them."

In a nutshell, that is the story of the tropics—great hopes for future finds, but few resources yet located. And one frequently hears, as if in way of an excuse, the tropics are poor because of their people. It is the people, they say—the people are lazy.

I spent an evening some years ago in the home of Francisco Brennand, a well-known Brazilian artist whose blue and white tile murals cover the exterior of Miami's Bacardi Building—a spectacular accent in the bland architecture of that city. His home was an old sugar plantation on the outskirts of Recife, a city of a million people in northeast Brazil, and as destitute a metropolis as I have seen anywhere.

Brennand said his ancestors were Irish. His great grandfather had emigrated there from Ireland in 1850 as a result of the potato famine. This caused one of the guests to comment that it was too bad the tropics had not had the benefit of immigration from northern Europe. It is a pity, the guest went on, that the northern Europeans had gone to the climatically more agreeable temperate zone. "Too bad," he said, "your Irish ancestors did not come here 200, rather than 100 years ago. Then maybe Recife would be quite a different place than it is today."

"I doubt it," Brennand's wife interjected. "My ancestors were Dutch, and they came here 400 years ago. In fact, this whole area was settled by the Dutch and they were responsible for bringing sugarcane cultivation to this part of the world."

It is wrong to blame the poverty of the tropics on the people who settled them—the Dutch are certainly not lazy, nor are the Portuguese who came later; after all, it was the Portuguese who opened up the Great Age of Discovery. No, there is little difference among the world's peoples in this respect, but there is a great difference in the local resources at their disposal.

Consider, for a moment, what the typical farmer in Latin America's low tropics must work with. First of all, he is highly limited when it comes to equipment: only a machete and a hoe. No tractor is yet available for him and he has no draft animals because the land will not support both them and his family. With his machete he cuts over the piece of land he intends to plant in the middle of the dry season—maybe two to five acres—depending on the number of machete swingers in his family who can help him. When the brush is dried out, he touches a match to it and burns over the whole piece of land he is going to plant.

At about that moment, a Peace Corps volunteer may happen along and tell him he should not be so destructive, that all the nutrients in the soil are going up in smoke. The farmer removes his hat, wipes the sweat from his brow, and says, "Okay, show me some other way I can clear my land."

In the process of burning over his land the farmer also gets rid of the underbrush, some weed seeds, some insect eggs, and fungi. A Mayan priest is no longer there to advise him, but he does have a modern calendar to help him pinpoint the best time to plant.

When that day comes, the peasant plants his corn by using a stick to make a hole and the heel of his foot to cover it over. When the rains come, everything—and I mean *everything*—bursts forth: every conceivable weed, insect, and pest, along with the corn.

The battle is on, man versus five acres of land. And it is soon apparent why the farmer cleared so few acres. With only a hoe and a machete he could not keep the weeds back on a parcel any larger.[1]

Finally the corn approaches maturity. Then come the weevils that begin eating the new kernels. So do the birds. Meanwhile, the farmer devotedly takes each stalk by hand and doubles it over so that each ear will hang down and the rain will run off it rather than into it. This "doubling" also makes it more difficult for the birds to perch on the ears and eat them.

Since the farmer last year produced little more than what he and his family ate, he now has no money with which to buy fertilizer. If he did have the money, it would not help too much because there is no fertilizer salesman nearby. Nor is there an agricultural technician to tell him what formula of fertilizer to use or how to use it. Ditto for herbicides, fungicides, and insecticides. Ditto for improved seeds. As a matter of fact, he probably uses the same seed his father had used and his father's father, and on back through the generations before the Spanish came.

How much corn does his land produce? Before going into the figures, I point to the miracle that the long-cultivated, burned-over acres produce any corn at all—not to mention the worn-out farmer himself. He probably has a bit of chronic malaria, also some amoeba and a variety of other debilitating "hitchhikers" festering in his system. Nevertheless, in the face of all these obstacles, the tropical land of this average Guatemalan or Mexican peasant farmer produces twelve bushels to the acre—about what his ancestors produced a thousand years ago.

This is not much of a yield compared to the United States where the average runs eighty-one bushels per acre.

Certainly it is a sad commentary on the actual wealth of the tropics.

But development planners and politicians and foreign aid men refuse to recognize the poor, worn-out quality of tropical land. Dirt is dirt, they say. There cannot be much difference in it. Hence comes their snap judgment that tropical agricultural development can be accomplished quickly, that it can attain in a few years the agricultural revolution achieved in the United States during the past half century.

In contrast to the farmer's tight work schedule in the tropics, here is the situation fifty years ago in the U.S. Midwest before the development of hybrid corn or herbicides. Tractors were still a distinct rarity. Because of the severe winter the temperate zone farmer would seem in worse straits than his tropical counterpart. Actually the cold snowy winter was a help because it served to suppress weeds and pests. Of equal importance, the land even fifty years ago was productive enough so the farmer could support himself, his family, and a horse. With the help of the horse he could cultivate a bigger piece of land than the tropical farmer. When he planted his corn (around the first of May), the soil temperature was about 50 degrees Fahrenheit. Germination was a slow process for both corn and weeds. This meant that plants grew slowly at first. Thus he could cultivate his fields several times before the soil warmed up, eliminating most of his weeds. By late June, when the hot weather arrived and the plants began growing faster, no further cultivating was necessary because the corn was now high enough to shade out any late-sprouting weeds.

He did not fertilize fifty years ago, but no matter. The nutrients had not yet been leached out of the virgin soil. And because of lower temperatures the organic matter was not broken down by soil organisms as it is in the tropics. Even with unimproved seed the Midwest farmer of fifty years ago averaged thirty-two bushels of corn to the acre, two and one-half times as much as the tropical peasant farmer of today. The latter can raise barely enough food to feed his family, while his northern neighbor of yesteryear had more than he could eat. This surplus was sold, and like tithes to the priesthood for the counted pebbles, part went to pay for agricultural colleges and research. Development of ever better varieties of corn and pesticides and fertilizers was the result, increasing the Midwest farmer's production and U.S. prosperity.

Thus while the temperate zone developed a prosperous family type farm, the tropics did not. The peasant in the tropics is condemned to poverty as long as he is unable to muster both the capital and the know-how needed to combat successfully the limitations of his land—the weeds,[2] the pests, the lack of soil nutrients.

In contrast, large plantations, which bring the efficiency of industry to the farm, can and do muster the money, equipment, and technology to conquer the limitations of the tropics.

Social reformers and politicians rant against the plantation system, calling it twentieth-century enslavement of the workers. In so doing they overlook the true burden of the system: the enslavement to a single crop, the inability to diversify. Plantation economies tend to be one-crop economies, unable to adjust to periodically glutted markets. Thus tropical countries with a preponderance of their foreign exchange coming from one or two crops always are in jeopardy of a collapse in their economy, a collapse which can destroy whatever economic progress they have achieved through years of hard work.

EARLIER I SAID THAT in a name there was a lesson for the development expert.

The lesson: to succeed in the tropical environment will, in most cases, require a large, well-financed organization. By any other name, such an organization will still be El Pulpo—hated and feared.

For, unfortunately, the modern day development priesthood has yet to discover the technology, the know-how which will permit simple, nonmechanized peasant agriculture to conquer the tropics.

No country wants to be dependent on one or two export crops for their foreign exchange. That so many countries are, is evidence we do not yet know how to solve the problems posed by the tropics.

TABLE 15.1

TROPICAL COUNTRIES DEPENDENT ON ONE
OR TWO EXPORT CROPS

Country	Product	Percent of exports (1966–1968)
Botswana	livestock	96
Gambia	peanuts	94
Burundi	coffee	84
South Vietnam	rubber	81
Chad	cotton	80
Burma	rice (55%) teak (22%)	77
Uganda	coffee (53%) cotton (23%)	76
Senegal	peanuts	75
Ecuador	bananas (53%) coffee (18%)	71
Cambodia	rice (41%) rubber (27%)	68
Dominican Republic	sugar (56%) coffee (12%)	68
Ethiopia	coffee (56%) hides (11%)	67
Sudan	cotton (55%) gum arabic (10%)	65
Ghana	cocoa (55%) wood (9%)	64
Honduras	bananas (49%) coffee (12%)	61
Equatorial Guinea	cocoa	60
Lesotho	wool/mohair	60
Colombia	coffee	60
Rwanda	coffee	57
Upper Volta	cattle	55

TABLE 15.1 *(continued)*

Country	Product	Percent of exports (1966–1968)
Nicaragua	cotton (39%) coffee (15%)	54
Panama	bananas	54
Ivory Coast	coffee (35%) cocoa (18%)	53
Philippines	coconuts (29%) wood (24%)	53
Guatemala	coffee (36%) cotton (16%)	52
Cameroon	coffee (28%) cocoa (23%)	51
Coasta Rica	coffee (36%) bananas (24%)	60
Brazil	coffee (43%) cotton (7%)	50
Malawi	tobacco (25%) tea (25%)	50
Dahomey	palm products	49
Congo (Brazzaville)	wood	48
Angola	coffee	48
Haiti	coffee	43
Thailand	rice (30%) rubber (12%)	42
Kenya	coffee (26%) tea (14%)	40

SOURCE: "Selected Economic Data for the Less Developed Countries," AID Publication, May 1970; Elmer E. Glaser, Office of Statistics and Reports, AID, September 11 and October 22, 1970.

TABLE 15.2

TROPICAL COUNTRIES DEPENDENT ON A SINGLE EXPORT MINERAL

Country	Mineral	Percent of exports (1966–1968)
Brunei	oil	98
Zambia	copper	94
Venezuela	petroleum	93
Liberia	iron	73
Mauritania	iron ore	73
Laos	tin	68
Guinea	alumina	64
Congo (Kinshasa)	copper	62
Sierra Leone	diamonds	57
Bolivia	tin	56

SOURCE: "Selected Economic Data for the Less Developed Countries," AID Publication, May 1970; Elmer E. Glaser, Office of Statistics and Reports, AID, September 11 and October 22, 1970.

The only sound means of getting rid of the plantation system is by a massive technological breakthrough in agricultural research. With the population explosion already rampant, making it all the more difficult for new technology to keep ahead of the threatening crisis, the need for a corps of scientists and technicians with a single-minded dedication to solving the problems of tropical farming becomes obvious. The preceding partial list of tropical countries relying on one or two crops or a single mineral for most of their foreign exchange illustrates how desperate the need is.

Science Is Our Leader

"Dumb is beautiful. . . . It's the smart guys who cause all the trouble in the world."

—GOLDIE HAWN

[C A M E O]

Everybody Loves a Gadget—
But It Must Be Scientific

ONE EVENING, *way back in the prepermissive society days of 1967, I had a group in for dinner. In the middle of normal dinner party conversation, between the soup and meat courses, I was startled to see one of the guests, vice-president of a university, take a squiggly plastic gadget from his wallet and hand it to the lady next to him. As host, I was caught off guard and had an uneasy feeling about how the guests would react because the gadget was an IUD. It was not a new invention, but it was only then attracting the attention of the world's population experts. Although no one else at the table seemed to recognize what it was, my puritan background made me react against the gadget's appearance. After all, this was neither a biology class nor a medical convention. Nevertheless, there it was, being passed from hand to hand.*

"It's the perfect solution to the world's population problem," he said. "Insert it into the uterus and conception does not occur. It works just as well if you can read and write or if you can't. You don't even need to teach a woman how to count on a calendar. It is guaranteed practically 100 percent to

179

do the trick. No one really knows how it works, but we know it does. It's a scientific discovery inspired by the Bedouin custom of inserting stones into the female camel in order to prevent pregnancy. Camel drivers for centuries have done that before a long caravan trip. It's very simple, really."

No one at the table blanched.

"Imagine! Really, science is wonderful. Let me look at that again," the first guest said.

"What an interesting gadget. I suppose the science of modern plastics made it safe for humans," said another.

"I wonder how science decided on this peculiar design? There's a reason for the shape, isn't there?"

"If you give science enough money, it can solve any problem."

"Let me have another look at it. How is it inserted?"

"How ingenious. Just think, such a simple little thing and yet so effective."

I marveled. No one resented the intrusion of the IUD. In the name of science one can get away with anything, even at the dinner table. Furthermore, if one is told that science is responsible for a new item, one automatically believes it is true— and no wonder. Science has accomplished so many miracles it seems the marvels will never stop coming. No need to understand them. How many know how a TV set works? Or how the trajectory of a moon shot is calculated? Belief in the wonders of science does not need to include understanding.

Since that evening in 1967 the IUD has achieved wide recognition and publicity. Some of my friends in development circles, wanting to em-

phasize the population explosion, now wear its squiggly design as a tie clasp or earrings.

But how about the hopes of 1967 for the IUD to slow the population explosion?

Alas, the bright hopes are already fading.

India, to mention just one example of a country where the IUD was expected to have a great impact, had a goal of 3 million IUD insertions for 1966, 6 million for 1967, and 25 million for 1969.[1] Instead of 25 million, however, less than ½ million were inserted in 1969 of which, statistics for India now show, only 54 percent were retained twenty-four months later.[2]

"Not surprising," a down-to-earth Women's Lib advocate has said about this disappointing record of the IUD. "It was invented by a man for women."

Referring back to my dinner party, I repeat that in the name of science one can get away with almost any subject today in social conversation and even pass the "scientific" IUD from hand to hand. However, I have yet to see anyone pass around the dinner table the not-so-scientific, but more effective worldwide (no side effects, easy to purchase, efficient), rubber condom.

Trying to Get Farmers
to Use Fertilizer

OF ALL THE PEOPLE ever to get mixed up in world affairs, Roswell Garst is one of the most improbable. The sudden ascent to fame of this Coon Rapids, Iowa, corn farmer was the result of an exchange of visits between him and Nikita Khrushchev. In 1959 the State Department, under the bright glare of television, brought the Russian leader to take a look at Garst's modern hybrid seed corn farm. (Garst's hefty kick in the pants to an interfering reporter, greatly to the delight of Khrushchev, was the highlight of the visit.) Then Garst went to look at Russian farming methods, also highly publicized.

Garst is a true extrovert and in no way a practitioner of the understatement. This, plus his new nation-wide publicity, brought him to Washington. AID rushed to accept him as an expert on the developing nations and sent him on a trip through Latin America. Recently I asked an AID staffer how the Latin American affair came about.

"As I remember it, it was essentially a junket," he said. "In Washington they looked on Garst as 'Mr. Corn in Iowa' because of the Khrushchev visit. Garst was convinced that modern use of fertilizer would increase corn production in Latin America. He then convinced Secretary of Agriculture Freeman that by using many small fertilizer demonstrations he could get the Latin Americans to increase corn production, just the way he said he had succeeded in getting Iowans to accept fertilizer in the 1930s." (Though the role of Garst in Iowa's wholesale adoption of fertilizer may have been of some help, a number of other factors were of greater significance: Roosevelt's New Deal to make agriculture economically viable, advances in soil science, hybrid corn, and the growth of the fertilizer industry itself.)

"Freeman told Gaud (then the AID administrator) he should listen to Garst and the next thing we knew—that was in 1964—Gaud had arranged for AID to pay Garst's way through ten Latin American countries to find the best one in which to try out his theory of small fertilizer demonstrations.

"At that time Ben Birdsall[1] was in Washington; he spoke Spanish, so was tapped to go along with Garst to keep him out of trouble and to act as tour guide in arranging interviews and translating for him. The trip was not to find out what should be done, but to sell Garst's views on how the use of fertilizer should be demonstrated. Garst had already told everyone what needed to be done. So he and Birdsall visited the ten countries, but El Salvador was the only one really receptive to the idea. The government there volunteered some extension service help. Birdsall apparently liked the idea of a return assignment to El Salvador before his retirement. So AID ended up sponsoring the project in that country with Birdsall as project director."

The resulting program, partly because of the personalities involved, quickly became widely known, and was soon hailed a great success. When I talked to Covey Oliver, assistant secretary of state for Inter-American Affairs, he said, "You must visit El Salvador and see the new techniques in mass fertilization, that is, the Garst technique." Oliver later sent me an internal memo describing the system.

The simplicity of the plan was its charm. Throughout the country thousands of small plots were to be planted by farmers who would be given free the best seed, pesticides, and fertilizers and instructions for their use. The results would be seen by all the neighbors. The following year one could expect those who had seen the plots would buy the improved seed, pesticides, and fertilizers so they, too, could take advantage of these profitable new techniques on their own farms.

Oliver's memo said that 14,385 of the mass fertilization demonstrations had already been "strategically placed in farm communities" in El Salvador. Corn and rice productivity in that country, the statement continued, has "increased significantly, as well as fertilizer consumption. The demonstration program has shown that with the use of fertilizer and other food practices and know-how, El Salvador can enjoy self-sufficiency for most food crops and could become an exporter for some commodities in a competitive world market."[2]

I later talked with Dr. Lester Brown, then head of the U.S.

Department of Agriculture's Foreign Agricultural Development Service. He strongly urged that I visit this Mass Fertilization Program. Reports to Brown from a number of his staff members in El Salvador had assured him of the success it had already demonstrated.

Newspaper coverage had called the results of the program "astonishing" and had quoted one AID official as saying, "Our experience proves beyond doubt that El Salvador . . . can provide all the food and feed requirements for at least five times its present population . . ."[3]

From the standpoint of my own research criteria for this book, the fertilization project was an ideal one. It was then more than three years old, it was small, and it was identified by high officials as a fine tool to help overcome El Salvador's agricultural stagnation. If, as claimed, the project had shown that El Salvador could "enjoy self-sufficiency for most food crops," it was clearly an important success story.

AID reports said the program began in 1965 with 3,200 corn demonstrations; soil tests were made to determine the best fertilizer to use; each participating farmer then received a bag containing a sack with twenty pounds of 20-20-0 fertilizer, a sack with twelve pounds of 33.5-0-0 fertilizer, one and one-half pounds of improved corn seed, and two and one-fourth pounds of insecticide with a small cloth applicator.

A report sent me by the State Department reviewing that first year of 1965 stated that 2,800 of the first 3,200 plots "were highly successful [and] yields were increased from a range of 5 to 15 bushels per acre to a range of 40 to 80 bushels," and that the increase in yields based on 1965 corn prices showed a return of from $3.00 to approximately $7.50 for every dollar the farmer invested in fertilizer seed and insecticide.[4] The report added that a farmer with such increases "is now a contributor to the national economy and not a parasite. . . . It is the first step in what we call community self help."

The entire program was carried out at an amazingly small cost. The Salvadoran government put up $1400 for staff support, as did the U.S. government. The sixty-eight tons of fertilizer and three and one-half tons of insecticide used were donated by local private industry.

The next year the corn program expanded slightly from 3,200 to 3,240 demonstrations, and a uniform system of planting the small plots was followed throughout the country. Rainfall was higher in 1966 than it had been in 1965, so the crop response to fertilizer was said to be even better. Although yields were apparently greater, I have found no published data as to how much return per dollar invested was received by the farmer that year.

In 1966 and 1967 private industry again contributed the fertilizer and insecticide, the AID contribution was the same as before, and Dr. Birdsall continued to be in charge.

A report supplied me by the State Department said that corn and overall production "has already increased significantly" due to this program. Because of this, fertilizer importation had gone up 50 percent and the department was expecting a 12 to 15 percent annual increase in the use of fertilizer on food crops. "From the experiences in the Mass Fertilizer Demonstration program in El Salvador, there is no reason why the country cannot expand its production of food and feed crops to meet its needs for many years to come . . . [it] has indeed been a successful Alliance for Progress program . . ."[5]

So much for my background information before I arrived in El Salvador.

Before calling at the AID offices, I stopped at the presidential palace to talk with the late George Westcott, a U.S. agricultural advisor. He said, quite frankly, that the entire U.S. agricultural program in El Salvador was in limbo awaiting the completion of a sector analysis study. "The U.S. government has supported an agricultural program here for twenty-seven years, but it has been a hit-or-miss thing. This new study which we are writing [eventually published in four volumes] should make the program straighten up and fly right," Westcott said. (Unfortunately, I could not help remembering that AID was also writing a study on Guatemala, and that a long-time technical advisor there had told me, "There is a sickness with AID in Latin America today and that sickness is an excess of planning.")

More clearly than any other person, Westcott expressed El Salvador's problem when he said, "This nation is on a suicidal course because the population is growing at 3.7 percent a year and its food production at only 3 percent. The only bright spot in the agricultural picture," he said, "is the Mass Fertilization Program."

The AID mission director in El Salvador, Paul Oecsli, was unique because he was then the only trained agriculturalist in Latin America heading such a mission and I immediately accepted him as well qualified to judge this particular development program. (He had been transferred from Ecuador and was scheduled to move on to India.)

PADDOCK: I have been told the Mass Fertilization Program is one of the most effective in Central America. But a former student of mine, now living in Salvador, told me last night it may be discontinued. Should not AID continue assistance to such a good program?

OECSLI: Most joint programs reach a point where AID support should be terminated in order to let the local people carry on. This is a good program and certainly has contributed to making Salvador self-sufficient in corn. We are not really stopping our support, it is just that Birdsall, who was the driving force behind the program when he was on our staff, has retired and his Salvadoran counterpart has quit the government to work for a fertilizer company.

PADDOCK: If the mass fertilizer demonstration technique was so effective in Salvador why don't all AID missions in Latin America have similar programs?

OECSLI: I don't know.

PADDOCK: Do you think AID should have a system for getting other missions to use a good idea when one like this is discovered?

OECSLI: We have. Look at this *(pointing to an eighteen-inch file of papers and reports)*. Every day someone comes in with a new idea but we can't try them all. We mission directors and our heads of agriculture get together and exchange ideas, but we can't try them all. What is good for one country is not necessarily good for all.

PADDOCK: Had you planned to try this Mass Fertilization Program in Ecuador?

OECSLI: No, we were using another approach—with farm cooperatives—which I think is one of the very best that has ever been tried.

PADDOCK: Are you going to try the cooperative approach in El Salvador?

OECSLI: We are not going to try a buckshot program here. We are going to undertake an agricultural sector analysis study first to determine what the country needs before we do anything. It wastes energy trying every new idea that comes along.

PADDOCK: But since the Mass Fertilization Program is so successful, would it not be possible to continue it, even though the sector analysis study has not been completed?

OECSLI: Actually, that program has had an inordinate amount of publicity for its real effectiveness.

With that I moved on to talk with the Salvadorans, one of the first being Ing. Francisco Osegueda, a product of the University of Florida Graduate School, who was head of the government agricultural school at San Andrés.

"How are the mass fertilizer demonstrations going?" I asked. "Not too well," he answered. "If they were going well, would you not expect their numbers to grow? Instead, each year there are fewer of them."

At extension service headquarters Ing. Guillermo Tamacas confirmed this. In 1965, 3,200 fertilizer demonstrations using corn were tried; in 1966, 3,240; in 1967, 2,600; and in 1968, 1,035. In 1969 no demonstrations were planted (due in part to the Soccer War with Honduras).

PADDOCK: Why is the number going down?

TAMACAS: The fertilizer companies are not giving the extension agency the fertilizer needed.

PADDOCK: But I note that in 1966, at the peak of the program, the entire cost of the 42,000 pounds of fertilizer used was only $2,105. Can't you find that much money?

TAMACAS: Not really.

The director of El Salvador's Agricultural Extension Service, José Pérez Guerra, drove me out to see some of the mass fertilization plots. Our resulting discussion showed a rather bleak picture. "Chepe," as he asked me to call him, began by praising the well-paved highway we traveled. Then he asked, "How can this highway be paid for if agriculture does not produce the products for export? Roads like this are being built with loans which must be paid back with dollars or the equivalent, and these dollars can come only from agricultural exports. Roads by themselves do not bring a higher income. I think much of what our land produces could be shipped just as profitably by oxcart, and then put the money saved into agricultural development."

I mumbled something about how the Mass Fertilization Program and other extension services might increase production enough perhaps to pay the bill.

Chepe said I was being too polite.

The Salvadoran government gives extension work only nominal support, he explained, which limits what can be accomplished. For the entire country, he said, there are only seventy agents. They earn an average of $140 a month. Even though they are for the most part only high school graduates, the better ones can get higher paying jobs after working with him for only a few months. Turnover is 50 percent a year. (This figure was confirmed later by Westcott who also said so few extension agents were employed that if each one contacted 100 farmers [an optimistically high number] a year it would take thirty-three years for them to see all of El Salvador's farmers once, that is, once in a lifetime for each farmer.)[6]

Chepe Pérez had worked nineteen years with the extension service and was self-confident about how to run it. I was told his greatest weakness as director was that he seldom delegated much authority, but with such a turnover in his assistants, to whom could he delegate authority?

While making a side trip to a colonization project near Zapotitán I met a young extension agent, Henri Alirio Menéndez, who was obviously a truly superb agent, and also unusual in that he was one of five extension agents in El Salvador with five years of service. But Alirio told me, "Next week I am resigning and going to work for the Coffee Institute." The reason: more money.

In 1969 (before the Soccer War had any effect) El Salvador had earmarked a mere 3.8 percent of its national budget, or $6 million for all agricultural operations, including salaries and the like. No new equipment was planned for. (Francisco Osegueda told me, "If I were ever minister of agriculture, I would change its name so it does not begin with the letter 'A.' Every time there is a budget cut, they always start at the top of the list and agriculture never escapes!")

The country's extension service was indeed poorly equipped. Only fifteen vehicles were provided, of which eight were able to function at the time of my visit. The jeep in which I rode part of that day was a 1953 model. That it ran at all was a tribute to the ingenuity of the Salvadoran mechanic. Pérez's own official jeep would not start, so for the rest of the trip he drove me in his personal car.

This poverty of the extension service explains how hobbled is the Mass Fertilization Program, a fact that soon becomes apparent when one studies it in the field rather than from its progress reports in the capital. Finding farmers who will use the fertilizer and seed, plant the plots, and take care of them is a job that must be done by an agricultural extension agent and it involves a lot of driving.

I was told to visit the town of Armenia because its extension office was much better than the average. There I reviewed the records kept on the Mass Fertilization Program and found them to be sketchy, to say the least. In 1968 seventy-six cooperators had used the hybrid corn seed and fertilizer. However the yield data for each of them was listed as fifty or sixty quintales (equal to 5,000 or 6,000 pounds), with an occasional forty quintales. Yields should be expected to vary much more than this. On questioning, it turned out the extension agent collected his data simply by asking the cooperators, "Was your corn production good or bad?" If it was good, he wrote down sixty quintales, if it was bad, he listed it as fifty, and if the cooperator said it was very bad he put it down as forty. Such data, of course, are next to valueless.

The Mass Fertilization Program was intended to educate the participating farmers by means of a one-time dramatic increase in their production. In the following year he was to operate entirely on his own resources. This implied, then, that each year only *new* farmers would be participating in the program.

The data at Armenia showed this was not the case. In 1967 the extension agent signed up twenty cooperators, all of whom were listed among the seventy-six for 1968, as were also those who had joined the program as cooperators in 1966. Thus almost all the cooperators with whom the agent was working were carry-overs from previous seasons.

When I asked if any training had been given to the extension agent about how to select cooperators, organize the trials, take the data, and report them, I received a one-word reply, "No." Similarly, when I asked how many of the cooperators would be carrying out the improved practices the following year, I was told, "We don't know."

One Peace Corps volunteer assigned to the extension service told me that 70 to 80 percent of the demonstration plots reported to have been planted actually never were, or else were planted so badly that nothing could be learned from them. This was obviously an off-the-top-of-the-head evaluation and I hasten to add that the demonstration plots I saw were well laid out and the difference between the fertilized and nonfertilized plantings clearly visible. Also, the cooperators with whom I talked seemed unusually capable men. Nevertheless when asked, "Are you going to use fertilizer next year?" their answer generally was, "I should like to, but I shall have to wait and see if I can buy it." I said, "But your production this year will be big enough to pay for it, won't it?"

The answer: "We'll see."

In fact, my question was not a fair one because the plots were very small, forty or fifty feet square, and any increased yield on such a small plot could not really be expected to pay for a significant amount of fertilizer for the following season.

I talked with the wives of five neighboring cooperators and was impressed by their lively personalities. One of them owned a sewing machine and two others had gone to the agricultural extension agent's office—a half-day trip—for instruction from the home demonstration agent on how to make a dress. They had learned enough to tell me about a dress they were making, explaining the intricacies of fittings and the placement of darts, and how to make a placket for the buttons and front opening.

All this led me to believe that if the fertilizer-improved seed approach really increased production, these farmers would be more than alert to take advantage of the process the next year.

I could not find, however, in either the field or extension offices a clear-cut answer to my question, "How much increased use of fertilizer or improved seed has resulted from the program?"

Chepe Pérez told me he felt 75 percent of the trials were successful and they had convinced the cooperators of the value of fertilizer and improved seed. But, he explained, since the plots were only one-tenth of an acre, the demonstrations could not themselves have much effect on their incomes.

However, loan facilities do exist for the small farmer and a separate Salvadoran agency has been established for his welfare and funded by a $5 million loan from AID. In 1968 some 5,000 loans were made to these small farmers for the purchase of such things as fertilizer, improved seed, and insecticides. Presumably the same number would be made in 1969 and the following years. Yet the bulk of the small farmers were not taking advantage of these facilities.

At the AID offices in the capital I was told that El Salvador, thanks in part to the Mass Fertilization Program, was importing from three to four times more fertilizer than it had some seven years ago.

In order to check AID's statement, I went to the agricultural section of the Customs House where I was pleasantly surprised to find an old friend who had once worked for me in charge. His records were precisely kept and were, I am sure, correct, but they contrasted directly with AID's information. Dozens of types of fertilizer are imported by El Salvador and records are kept for each type. The following showed the importations for 20-20-0, the type most used and that recommended by the Mass Fertilization Program.

The year ⎤	1964	6 million kilos
Mass Fertilization ⎬	1965	2 million kilos
Program began ⎦	1966	0.5 million kilos
	1967	1.6 million kilos
	1968	3.8 million kilos

These figures scarcely bore out the AID claim, nor did a conversation I had with the man who handles sales to small farmers for a major fertilizer company. The salesman had a "gut feeling" that mass demonstrations had increased sales, but he admitted no statistics backed this up. Then, too, he pointed out something I had not realized, namely, that cotton growers use a great deal of the 20-20-0 fertilizer. For example, he knew of one farmer who had bought 1.5 million kilos of this fertilizer the previous year. Visits to other fertilizer companies confirmed what he had told me. Thus any report going back to Washington stating the Mass Fertilization Program had increased fertilizer use in El Salvador was based on nothing more than AID's own "gut feeling."

While pursuing this question, I learned that the fertilizer companies were no longer willing to donate to the Mass Fertilization Program. This seemed paradoxical because if the companies could get the government to set up demonstration trials all over the country, and the trials increased their sales, one would assume the companies would be eager to donate a few thousand dollars worth of fertilizers for such promotion.

Ing. Humberto Toval, in charge of sales for Fertica (a fertilizer company), told me that while the demonstration trials were excellent and they were a good educational tool, they had had "little influence on El Salvador's corn and bean production." The reason: the plots were too small for the farmer to be able to buy fertilizer and either no credit was available or he did not have enough interest to use what credit he could obtain. Thus the demonstrations may have convinced a group of farmers of the need for fertilizer, but they did not then make use of this information. The program seemed to have concentrated on farms with less than two acres of land (190,000 in the country), at best a marginal economic group, and the fertilizer companies did not consider them good potential customers. Another fertilizer salesman said 95 percent of his company's product was used for coffee, cotton, sugar cane, and some rice. Thus, he said, it would be quite difficult to measure the impact of the Mass Fertilization Program on the 5 percent of their sales for corn and beans.

My efforts to determine if the program had increased the use of improved or hybrid corn were equally disappointing. While all the small farmers with whom I talked recognized the influence of fertilizer on their production, they were all indifferent to the advantages of hybrid corn.

Later in Nicaragua I met with Dr. Angel Salazar who represented the DeKalb Corn Company, a major American producer of hybrid corn seed. He is one of the few real authorities on the general status of corn production throughout Central America. Speaking of the Mass Fertilization Program, he said El Salvador plants about 30 percent of its corn land with hybrid seed—twice the figure of Mexico, and possibly more than any other Latin American country. But virtually all of El Salvador's hybrid corn is used by the large farmers. Only 5 percent of the corn is fertilized, and all of this, again, is by the large farmers.

"If the increase in corn production in El Salvador is due to the big farmer, if he is the only one who uses the hybrid seed and fertilizer, why then do we hear all this talk about the wonderful impact of the Mass Fertilization Program?" I asked Salazar.

"It is simple," he said. "Everyone knows it is the big farmer who uses the new technology, but," he added, "it is more poetic to say you have helped the *campesino*."

Another puzzle is: why has the number of demonstration plots been falling? Birdsall, who had originally made the trip with Garst in 1964 and had then been assigned to El Salvador to operate this program, has retired. He was a persuasive, hardworking agronomist. By the sheer force and will of his personality he made the program live. A Peace Corps volunteer told me Birdsall would be out at 7:30 A.M. and would make sure the extension agents were, too. It was not unusual for Birdsall to phone an extension agent in a town two hours' travel from the capital that he would see him in a cornfield at 7:30 A.M. the next morning. He would be up and out of the capital by dawn and when the extension agent arrived in the field he would find Birdsall already there.

He pounded on doors to get the fertilizer and pesticides donated. It was useless to give him "no" for an answer, because he would still stand there with his hand out.

When Birdsall retired, AID did not bother to replace him. And so the program died. In fact, one fertilizer company told me quite frankly, "We gave all the fertilizer and help needed as long as we had confidence the demonstration trials were carried out properly. We had confidence in Birdsall. But with him gone, who knows? We have not cut down on our donations since he left, but now we give our fertilizer to help the agricultural school."

Still, this seems an inadequate answer.

My own conclusion is that the fertilizer practices proclaimed by Roswell Garst may have been valid for Iowa, but it was quite false to assume we knew how they could be transferred, without adaptation, to Latin America. Fertilizers, pesticides, and improved seeds can, of course, double or triple production of the small farmer, but it is questionable whether the increased production will really justify the cost, that is, make the new technology economically profitable.

Without preliminary trials, AID accepted the "Garst technique" as a science-based device that would "have a strong impact on increasing productivity from an average of 15 bushels to the acre to about 40 in El Salvador in just a few years."[7] Thus AID had not learned from its accumulated two decades of development experience that crash programs without proper preliminary groundwork can be expected to fail.

"Four Cents Worth of Zinc"

ONCE UPON A TIME, or so I have heard it repeated in development circles, there was a nice, neat little Mexican valley on the other side of Querétaro. The valley was deeply isolated within a rim of mountains. The people there were forlorn and sad because they were so poor, and there was nothing to grow except corn and beans.

Then suddenly the Campbell Soup Company appeared. Scientists from the company tested the soil and found it good for growing other things, including vegetables used in soups, provided just one chemical was added—zinc—only four cents worth for each acre. Having discovered this, the company built a soup factory in the valley. The people were happy because the company taught them the secret of raising high-quality tomatoes for which it paid them lots of money. And the people in the valley lived happily ever after.

"This is a classic case of a company bringing in new technology and revolutionizing an economy," William Spruce, our commercial attaché in Mexico, told me.

"It is an example of what American industry can do to industrialize, in the best sense of the word, a community's food processing business," said Aaron Altschul, special assistant to the U.S. secretary of agriculture.

Our former ambassador to Mexico, Thomas Mann, urged that I visit the Campbell plant to see how American capital and know-how can operate at its best. This company, he said, "ran soil analyses, found what was deficient, supplied the fertilizer, and guaranteed growers a market. It provided county agent-type advice: when to plant, how to harvest."

Actually I had been hearing these same statements about

Title of the chapter taken from an article in *Campbell's News and Views*, Fall-Winter, 1963, p. 3.

Campbell's in the shoptalk among development personnel for several years.

After such praises, naturally, I wrote to the company, saying I had "heard a great deal about the contributions which Campbell Soup had made in Mexico and about its effect on the community in which it has been working" and asked whom I might see in Mexico to learn more about it.

No answer.

I wrote again and finally received a reply saying the delay was "involved in seeking permission to have you contact our Mexican plant. It has been established now that it would be satisfactory for you to do so. It was also determined that use of information on Campbell Soup Company in your forthcoming book would be contingent upon clearance by Campbell Soup Company in Camden, New Jersey."[1]

I was a bit put off by the implied threat of censorship, or "controlled" publicity (I have not cleared this chapter with New Jersey), but not enough to dampen the anticipation of a visit to the Querétaro region which I had first seen when I was eleven years old. I had not been back for twenty years.

Driving south from the border city of Laredo, the countryside was the same semidesert as always. The urban areas of the cities of Monterrey and Saltillo and to a lesser degree San Luis Potosí, however, were greatly expanded. The good motels and hotels, spaced at convenient intervals, were new, as was the highway itself over which six-wheeled semitrailers zoomed night and day.

But the biggest surprise was Querétaro. That nimbus of modern civilization, smog, could be seen for miles as I approached, the factories belching smoke. Along the new superhighway, the factories of today's corporate elite were lined up like a guard of honor: Singer Sewing Machine, Massey-Ferguson Tractors, Joy Manufacturing, Gerber Baby Foods, Carnation Milk, Kellogg's Breakfast Food, Link-Belt, Chicago Bridge and Iron, Ralston Purina, and that old capitalistic pioneer, Coca-Cola.

This fantastic growth of Querétaro has been stimulated at both the national and state levels, primarily by the policy of using tax concessions to encourage new industries to locate there, away from overcrowded Mexico City. The Mexican government has even gone so far as to build a four-lane turnpike between Querétaro and the capital to help this process along. Of course Querétaro had always been the principal city of the agriculturally rich Bajío, a wide valley (really a plateau) covering several hundred square miles. The Bajío has long been known as the "Breadbasket of Mexico."

As a youth, I had visited the Hill of the Bells outside Querétaro, and had my picture taken, blindfolded, as I stood with my back to the same wall where the ill-fated Emperor Maximilian had stood and been executed by the victorious troops of Benito Juárez. I had reached the hill by walking a mile or so across pastures and hopping over irrigation ditches. Afterward, I returned to the city in a horse-drawn streetcar that wandered about the countryside in a delightfully bucolic fashion.

Today the Hill of the Bells is sandwiched between a residential area on one side and an industrial park on the other. Behind the little chapel that marks the execution site stands an enormous statue of Juárez, with red warning lights for airplanes blinking from his ears. The artist, in his attempt to emphasize that Juárez was an Indian, made him into a sort of frock-coated Neanderthal man. It is one of the ugliest statues I have seen.

In a way, though, it is a fitting monument for this new industrial complex which has everything today's "new" Mexican wants his country to have: power lines, smokestacks, and rows of little houses and apartments for people who have just scrambled up the hard slope of success from their former adobe huts with dirt floors. Nor should one belittle this. It is what all the undeveloped world wants.

Driving along the superhighway outside Querétaro, I had planned to continue on to the Campbell valley, reportedly some thirty miles west, for a quick reconnaissance before returning to find a hotel in the city. So, whizzing along at seventy miles an hour, I suddenly passed, completely without warning, a large water tower labeled "Campbell's."

I was dumfounded. Could this be the nice, neat little isolated valley? The Bajío!

I had even been here in 1951, practically across the fence from where the Campbell plant now stands, when with the Colombian minister of agriculture and others I had visited the seed plant the Mexican government had just built to process the hybrid corn which the Rockefeller Foundation had developed.

The Bajío is the agricultural heartland of Mexico. It is the nation's cradle of liberty, too. A few miles to the north Father Hidalgo had issued his ringing *Grito de Dolores* call to freedom; ten miles to the east he had been proclaimed commander-in-chief of the revolutionary army of 1810; and here Emperor Maximilian had made his last stand in 1867. But somehow all of this had been left out of the Campbell Soup story about the "small, isolated valley." Actually, the plant is located within sight of two major trunk highways and a railroad. Nothing could be less isolated. Immediately obvious also was that this one new plant of Campbell's, in and of itself, could scarcely have led to the revolutionizing of the area.

I asked George Goodrich, the plant manager and a man with forty years experience in Mexico, about its history. In 1959 Campbell began looking around for a factory site in Mexico, he said. As a preliminary, the firm sent Dr. William A. Schmidt, an agricultural scientist, to run some tests to find out what could be grown in the Querétaro area. He learned it was impossible to grow celery in the Bajío without adding four cents worth of zinc per acre.

But this discovery, though it has been widely repeated as part of the Campbell story, was of little or no importance in locating the Campbell plant here. "The major reason," said Goodrich, "was that it is centrally located. Some 60 to 70 percent of all consumer goods produced in the country are sold in the surrounding area and in the Mexico City region. We have a market of 12 million potential customers located conveniently nearby."

Most important, the processing of vegetables was already well established in this region. In fact, this was the biggest surprise of my visit. As development people tell this story, no mention is made of Heinz or Libby or Del Monte.

Actually Libby was the true U.S. pioneer in the Bajío. It had started a plant here thirty years before Campbell arrived; later, Heinz bought the factory and is still operating it today. Also Del Monte began its research activities at nearby Irapuato in 1959 and there built Mexico's largest canning plant, one that is at least twice the size of Campbell. And, of course, the flow of vegetables from the local farmers into these well-established plants has long been routinely organized.

Furthermore prosperous farming was nothing new here. As I have already indicated, the Bajío was intensively cultivated far back into prehistoric times. Today part of the land is irrigated and some of the farms are mechanized. With the exception of the irrigated lands in the Northwest, no part of Mexico has any better farmers than the Bajío. The story of Campbell introducing modern science in the form of zinc fertilizer and thereby making possible the growing of vegetables in this area is an exaggeration of fact.

While it is true that zinc fertilizer does increase celery production, I was told the zinc deficiency is not a major factor affecting the raising of other vegetables in the Bajío. Tomatoes, for instance, are the chief crop used by all three canners, and are also shipped in large amounts to the United States. But tomatoes have been raised here by the Indians for several thousand years.

A former American agricultural attaché in Mexico, in writing to me about Campbell's "considerable" contribution to the economic development of the area and its "extensive research" to determine the varieties of vegetables adapted to it, had said, "Also, as is normal in the United States, but quite unknown in Mexico at the time, the company entered into contracts with growers to purchase their production, provide the required seed and other ingredients for successful production and kept their [the company's] field man out working with farmers to provide all the help and advice needed."[2]

Campbell's Mexican staff were most open about their operations and made no claims at all about any local impact by the plant. Their main problem, as at Campbell plants in other parts of the world, is to ensure a reliable flow of vegetables, especially tomatoes, that meet company standards of quality. Whatever technology the company has introduced is focused on achieving this result. At the time of my visit the company employed five agronomists, three working on research problems and two seeking out farmers with whom the company could work and to whom they would then offer some technical assistance. All the men were Mexicans; each of the two field men had an assistant who was a high school graduate and who had had no further training.

I asked the company men about the "great number" of farmers benefiting from Campbell's operations. Although I received varying answers, it appeared that Campbell had contracts with twenty to thirty growers. Each of these used from 25 up to 375 acres of land to fulfill his contractual obligations to Campbell. The total acreage affected by the Campbell plant was about 1,000 acres. That produces a lot of vegetables, of course, and if this were centered in one small valley the economic result would be important. But in the huge Bajío the effect is negligible.

Has Campbell's technical assistance affected the tomato yield of its farmers under contract? This I could not determine. The yields are less than would be expected in the United States (twelve to fifteen tons per acre versus an average of eighteen in California).

But Campbell also pays its growers less than it does in the United States ($22 to $24 per ton versus $30 to $36 in New Jersey).

Interestingly, its tomato soup sells for 40 percent more in Mexico than in the United States (23¢ per can versus 16¢).

Even so, Campbell has one outsized headache: it is losing money in Mexico and the plant is operating at only half capacity.

ODDLY, a more valid success story is just down the road from Campbell's. There, another American firm, Del Monte, has a canning plant which has operated in the area as long as Campbell, employs twice as many agronomists, uses produce from five times as much land, and operates at a profit. But nobody in the development field has ever heard of this establishment.

It was nearly impossible for me to catch Del Monte's busy manager for an interview. I finally met up with him while he was en route to the bank to make, perhaps, a company deposit. "It's okay with us if Campbell gets the publicity," he said, as he disappeared into the bank.

WHY, then, is Campbell cited as an illustration of how outside science and technology has revolutionized a local economy when there is so little to publicize—four cents worth of zinc? Perhaps the answer is nothing more than success through association, to wit: Since 1943 the Rockefeller Foundation has conducted an agricultural program in Mexico and because it has achieved worldwide recognition, it has been visited by large numbers in the development profession. Campbell's cannery is next door to the plant which processes seed from the foundation's corn program. Campbell offices in Mexico City are on the floor below those of the foundation. The president of the Rockefeller Foundation is on the board of directors of Campbell Soup Company in Camden, New Jersey.

The Rockefeller Foundation:
Prophecy of Plenty

As ONE GROWS OLDER, it is a pleasure to meet an old friend you have not seen since the carefree days of long ago and to learn he has become a success in the world. He has a big house, a flashy car, an expensively dressed, beautiful wife, and that wonderful air of assurance that self-achievement brings. The encounter is particularly delightful if, back in the old days, the guy had been the happy-go-lucky sort you thought would never have two dimes to rub together.

That was my reaction to my old friend Mexico. Never in the wildest flights of cantina conversation during the 1930s did anyone forecast that charming, lovable, tatterdemalion Mexico would in three decades become an industrialized, prosperous nation, highly respected throughout the world.

On this, my first trip back in many years, it was a constant surprise to keep discovering new, unexpected evidence that the material things of the world have become available to a goodly percentage of the Mexican people. Of course the nation has not reached Nirvana. The evidence of terrible poverty is still omnipresent in both cities and countryside. But no one from the United States, aware of his own country's shortcomings, can cast stones at his neighbor Mexico.

For Mexico has attained the statistical hallmark of modern success. Its gross national product (GNP) has increased annually over the past ten years at the rate of 7 percent, one of the highest growth figures in the world. In the last twenty years the nation has tripled its output of goods and services; real per capita income has increased 75 percent.[1]

Many complex reasons are credited for the great surge in industrial output.

Regarding the growth in agricultural production, however, the public, the officials, and the economists are virtually united in giving credit to a single institution, the Rockefeller Foundation, saying it has:

—increased Mexico's total agricultural production

—introduced new technology that has substantially increased farm profits

—made Mexico self-sufficient in wheat and corn, thereby saving the nation significant foreign exchange

—made Mexico a grain exporter.

Here are typical comments (made during interviews):

"Of all development efforts in Mexico, the Rockefeller Foundation's has been by far the most successful"—Thomas Mann, former assistant secretary of state for Latin American Affairs and former U.S. ambassador to Mexico.

"The Rockefeller Foundation has had an enormous impact on my country"—Hugo Margáin, Mexican ambassador to the United States.

"Mexico's agricultural success is largely due to the Rockefeller Foundation"—Fulton Freeman, U.S. ambassador to Mexico.

When I asked the foundation's president, "Which, in your opinion, are the most successful agricultural programs which have been made possible by the Rockefeller Foundation support?" I was encouraged to visit the wheat improvement program, centered in Ciudad Obregón in northwest Mexico. In later talks with members of the foundation's staff in New York, Mexico City, and elsewhere, it was clear they also believed this to be one of their most outstanding operations, that the agricultural revolution in Mexico has paralleled the history of this project, and that the credit for its success is due to Dr. Norman Borlaug, a long-time foundation scientist.[2] In 1970 his work received worldwide recognition when he was awarded the Nobel Peace Prize.

Borlaug began his research at Ciudad Obregón in 1945, releasing to Mexican farmers his first rust-resistant wheats in 1947. In the late 1950s he began work on dwarf wheats and was able to release these in that area in 1961. These were labeled "wonder wheats" and were quickly introduced into India and Pakistan. These dwarf wheats were soon followed by the "miracle rice" (developed in the Philippines with Rockefeller and Ford foundation money and guidance), and together they formed the basis for what soon came to be known as the "Green Revolution."

Dr. J. George Harrar, then president of the Rockefeller Foundation, stated at the end of 1969 that the Green Revolution offers the hope "of gradually eliminating hunger, malnutrition and the all-too-frequent famines from regions where they have long been ever-present threats to society."[3]

No single event in economic development has received so much publicity as this Green Revolution. Hopes have skyrocketed that the threat of famine has indeed been removed from the hungry nations of the development world for the foreseeable future. "For the majority of mankind suffering from chronic hunger and malnutrition, development of the 'miracle' wheat and rice is a far more meaningful achievement than the landing on the moon."[4]

The worldwide publicity given to its dwarf wheat project has redounded to the credit of the Rockefeller Foundation in all its other work, so that today it is the unquestioned leader for those advocating agricultural research as the key to a decent future in the undeveloped nations.

All this echoed my own earlier reactions. In 1952 I wrote an article for the *Saturday Evening Post* on the Rockefeller Foundation agricultural research program in Mexico. It was so complimentary that Warren Weaver, then vice-president of the foundation, protested in a letter (May 8, 1952) against "the brilliance of the illumination which you turn on us!" Others told me my article was the first mass-media publicity given to this Mexican program.

Through the years I had read only praise about the foundation. Now, seventeen years after writing that article, I was returning for another look at the foundation's work. There was no reason to believe my observations would not be equally laudatory.

IT IS EXCITING to drive into Ciudad Obregón from the airport, and to see the productiveness of this region. The land is tabletop flat. Wheat fields stretch away in every direction to the horizon. In April the harvest was under way and self-propelled combines rolled out into the distance and disappeared. Although this country has a per capita GNP of only $572[5] and is classified by most as a developing nation, this particular temperate zone region of Mexico looked like Kansas—only better!

In the popular mind all this progress of northwest Mexico dates from 1945 when Borlaug took over a run-down agricultural experiment station just outside Ciudad Obregón.

When he arrived, the town itself was only twenty years old, having been laid out in 1925 in the center of a new irrigation area in the delta of the Yaqui River. This date is important in the understanding of the region's development. Not only had its boom begun before the arrival of the Rockefeller Foundation, but it was already developing outside the traditional Mexican cultural, economic, and agricultural patterns as the following bit of history shows.

The favorable features of the Yaqui Delta for irrigation were first recognized by Carlos Conant, a Mexican. Toward the end of the nineteenth century he received from President Porfirio Díaz the concession for the entire district, then virtually uninhabited, and began the first engineering works. Because of circumstances beyond his control—floods and attacks by the unpacified Yaqui Indians—he went broke. The concession was picked up by an American, Davis Richardson, who in 1903 persuaded two New York financiers, John Hays Hammond and Harry Payne Whitney, to put up $12 million for its development. By 1923 some 15,000 acres were under cultivation, but more floods and new financial troubles slowed down the operation.

About this time Alvaro Obregón, president of Mexico, and himself a native of Sonora, acquired 7,500 acres of the original concession to use as his retirement ranch. In addition to Obregón, the area produced another Mexican president, Plutarco Elías Calles, who succeeded Obregón. When Calles' term was over, Obregón was reelected but was assassinated before he could take office. The Congress then appointed Emilio Portés Gil as interim president but he turned out to have virtually no power so that Calles remained the de facto president. Thus, this small, sparsely populated region of Sonora was blessed with fourteen years of presidential attention and largesse.

In 1926 the Yaqui Indians in the area, who had continued to be a warlike crowd, attempted to kidnap Obregón by attacking a train he was on. Furious, he launched a campaign against the Yaquis which ended their careers as troublemakers, and for the first time enabled the delta to be developed in peace.

Obregón had recognized the tremendous potential of the Richardson concession. New land tenure laws had been enacted during the revolution (the concession was subject to them) which had the net effect of forcing foreigners out of this coastal area. Obregón arranged to have the Mexican government buy out Richardson and his American partners.

The land was now distributed by the government as part of

its national land reform program. Unlike elsewhere in Mexico (i.e., Papaloapan and Atotonilco) the farmers received sizable acreages because the land was primarily barren semidesert. Without irrigation, it could not be cultivated. About half the land went to *proprietarios pequenos*,[6] the government classification, of a group which, translated literally, means "small farmers." But, in actual fact, this group includes some of the nation's biggest and most prosperous farmers. They received from 47 to 247 acres each. When irrigation canals were constructed later, these farms became extremely valuable. One hundred acres of irrigated land is a big farm by anyone's standards anywhere!

Thus when one refers to the wheat program in northwest Mexico as benefiting "small farmers" he is referring to this misleading government classification and not necessarily to any sort of peasant agriculture. Likewise the land here which went to those classified as *colonos* and *ejidatarios* was in acreages larger than the Mexican average.

In 1942 (three years before Borlaug arrived) the government began a massive public works program for the Yaqui Delta. Tens of millions of dollars were poured into the area; $35 million went into two big dams alone, one started in 1942 and the other in 1952, and the amount of irrigated land swelled to over 560,000 acres. Additional millions went into irrigation canals, roads, power lines, telephones, and the like. It was part of the government's massive effort to help agriculture throughout all Mexico. One result was an increase in farm loans by 400 percent in the decade of the 1950s; nearly three-fourths of these went to farmers in northern and northwestern Mexico.[7] Financing for the farmers in the Yaqui area continues to be readily available. "It's really too easy to get a loan," said one local farmer to me; he was not, however, typical—he commutes between his farm and Ciudad Obregón in his own twin-engine plane.

The farmers of this thoroughly nontropical area around Ciudad Obregón prospered. Note that:

—they received the lion's share of Mexico's agricultural development money
—they own large acreages of fertile, newly irrigated land
—they are not bound to traditional peasant agriculture
—they have the money to risk on innovative ideas.

Thus, Borlaug, when his new wheats were ready for release, was not dealing with the traditional subsistence farmers. They were, by comparison with the rest in Mexico, already booming and prosperous.

NORMAN BORLAUG was not originally hired to work on wheat at Ciudad Obregón, but on a variety of crops near Mexico City where the Rockefeller Foundation was concentrating its agricultural work. Although wheat was widely grown in the plateau area of central Mexico and in the northern districts, the total amount produced, relative to corn, was not large.

Borlaug soon realized the need for a wheat research program in the expanding area of northwest Mexico and with some difficulty, I was told, managed to get the foundation to agree. In 1945 he took over a small, disused experiment station a few miles outside Ciudad Obregón owned by the government; he repaired some broken windows and went to work. Borlaug faced many pesky inconveniences. Although working conditions were difficult, the hardest part, Borlaug told me, was that no one seemed particularly interested in what he was doing.

At first he spent a great deal of time talking with the local wheat farmers about their problems. He learned their chief worry was rust, a disease caused by a fungus to which all the world's wheats were susceptible (although some wheats had more natural resistance than others). The varieties then grown in the Yaqui Delta had almost no resistance, thus endangering each year the farmers' chances of a profitable crop. Borlaug, with his characteristic enthusiasm, launched an intensive program to breed and select rust-resistant varieties for the region. The techniques were well known, having been worked out in the 1920s in a number of laboratories around the world.

In order to speed up his work Borlaug opened a second research center in Toluca, 550 miles further south and 7,250 feet higher. He planted, bred, and tested his new varieties in Ciudad Obregón during the winter; then, during the summer when wheat cannot be grown there, he moved his experiments to Toluca. This double timing of the pace of his research by working in two areas in a single year was not original. But this was, I believe, the first time it had been applied systematically in wheat research.

In addition to making it possible for the work on rust resistance to go twice as fast, the technique offered another, previously unsuspected advantage: Borlaug was selecting varieties of wheat that did well both at Ciudad Obregón and Toluca, and he ended up with wheats adaptable over a far greater range of latitudes than any previously developed. Without planning it, he had developed wheats with a new and valuable characteristic: insensitivity to the length of day. Perhaps more than any other factor, this was to be the reason why his dwarf wheats could be planted so effectively and extensively years later when they were sent to Asia. The importance of this characteristic in the global fight against hunger was not to be recognized, however, until about 1957 when new data on all types of wheat were developed through field trials conducted around the world. These trials showed that wheats developed from research in the United States and Europe (where day length is long during the growing season) are practically worthless when planted nearer the equator (where the day length is shorter and where the food-hungry nations are located). In contrast, Borlaug's wheats grew beautifully.

Simultaneously with the release of his first rust-resistant wheats in 1947, Borlaug made available the data from his research on more efficient use of fertilizer and irrigation water. Taken as a package (the new varieties plus improved farming techniques) his recommendations enabled the local farmers to achieve sizable increases in their production.

In 1956 Borlaug began experimenting on a new short-stemmed type of wheat. As a result his work achieved an entirely new dimension of importance.

The origins of this dwarf wheat plant date from 1946 when C. S. Salmon, a U.S. Department of Agriculture scientist assigned to General Douglas MacArthur's staff, noticed a wheat plant growing in Japan that was only ankle high. Intrigued by the small size, he collected its seed and sent it to the U.S. Department of Agriculture plant quarantine nursery at Yuma, Arizona. A year or so later, Orville D. Vogel, a wheat breeder from Washington State University at Pullman, visited the nursery, recognized the uniqueness of the dwarf wheat, and took some of the seed back to his university research station. In 1949 he began to cross it with standard wheats and within a few years proved that the height of a wheat plant need not be a decisive factor in producing the carbohydrate needed for large wheat yields.

This was an important scientific breakthrough. Word of it traveled fast among wheat breeders. Borlaug, along with others, obtained seed from Vogel and began to cross it with his Mexican varieties.

Several other scientists were also experimenting with these dwarf wheats. However Borlaug became the first to develop a usable variety, mainly because he was "double timing" at Toluca and Ciudad Obregón. Another element in his favor was his goal to produce a wheat that would be acceptable to the Mexican market, not to the U.S. market. Since in Mexico there is less concern over quality of grain (its uniformity and its milling and baking qualities), Borlaug could concentrate on giving the Yaqui Delta farmers a higher-yielding variety while being relieved of the time-consuming task of selecting for high quality.

With this competitive edge, Borlaug was able by 1961 to release his dwarf wheat to the Mexican farmers. It had three important advantages:

—it made particularly efficient use of fertilizer
—it remained erect until harvested (most wheats, if heavily fertilized, tend to fall over as harvest time approaches and lose much of their grain)
—it had the same insensitivity to day length as that of his earlier rust-resistant varieties.

The rest is history. Borlaug's dwarf wheats immediately became the dominant variety in northwest Mexico and from there the seed was taken to India and Pakistan where they contributed to a dramatic increase in yields.

VISITING Borlaug's research center and watching him in action is quite an experience. He is a stimulating person, one who inspires intense loyalties in the people around him, including, almost instantaneously, the flood of visitors who today make a pilgrimage to this shrine of the development world. He makes a vivid salesman for his wheat program, talking in quick, short sentences. Tight-lipped, though always with a ready grin, he has a little-boy look about him as he threads his way back and forth across the hundreds of intricately laid out breeding plots.

He explains his program in terms of a football game, emphasizing to the rapt visitors that success depends on training students to become good ends who can be counted on to catch the ball and stressing that he also needs the support of all the tackles and guards he can get. He wants his linemen to tumble all over the opposition. His strategy, he says, is dictated by the fact that many of his ends are green and unskilled, but he must throw the ball to them anyway. No matter what else happens, a good end, despite all tackling, must hang onto that pass and run with it. Each man, says Coach Borlaug, must pick up his portion of the wheatbreeding program and carry it over the goal line, even without advice from the bench.

His listeners, whether high officials, acolyte students, or pagans who have never seen a football game, are swept along by his enthusiasm. They, too, yearn to be ends and tackles and to become part of the winning ball club in this vital contest against world hunger.

When he is expounding his program, Borlaug never really listens to anyone else; he is too intensely wrapped up in explaining his work and its results. Interruptions, to tell him about an aspect of another program or even to comment on his own program, pass unnoticed. Immediately, he picks up where his last sentence stopped and plunges ahead with his mile-a-minute discourse. He loves his work.

In 1968, following a highly profitable sale of wheat seed to India and Pakistan, Ciudad Obregón named a street in his honor, with a marble monument in recognition of his accomplishments. A testimonial luncheon was given for him, one of the most publicized local events in years and "everybody" was there. Typically, I was told, Borlaug arrived straight from the fields in mud-spattered boots. He listened with unaccustomed patience to the series of flowery speeches in his praise. When his turn came to speak, it dawned on him that here was a fine opportunity, not to be missed, to act as coach for his assembled players. He scolded the farmers for their truancy saying, according to my informant, something like the following:

"How did it happen you fellows failed to put in your irrigation water on time last year? Because you didn't, you lost some of your wheat. The reason you failed was that you were running around the countryside in your pickup trucks, playing with your radio-telephones, and yapping at your foremen. You're so busy with your gadgets you don't go out to the fields anymore to find out what's happening. I've just now come from there. A lot of aphids are developing, and you people are going to lose some of your wheat because you don't even know this is happening. You've got to get out into the fields the way you used to, before you made so much money off your wheat. We've got the wheat problem licked, but we don't have your complacency licked!"

Needless to say, this badgering delighted the audience and Borlaug's reputation soared even higher.

To SAY the Rockefeller Foundation has achieved a near-omnipotent reputation for success in the development field, a reputation with global implications, is no exaggeration. The foundation has believably, has indeed rolled the rock of adequate food supplies by the gods forever to roll a heavy rock up a hill without ever having the strength to push it to the top, who, suddenly and unbelievably, has indeed rolled the rock of adequate food supplies up to safety. People now widely believe that the Rockefeller Foundation has shown the way to accomplishing what before was regarded as impossible, that the enormous and complex task of feeding all the hungry of the world can be solved.

Much of the foundation's recent reputation stems from Borlaug's Mexican wheat program, which is reputed to have made wheat growing possible in northwest Mexico, and also to have:

—increased Mexico's total wheat production

—created prosperity for the wheat farmers in northwest Mexico

—made Mexico self-sufficient in wheat (thus saving the nation considerable foreign exchange)

—enabled Mexico to become a wheat-exporting nation.

As a result of my studies for this book, I have found myself in the unexpected and, to me, startling situation where it is necessary to challenge each of these popular beliefs.

DID ROCKEFELLER RESEARCH *make wheat growing possible in northwest Mexico?*

The popular legend includes the belief that the foundation's research has made it possible to grow wheat in this region for the first time. This is not true. In 1911 wheat was regarded as the most important crop there from the standpoint of acreage and this has remained unchanged. For a few years rice occupied more land, but that ended abruptly in 1952 when the new dam cut off the flow of silt needed to fertilize rice inexpensively.[8] In 1940–41, just prior to the foundation's arrival in Mexico, wheat accounted for about half the acreage planted in this area, the same figure as for the years 1950–58 and, as far as I know, for today. Thus in northwest Mexico wheat was a major crop long before Borlaug began his research.

Prior to Borlaug's arrival the delta grew imported wheat varieties (the raising of wheat seed to send to Mexico was then an important business for California's Imperial Valley) and the U.S. government had paid for some earlier wheat research.[9]

Nevertheless it is frequently stated or implied that in northwest Mexico true wheat production began only with the advent of the Rockefeller Foundation. For instance, E. C. Stakman, a world authority on wheat rust and a member of the team which planned the original Rockefeller Mexican program, wrote that in northwest Mexico "wheat growing was a gamble with rust and most growers in that area had been wise enough to stop gambling with it."[10] Similarly, agricultural economist Whitney Hicks refers to the wheat resulting from Rockefeller research as a " 'new' crop [which] was introduced in northwest Mexico."[11]

To what extent *has Rockefeller research increased wheat production in Mexico?*

"The power of the improved, high yielding . . . varieties in revolutionizing agricultural production is clearly shown by the acceleration of wheat production in Mexico . . ." says a recent CIMMYT report.[12]

Mexico's wheat production has indeed increased dramatically during the past twenty-five years. Popular opinion as well as nearly all development specialists credit this entirely to research by the Rockefeller Foundation. For example, the two definitive papers on the subject both dramatize the wheat story with the table *and* heading that appears on page 212. The table heading implies that research has been entirely responsible for increasing Mexico's per acre wheat yields from 750 kg/hectare to 2790.

Crediting the increase in wheat production throughout all Mexico to "the impact of research" is an oversimplification if not a misstatement. Research has been important. Three additional reasons for this increase, each of which may be of equal or greater importance than the research itself, are newly irrigated land, increased use of fertilizer, and subsidies.

1. *Newly irrigated land.* The table says nothing about the difference in the quality of land used before and after Rockefeller research began. New, irrigated land can easily outproduce long-farmed, deteriorated soil. Before the foundation arrived, average wheat yields of the Ciudad Obregón area were already twice that of the nation as a whole. The reason: Ciudad Obregón land was new but most of the rest of the nation's wheat was grown on depleted soils in the region known as the Bajío in central Mexico.

Exactly coinciding with the Rockefeller period in Mexico, but for reasons unrelated to the foundation, wheat growing was moved off the poor soils of the Bajío. For it was during this period, 1946

TABLE 18.1.
THE IMPACT OF RESEARCH ON MEXICAN WHEAT
PRODUCTION

Year	Cultivated Area (10³ hectares)	Yield (kg/hectare)	Production (10³ metric tons)
1945	500	750	330
1946	520	800	390
1947	550	820	430
1948	590	850	500
1949	600	880	560
1950	625	900	600
1951	635	920	640
1952	650	940	710
1953	670	960	770
1954	680	980	800
1955	790	1100	850
1956	780	1200	1200
1957	770	1352	1200
1958	840	1592	1337
1959 (a)	937	1351	1265
1960	840	1417	1200
1961	816	1700	1373
1962	777	1800	1400
1963	787	2200	1800
1964	846	2600	2200
1965	668	2368	1565
1966 (b)	723	2250	1627
1967	860	2790	2400

SOURCE: Norman E. Borlaug, "Wheat Breeding and Its Impact on World Food Supply," *Third International Wheat Genetics Symposium Proceedings, Canberra 1968*, Australian Academy of Science, p. 7. The same table appears in the earlier publication: "Wheat, Rust and People," *Phytopathology*, October 1965, p. 1090.
(a) A year with heavy losses from infestations of the English grain aphid.
(b) Considerable loss from frosts and severe leaf rust.

to 1964, that Mexico increased the number of its irrigated acres from 2 million to 6 million.[13] Today only 17 percent of Mexico's wheat is grown in the Bajío.

University of Missouri's Whitney Hicks shows that 87 percent of all Mexico's increase in wheat production has occurred in the Northwest and that two-thirds of this increase was due to increasing the amount of irrigated land.[14] Economist Henry Hopp of the U.S. Department of Agriculture says that "the increase in the irrigation, especially in the Northwest, has been as important as . . . research advances."[15]

2. *Increased use of fertilizer.* From the beginning, Borlaug's research looked for and encouraged efficient use of fertilizer. As

wheat production has expanded in Mexico, fertilizer use also has increased—but only in part due to research.

Desert land, when cleared of vegetation and irrigated, does not at first need fertilizer.[16] However, once the land (such as that developed for irrigation during the 1940s and 1950s) has been farmed a few years, the original nutrients are reduced and fertilizer is required. Fertilizer consumption then goes up.

The foundation's new wheat varieties *must* have fertilizer to achieve their yields. Fortunately, during the period of Borlaug's research, Mexico's petrochemical industry greatly expanded, making fertilizer far more accessible to agriculture. Hicks says a third of the increased production in the Northwest during the last twenty-five years comes from improved varieties *and* fertilizer.[17]

Studies conducted by Reed Hertford, U.S. Department of Agriculture economist, show that from 1953 onward, well over half the total change in Mexican crop yields has been due to the increased use of chemical fertilizer.[18]

3. *Subsidies.* It was like tripping accidentally over a top secret document when I discovered the role subsidies have played in increased wheat production in Mexico.

Dr. Oscar Brauer Herrera, dean of the Graduate School of the National School of Agriculture. first referred to it in a general interview, saying, "If there were no price support program, no wheat would be grown in Mexico." Later I came across an Iowa State University study which stated simply that an increase in wheat production in Mexico will occur *only* if a pricing [subsidy] program is carried out.[19] I investigated and found that Mexico pays its wheat farmers $1.99 a bushel or 33 percent above the approximate $1.45 world market price. (Wheat was actually costing $2.61 a bushel in Mexico City when I was there.)

When I asked the Rockefeller staff about this, they said this high subsidy is justified on the basis that the Mexican wheat farmer must pay 100 percent more for his fertilizer than the U.S. farmer. However, I found no evidence to support this point. For example, farmers were paying $135.20 per ton for anhydrous ammonia in Sonora at the same time farmers were paying from $148.50 to $176.00 in the wheat-growing areas of Montana, Wyoming, Idaho, and Washington. The Chamber of Commerce in Ciudad Obregón said quite frankly the government subsidizes the cost of fertilizer. Reed Hertford's 1967 study concludes, "until recently [the government] has sold chemical fertilizers at below apparent production costs."[20]

In the United States I have never seen wheat grown under irrigation because the cost is too high. In Mexico, on the other hand, the wheat farmer does not have this problem. Since 1940 the Mexican government "has completely underwritten all irrigation projects involving gravity-fed water." In addition, it has subsidized, or paid for, 46 percent of the operating expenses.[21]

To WHAT EXTENT *has Rockefeller wheat research increased farm incomes?*

"These varieties have suddenly made wheat production highly profitable in many areas of the world for both the farmer and the country as a whole," says a CIMMYT report.[22] Speaking of the Ciudad Obregón area, one Rockefeller scientist told me emphatically, "Wheat has built this area."

Wheat is important to the economy of northwest Mexico. But just how important?

In 1966–67 a group of Ciudad Obregón farmers made a sizable profit—a real killing, I was told—on the new Rockefeller wheats. India and Pakistan were on the verge of famine because of poor crop yields the previous two years; the U.S. government was keeping 60 million Indians alive by shipping enormous amounts of its food stocks to India. Borlaug had already demonstrated that when fertilized and irrigated the Mexican dwarf wheats did extremely well in Asia. The result was that India and Pakistan sent buyers to Ciudad Obregón; they returned with 60,000 tons of wheat seed[23] and left behind a bonanza in the premium prices they had paid.

But this was an unusual situation wheat growers said, unlikely to be repeated.

The head of Ciudad Obregón's Chamber of Commerce told me, "In spite of the high support price, farmers here really can't make money on what they are paid for wheat." While I was visiting the area, a delegation of wheat farmers left for Mexico City to ask the government to raise their wheat subsidy still higher. This may have been only a ploy to keep pressure on the government and to prevent it from lowering the subsidy. Yet the U.S. Department of Agriculture's Vernon Harness, who has studied the 1969 income of these farmers, concluded that the "man with average yields is not making much of a profit." In the Ciudad Obregón area the average wheat farmer made $12 an acre while in adjacent Sinaloa, he lost $12.[24] In talking with these farmers I learned nearly all of them considered their most profitable crop to be cotton, then soybeans, and finally wheat. Wheat appears to be grown largely because it is the only crop which they can plant during the winter. Therefore it is useful in that it can absorb some of the farmer's overhead during his off-season.

Thus to believe that the booming agricultural complex of northwest Mexico is the result of wheat is incorrect. The crop is not that profitable.

DID ROCKEFELLER *research make Mexico self-sufficient in wheat?*

If the answer is "yes" then the corollary is that Mexico has been able thereby to save the foreign exchange it otherwise would have spent for wheat imports—an important advantage to any undeveloped country.

At a congressional committee the president of the foundation said, "The Rockefeller Foundation was *invited**** [italics mine] in 1941 by the Government of Mexico to establish a cooperative program designed to eliminate the gaps in the national food budget, particularly wheat, corn, beans and potatoes. Mexico at that time was spending some very difficult to come by, hard won, foreign currency to buy what might be called bread from abroad. I mean wheat and corn . . . The deficits were rather large at that time. But it was by identifying the problems, selecting the priorities, and attacking the problems right at their roots that by 1955 Mexico no longer had to import . . . wheat . . ."[25]

---

* In discussing its work abroad, the Rockefeller Foundation stresses that it works by "invitation" only. In contrast, it is said, the U.S. AID program operates in a host country by its own initiative. The difference in approach is credited by many as being one reason why the Rockefeller Foundation supposedly has greater success than does AID in its foreign assistance programs.

In looking at the Mexican record, however, Rockefeller's 1941 "invitation" would appear to be nonexistent—or at best, an afterthought. In fact, the foundation began working in Mexico nine months before there was an agreement with the Mexican government and the *entire* initiative came from the foundation.

To check on this I asked the foundation for a copy of a document it had prepared entitled, "The Beginnings of the Mexican Agricultural Program" but was told that it "has recently been assigned to archives" and that it would be available to responsible scholars after processing which "will require several years" (letter to William Paddock from Henry Romney, head, Information Service, November 20, 1970). I was, however, referred to the book, *Campaigns Against Hunger* by Drs. Stakman, Manglesdorf, and Bradfield, the three men who planned the foundation's agricultural program in Mexico. The book gives the following chronology:

However figures supplied me by the U.S. embassy show that Mexico imported only 1,225 tons of wheat in 1940[26]—hardly enough, it would seem, to give it such high urgency in 1941. Thereafter imports did rise quickly and were 288,301 tons in 1943.

This considerable surge of wheat imports apparently was due largely to the war. Mexico was finding a ready market for anything it could move across the border to shortage-plagued United States. Dollars in quantities previously unheard of were flowing in and the economy enjoyed a wartime prosperity. Thus thousands of Mexicans for the first time could afford to buy wheat, or could afford more of it.

In stressing the need for wheat self-sufficiency, I wonder whether the foundation has put its wheat research program in true perspective with the other agricultural problems of Mexico awaiting solution. I raise the point because in comparison to the country's basic foods—corn and beans—wheat has always been a relatively costly food, in fact, a luxury food.

Along with most other observers I, too, was caught up in the

February 3, 1941. Rockefeller Foundation President Raymond B. Fosdick and Dr. John A. Ferrell of the Foundation's International Health Division met with Henry A. Wallace who suggested they work on agricultural problems in Mexico. (p. 19)

February 18, 1941. Fosdick appointed a committee to investigate the advisability of a Mexican agricultural program. The committee then set up a "Survey Commission [consisting of Stakman, Bradfield and Manglesdorf]." (p. 22)

June 5, 1941. The Survey Commission was told: "Go to Mexico and find out whether you think the Foundation could make a substantial contribution to the improvement of agriculture and, if so, how?" (p. 24)

October 14, 1941. After spending two months in Mexico the three-man Survey Commission (plus a graduate student who spoke Spanish) submitted their report; they wrote of themselves: "In retrospect it appears that the Commission must have worked hard and with some degree of intelligence, for the recommendations were adopted unchanged by the Rockefeller Foundation's Board of Trustees as 'the guideline for an action program in Mexico.'" (p. 34)

1942 (date not given). J. George Harrar was hired to head the Rockefeller Foundation's Mexican program but he did not go to Mexico until the following year. (p. 37)

February 1, 1943. "The Rockefeller Foundation agricultural program in Mexico began"—as Harrar arrived in Mexico on that date. "Subsequently, working with Dr. H. M. Miller [of the Foundation], a memorandum of agreement was developed and presented to the Secretary of Agriculture of Mexico." (p. 37)

October 1943. "The Mexican Minister of Agriculture authorized the establishment of [a cooperative organization] comprising experienced scientists of the Foundation's staff and aspiring young Mexican associates or interns selected jointly by the Mexican Ministry and [the program's] director [a Rockefeller Foundation employee]." (p. 39) pleasant phrase "self-sufficiency in wheat," and commented favorably about this situation in a previous book, *Famine—1975!* Fortunately there is always an honest skeptic waiting to spring on careless writers. The late William Vogt, a marvelously astute conservationist, wrote me, "One thing [about your book] *does* dismay me: your acceptance of the Rockefeller line that 'Mexico was self-sufficient in wheat.' You mean there were no more people who wanted it? Or do you mean there were no more people able to pay the price? Malnutrition is wide-spread."

Vogt's friendly, but deadly, rejoinder to me was, "I'm afraid you've been had, me lad."[27]

And, indeed, the government's effort to close the gap between supply and demand by paying high subsidies to farmers priced wheat out of the reach of many. Mexico, with a per capita GNP 87 percent lower than the United States, pays a wheat subsidy 40 percent above that of the United States. Nevertheless, the foundation's president stated in 1967, "Mexico became self-sufficient in wheat [and] . . . now has a wheat surplus and is beginning to devote some of its wheat lands to other food crops."[28]

The picture on the other side of the coin: "A surplus follows a high support price like the night follows the day . . . [this] is economic orthodoxy."[29]

HAS ROCKEFELLER *research made Mexico a wheat-exporting nation?*

Parallel to the nice phrase "self-sufficiency" is the delightful prospect of being a "wheat-exporting nation." This, too, is often repeated today. For example: "[Mexico] has brought its wheat production up to and beyond the point of self-sufficiency, and now looks for customers beyond its own borders."[30]

Perhaps only a skeptic would analyze (because, of course, it is taken for granted that everybody everywhere is wild to export everything) whether or not Mexico wants to export wheat.

I asked Juan Gil Preciado, minister of agriculture, and Antonio Carillo Flores, the foreign minister, about wheat exports. Both said candidly that exporting wheat was poor business. Indeed, they said, when Mexico ships wheat out of the country, it does so at a financial loss.

Few things are as difficult to work out as export prices for wheat. There are so many different grades of wheat, under-the-counter arrangements, and the like, that generalized statements must contain some inaccuracies. But consider the economics of the following transaction and it is obvious why the ministers of agriculture and foreign affairs spoke as they did.

In August 1969, Mexico exported wheat at $48.64 a ton FOB. Since the Mexican farmers had been paid $73.00 a ton (the support price) and inland freight added another $5.00 to the cost, Mexico thus lost $30.00 a ton, or 80¢ on each bushel exported.[31]

To SUMMARIZE, the Rockefeller Foundation has conducted an effective wheat program in a developing nation; it has produced new wheat varieties as well as the agronomic information to go with them. The result is that wheat farming is now a more reliable business than in the past.

On the other hand, the impact of the wheat program in Mexico has been exaggerated. The result has been a distortion of this quite valid accomplishment into the belief the Rockefeller Foundation offers a prophecy of plenty,* a prophecy which other development organizations (AID, Peace Corps, etc.) cannot fulfill.

Unfortunately neither can the foundation, a conclusion which should not be based solely on the wheat story.

A better illustration of the complexities and uncertainties of agricultural research is the Rockefeller program in Mexico on corn. In fact, it was the corn program which first brought worldwide acclaim to the Rockefeller agricultural program. Corn is the country's staple grain and is grown by forty[32] times more farmers than wheat farmers on eight times the acreage of wheat. Thus the potential impact of successful corn research on the economy of the nation would have been truly revolutionary had it succeeded.

But it did not.

-----

* Note how the Nobel Committee chairman continued the exaggeration when announcing Dr. Borlaug to be the Nobel Peace Prize winner in 1970 by citing him for a "technological breakthrough which makes it possible to abolish hunger in the developing countries in the course of a few years. In short," the chairman said, "we do not any longer have to be pessimistic about the economic future of the developing countries." *Washington Post*, October 23, 1970.

The Rockefeller Foundation:
Two Vital Crops

"WHY DO YOU WISH to see the terrible Oz?"
asked the man.

"I want him to give me some brains," said
the Scarecrow eagerly.

"Oh, Oz could do that easily enough," de-
clared the man. "He has more brains than he
needs . . . Oz can do anything . . ."

Next morning the Scarecrow said to his
friends: "Congratulate me. I am going to Oz to
get my brains at last . . ." Then he said good-
by to them all in a cheerful voice and went to
the Throne Room, where he rapped upon the
door.

"Come in," said Oz . . .

"I have come for my brains," remarked the
Scarecrow, a little uneasily.

"Oh, yes, sit down in that chair, please,"
replied Oz. "You must excuse me for taking
your head off, but I shall have to do it in order
to put your brains in their proper place."

"That's all right," said the Scarecrow. "You
are quite welcome to take my head off, as long
as it will be a better one when you put it on
again."

So the Wizard unfastened his head and
emptied out the straw. Then he entered the
back room and took up a measure of bran,
which he mixed with a great many pins and
needles. Having shaken them together thorough-

*ly, he filled the top of the Scarecrow's head with
the mixture and stuffed the rest of the space
with straw, to hold it in place.*

*When he had fastened the Scarecrow's head
on his body again, he said to him, "Hereafter
you will be a great man, for I have given you a
lot of bran-new brains."*

*The Scarecrow was both pleased and proud
at the fulfillment of his greatest wish, and having thanked Oz warmly he went back to his
friends . . .*

*Oz, left to himself, smiled to think of his
success in giving the Scarecrow . . . what he
wanted. "How can I help being a humbug," he
said, "when all these people make me do things
that everybody knows can't be done? It was easy
to make the Scarecrow . . . happy, because he
imagined I could do anything."*[1]

BY NOW, almost everyone connected with development—both re-
ceivers and donors—are, in their frustration, like the Scarecrow,
eager to believe and to follow any wizard who announces he has a
cure.

Currently, the Rockefeller Foundation is regarded as the
Grand Panjandrum himself who, "everyone" says, has the knowledge and the power, the "open sesame," to create successful development, or at least the agricultural part of development. Is the
Rockefeller Foundation the true oracle of agricultural development knowledge, or is it the Wizard of Oz letting the world believe it knows how to do things which, in fact, cannot be done?

DURING THE 1930s the Rockefeller Foundation had a medical program in Mexico involving some sixty people which was rated
effective by those I questioned. Then in 1940 Vice-President Elect
Henry Wallace went to Mexico for the inauguration of the Mexican president, Manuel Avila Camacho. Forgotten today is the
fact that Wallace, at that time, was a symbol of the dynamism of
U.S. scientific agriculture. In the Corn Belt he had sparked a true
agricultural revolution by being the first to produce hybrid corn
seed commercially. In Mexico his prolonged visit and infectious

enthusiasm inspired the government to establish a corn breeding and improvement program at León in the Bajío.

The following year Wallace told Raymond Fosdick, president of the Rockefeller Foundation, "If anyone could increase the yield per acre of corn and beans in Mexico, it would contribute more effectively to the welfare of the country and the happiness of its people than any other plan that could be devised."[2] This led the foundation to mount in Mexico its first agricultural research effort outside the United States. Through the years this eventually embraced, in addition to the original beans and corn, a variety of activities ranging from student training to poultry production and including the famous Borlaug wheat program and the successful Niederhauser potato program.

But to measure the uncertainties of agricultural science in its efforts to solve a specifically designated problem in the hungry world one should look not at its impact on these secondary crops but look at how well the foundation achieved its original goals for beans and corn, the two crops most vital to the country.

The bean program was initiated in 1944 and several new bean varieties were released, but rather soon it drifted out the window. This may seem surprising, since beans are the principal source of protein in the Mexican diet and should rate the highest priority in any continuing agricultural development program there.

Quick impact from bean research is extremely difficult because of the attitude of Mexican consumers. Probably more than a thousand varieties of edible beans are grown in Mexico and a person tends to favor strongly the flavor and consistency of the beans with which he grew up. Thus any improved bean variety generally has a rather narrow consumption and will affect only a limited number of farmers.

Whatever the reason, when Dr. William D. Yerkes who had headed the bean program resigned in 1960, the foundation did not replace him. Little has been heard of it since then. Nevertheless merely by increasing the acreage planted in beans, Mexico's bean production has kept pace with its population growth (currently 3.4 percent a year), although yields per acre (averaging 2.7 percent from 1940 to 1969) have not.[3]

When I asked a world-famous bean specialist familiar with the program (but unwilling for me to use his name), "Why didn't the foundation push the bean program?" he said, "I never could figure out why. Perhaps it was because progress in a bean breeding program is slow and possibly they [the foundation] realized it is more difficult to get the same type of publicity on this crop as on corn or wheat."

When the foundation faded out of the bean program in 1960, Mexico's average bean yield per acre had been falling for several years at the rate of 4 percent a year.[4] Be that as it may, in 1969 the president of the Rockefeller Foundation told a congressional committee that "beans have about doubled" in production during the foundation's period in Mexico,[5] strongly implying, as I read it, that the foundation was largely responsible for this statistic; in fact, the cause had been primarily merely one of increased acreage.

The Rockefeller corn program was an apple off another tree.

The goal set for it was nothing less than "to revolutionize Mexico's corn production as hybrid corn has already revolutionized corn production in the United States."[6]

The advantages of hybrid corn had been known since the 1920s, but it was not until the 1930s that it came into commercial use. Soon it was being raised by all our midwestern corn farmers. Most Americans have now forgotten what a phenomenal stimulus it was to our farm economy. In Mexico, where corn is king (in the diet, in acreage, and in monetary value), it was logical to hope the development of hybrids would have an even greater impact than in the United States.

No one questioned the ability of the foundation to develop hybrids. The techniques to be used were well known and it was certain that research could produce high-yielding hybrids for Mexico. The foundation hired a well-qualified corn breeder, Dr. E. J. Wellhausen, and gave him a staff larger than for any other segment of their work. He moved fast. Eight hybrid corns were soon released. In speaking of this period, a history of the program written at the request of the Rockefeller Foundation states, "In 1948, five years after the beginning of the program, Mexico, for the first time since the Revolution of 1910, had no need to import corn. This first success was soon followed by others. The social revolution was on the way to becoming an agricultural revolution."[7] By 1950 the foundation's president was able to say that enough hybrid seed corn had been produced "to plant approximately 1,500,000 acres of Mexico's total corn acreage, or nearly eight per cent of the national production. At this rate of acceleration, it is only a matter of time before the improved varieties and hybrids will completely supplant the less productive stocks."[8]

Now, twenty years later, this dream remains unfulfilled.

In 1967, when the three scientists who planned the foundation's agricultural program wrote a history of the work (one reviewer said the authors are so highly complimentary they "gush like a school girl"),[9] they acknowledged that the Rockefeller hybrids "which have been available for 18 years, have come to occupy only 14 percent of Mexico's corn acreage, and this is a real disappointment."[10]

More recently Reed Hertford, writing a doctoral thesis in Mexico for the University of Chicago and a somewhat more objective observer, wrote, "At present only about 10 percent of all corn land is planted with improved varieties."[11]

Prior to Borlaug's dwarf wheats becoming so well known and taking center stage, this corn program had been the most publicized single development effort in Latin America. Because the impact of the program apparently peaked out a decade ago, now would seem to be a good time to judge some of the claims that were then, and still are attributed to it. The foundation's research has been credited with:

—a substantial increase in Mexico's *total corn production*

—an increase in *profits* from corn raising

—*self-sufficiency* in corn, thereby eliminating costly outlays of foreign exchange to import corn.

I have examined these allegations and must, I regret, call them myths.

THE MYTH *that Rockefeller research has caused Mexico's increased corn production.*

The Mexican corn myth can be summed up in two statements:

Harvard University's demographic high priest, Roger Revelle, has said without equivocation, "The Rockefeller Foundation has been responsible for doubling the corn yields of Mexico."[12]

The foundation's president, J. George Harrar, has said, "In 1941 the Mexican Government asked the Rockefeller Foundation to help improve annual corn yields . . . Today Mexico can produce all the corn it needs on *less land* through the use of synthetic hybrid varieties, even though its population has almost doubled since 1943.[13] (italics mine)

But it has not been on less land. When the Rockefeller Foundation began its agricultural research in Mexico in 1943 that country planted only 8.4 million acres with corn; now it plants 20 million acres.[14]

Mexico would be in serious trouble today without this increase in acreage because from 1940 to 1962 Mexico's yield per acre grew at a compound rate of only 1.7 percent[15] (though some calculations show the growth to be 2.3 percent), while population grew at 2.9 percent.[16]

What was the reason for the increase—modest though it was— in corn yields? I consider the major factor to be Mexico's price support program which began in 1937.[17]

This stimulated corn production almost immediately (by making it profitable to plant corn on better land). During the next ten years, a period in which the foundation's corn-breeding program could not be expected to have any significant influence, average corn yields went up 30 percent. In the two subsequent ten-year periods, when the foundation's corn varieties were available, yields continued to improve but at a no faster rate (21 and 30 percent respectively).[18] The subsidy for corn raised on non-irrigated land at this writing is $1.93 per bushel (versus $1.05 in the United States and a world market price of about $1.25).

THE MYTH *that Rockefeller research increased the profits of corn farmers.*

Hugo B. Margáin, former Mexican ambassador to the United States, was candid in assessing for me the political significance of the corn subsidy program. "It does make corn expensive. This is poor economic business, but it is good social business," meaning that it brings more income into the seriously depressed rural areas, much of which is tied to a subsistence corn economy.

The difficulty the government faces in these dispirited and tradition-bound rural communities is indeed immense. "The government here wishes the farm problem would just float away and disappear," one official of the U.S. embassy said to me. "All systems in Mexico are go except for agriculture."

With the benefit of hindsight, I suggest the Rockefeller Foundation made two basic mistakes with its corn program. Both mistakes were natural and are not mentioned here in any sense of criticism. They are included to show that the foundation is, after all, only human.

First, it decided to concentrate on developing *hybrid* corn. The decision to do this was logical in view of the then recent impact of hybrids on the U.S. Midwest. But in Mexico corn is raised throughout a vast diversity of climate and terrain; it would be difficult to imagine a greater contrast to the conditions of our

Midwest. Hybrid corns have a narrow adaptability, so generally each hybrid can be used for only one locale. To have hybrids used throughout Mexico, then, would have required developing dozens of varieties. Even more important, farmers cannot save the seed of their hybrids, but must each year *buy* seed from a company equipped and able to produce it through controlled pollination. For small farmers this can be a difficult procedure.

Second, through foundation guidance and encouragement Mexico opted to produce the new hybrid seed corn through an especially established government corn commission commonly called today "Productora." Thus private enterprise was denied the opportunity to build on Rockefeller research and to use its talents to produce quality seed. Hybrid seed corn production is big business in the United States where intense competition between seed companies has resulted in continually better varieties. Henry Wallace became a wealthy man producing it and his company, the Pioneer Seed Corn Company, today employs fifty geneticists so that its seed can be constantly improved and either kept on a level with or ahead of its competitors.

Productora, in contrast, is a government monopoly. I myself heard nothing but complaints about Productora from one end of Mexico to the other, including stories of graft, corruption, and venality. A typical complaint, not verified but repeated so often I came to believe it, was that Productora often buys contaminated and even open-pollinated (nonhybrid) seed from politically favored friends and then sells it to the farmers as genuine hybrid seed.

When I inquired why Productora is allowed to continue, the most common reply was some variation of the fact that this monopoly is now so entrenched in the bureaucracy that any constructive change is impossible. Of course in no country do people enthuse favorably about the efficiency of their government agencies; perhaps Productora is not as bad as some say, but the evidence at hand indicates it is.

So why do some farmers buy its seed? Why do they not go on growing their own cheaper unimproved corn varieties? The primary reason, apparently, is that in order to get a government loan a corn farmer must agree to buy his seed from Productora.

Whenever possible I stopped to talk with farmers along the road to ask about their problems. The following is a conversation I had with a farmer I found near Veracruz. In his dirt-floored patio surrounded by a crumbling adobe wall patched with sticks, he was sorting through one of his two piles of corn.

"What kind of corn do you have?"
"Both criollo *(native, unimproved) and hybrid."*
"Which do you like better?"
"Criollo."
"Why?"
"The weevils do not get into it so badly and so it keeps better."
"Why do you also have hybrid corn, then?"
"Because my neighbor used some and let me have 500 pounds."
"What is better about the hybrid?"
(blank look)
"I am an agricultural scientist and interested in corn. Tell me what is better about hybrid."
"Hybrid produces a little more—maybe three tons. I get about two and one-half tons with criollo."
"Are you sure?"
"No, but that is what people say about the hybrid."
"If the *criollo* is almost as good as the hybrid, why does your neighbor use the hybrid?"
"Because he has a loan from the bank, and the bank will not give him money unless he plants the hybrid."

This apparently government-enforced (via a condition to get a loan) use of the hybrids casts doubt on those reports which praise their value and acceptability.

Throughout the 1950s the acreage planted to improved corns had stabilized at about 4 percent of the total. Then the figure suddenly doubled between 1961 and 1963 as shown:[19]

Year	Percent of Acreage Planted with Hybrid Seed
1955	4.1
1956	3.5
1957	3.1
1958	4.1
1959	4.8
1960	4.4
1961	5.6
1962	8.0
1963	11.8
1964	12.6
1965	13.0

Our own Department of Agriculture which compiled these data has no explanation for this spurt in the use of the improved corns, and while I was in Mexico I learned of no new varieties which would have unusual acceptability. Accordingly, my unverified hypothesis is that in 1961 Productora must have worked out the arrangement with the government's Farmer's Bank to require borrowers to buy its seed. (Perhaps this related to the $25 million loan which U.S. AID made to the National Bank of Mexico in 1962–63 specifically for lending to the small farmers.)

Dr. Oscar Brauer Herrera, dean of the Agricultural University Graduate School in Chapingo, told me that in Mexico the hybrids must be grown under irrigation or at least on land with very good rainfall in order to get satisfactory results. This, he said, restricts their usefulness to the best farmers, and eliminates the poor, marginal farmers.

Roberto Quesada, owner of a large farm in Hidalgo, told me he preferred the Rockefeller hybrid corns. Nevertheless he claimed his corn production was unprofitable and consequently he was not planning to raise more in the future. This reminded me of a comment by a foundation scientist, Elmer Johnson, "No one here is making a mint of money on corn." Quesada pointed out that some large-scale, mechanized farmers prefer the graded seed from Productora because it works better than ungraded corn in their mechanical planters. This further explains why hybrids benefit primarily the big farmer.

As a matter of fact, the foundation did design its hybrids specifically for the big grower. When it began research on corn, it wanted to make the fastest progress possible; thus it concentrated its efforts on helping the large, prosperous farmer, the farmer with the best land and with money to spend on seed, fertilizer, and pesticides. This was a valid goal, but it left the peasant farmer outside of its research interest.

THE MYTH *that Rockefeller research has made Mexico self-sufficient in corn.*

No example to illustrate the efficiency of the Rockefeller approach is more often repeated than that it has made Mexico self-sufficient in corn. After first visiting the Rockefeller corn program in 1951, I repeated what I had been told, saying a new era was on the horizon for Mexico, an era that had begun in 1948 when no corn was imported. "Mexico can now be said to be self-sufficient in corn in normal years . . . thanks to the Rockefeller Foundation . . ."[20]

Congressional committees have heard the same story many times. In a statement before the House Ways and Means Committee the foundation's president pointed out that since his organization began to work there, "Mexico has become self-sufficient in corn production, even though its population has risen some 60 percent."[21]

However, in Mexico today I found less emphasis on this self-sufficiency in corn. Questioning a key official in our embassy, I was told, "The Rockefeller Foundation tends to exaggerate the importance of this so-called self-sufficiency." Later I had a candid conversation over lunch in Mexico City's University Club with two of the foundation's corn breeders.

"What has been the impact of the Rockefeller corn program?" I asked.

"What do you mean by 'corn program'? Our work on fertilizers, our agronomic studies, or our breeding program?"

"Let's limit it to the breeding program. That is what Rockefeller has become famous for in Mexico, isn't it?"

"Yes."

"What has caused Mexico's self-sufficiency in corn?"

"Increased acreage, certainly, is one reason and the increased use of fertilizer. Another factor that cannot be ignored is price support. The increase definitely has not been due to our hybrid seed coming out of Productora, but to other things."

For the record, in 1941, the year the Rockefeller Foundation was "invited" to work in Mexico and before it had released any new varieties, Mexico imported only twenty-four tons of corn, certainly as close to self-sufficiency, at the prices then existing, as a country can ever be.

So WHAT has been the overall impact of this well-publicized corn program?

The following were the compound rates of growth for the nine principal crops in Mexico from 1940 to 1962 (I do not have more recent figures):[22]

	Production	Yield/Acre
Corn	3.3%	1.7%
Rice	3.5	0.8
Beans	3.8	2.7
Sugarcane	3.9	0.3
Henequen	4.2	1.9
Wheat	6.1	3.4
Tomatoes	8.8	3.5
Coffee	9.2	4.8
Cotton	10.9	3.5

Of all these, corn made the least gain in production and a comparably poor figure was given for beans.

"OZ CAN DO ANYTHING," or so thought those who listened to the Wizard.

If one accepts without question the accomplishments so widely attributed to the Rockefeller Foundation, one likewise has the impression it can do anything.

And it has indeed done much.

In Mexico the disease-resistant varieties of wheat have taken most of the risk out of production. The foundation has not revolutionized the corn industry, but it has assisted the large commercial farmers, many of whom have found the improved corns useful. On the other hand, no significant help has been given to bean producers. Yet the foundation has aided Mexico in other ways not discussed in these chapters, such as paying for an agricultural graduate training program involving a large number of Mexicans.

But an element of the Wizard's humbug is manifest in the foundation's unwillingness to admit its failures, its unwillingness to let its successes speak for themselves, and its tendency to exaggerate its role in the agricultural development of Mexico. In this it is no different than AID, the UN agencies, the development banks, and the other private foundations. They similarly tout their programs with a fog of self-praise through which it is difficult to get at the facts. Their failures become successes and their successes become stupendous achievements.

There would be no harm in this except most Americans believe that somewhere, someplace, exists the key to developing the hungry world, and that somehow and sometime American ingenuity will save the day by discovering that key.

By overstating its own case before congressional committees and at conferences and symposia (which at times are quietly paid for by itself), the Rockefeller Foundation has convinced most of those involved with assisting the hungry world the key to development does exist and, eureka! the Rockefeller Foundation has it.

This encourages Congress to believe that with still another appropriation to AID (or the Inter-American Development Bank, or FAO, or Peace Corps, etc., etc., etc.) it too can find that elusive key. For it is always worth hunting if you know that what you are hunting for actually exists.

This is part of the reason Congress continues its appropriations for AID and ignores the overwhelming evidence of the ineffectiveness of that agency to date.

New Foods versus Old Taste Buds

As EVERYONE is suddenly shouting, there is not enough food in this world to feed us all as we should be fed. The world's population today is 3.7 billion; at least 2 billion, including several million in the United States, do not have the food their bodies need. To solve this problem is much more complex than merely growing more food. It involves having available the right kinds of foods and the people having in hand the money—and the desire—to buy that food.

The most critical shortage in world diets is protein. It is also the most expensive item in one's food budget—another way of saying it is the scarcest. The development professionals have turned, for the most part, to the scientist to solve the shortage of protein. One such solution involving conventional agriculture was the discovery during the 1960s of the opaque-2 gene which increases the lysine-protein content in corn. We now are waiting to see what the commercial results of this discovery are to be. But the head of the nutrition department of the Massachusetts Institute of Technology says, "While scientific agriculture will greatly increase yields per unit of land and total production of food crops, as well as animal protein sources, there is little likelihood that such increases will keep pace with the present rate of population rise. We must, therefore, look to unconventional sources of protein produced through the application of science and technology to supplement those coming from conventional sources."[1]

Science has learned how to synthesize several amino acids (protein components) which can be used to enrich foods. In addition, several new foods spun from vegetable protein are on the market today and are reasonably close to the taste and chewability of meat.

In the effort to alleviate the world protein shortage, the project

231

receiving the most serious discussion and publicity centers around formulating new foods by combining inexpensive cereals with inexpensive cottonseed or soybean protein concentrates. If proven successful, these new foods would represent a major scientific end run around the population/food crunch.

The granddaddy of these fortified foods is "Incaparina," a product developed in the mid-1950s by INCAP (Nutrition Institute for Central America and Panama) located in Guatemala City and supported primarily by U.S. money. Repeatedly government officials and development specialists urged that I study Incaparina as an example of an unusually successful product well documented by a widely known story, a story covered in a hundred popular and scientific articles. Hopes have run high for Incarparina from the beginning. One early article about it, for instance, began:

> On August 25, 1959, the picturesque little town of Palín in the highlands of Guatemala became the center of a new kind of revolution—a revolution that could well overthrow one of the oldest enemies of the underdeveloped countries: malnutrition, particularly among younger children. A small cellophane-wrapped package containing a powdered substance called INCAPARINA, which went on sale for 3¢ that day in Palín, is the major weapon.[2]

John Balcomb of UNICEF, writing about Incarparina in 1962, said, "To save thousands of children from sickness and early death, international research workers in Guatemala had to find a cheap, high-protein food that mothers could prepare as simply as cornmeal gruel—and they succeeded."[3]

Of what was this new food made?

Searching for a vegetable substitute for milk, INCAP developed a powder consisting of ground corn, sorghum, cottonseed flour, a pinch of Torula yeast (for vitamin B), a dash of calcium carbonate, and some vitamin A, and called it Incaparina. It is a very nutritious and inexpensive baby food. Immediately INCAP scientists were credited with a major achievement and, indeed, it was revolutionary. Although for years animal nutritionists had been using a similar formula to nourish calves, pigs, and chickens, human nutritionists had not used this approach on food for children.

Incaparina ought to have been a success immediately. Not only is it nutritious but it meshes beautifully into the Guatemalan diet. To prepare it, one cooks it with water and sugar for fifteen minutes. The result is a thick milklike drink similar to *atole,* a common Guatemalan drink made from corn. *Atole,* it is true, tastes yucky to a gringo, but Guatemalans love it. Thus acceptance of Incaparina should have been rather simple. Scientists point out that Incaparina has the nutritional value of a glass of whole milk, whereas *atole* has only the nutritional value of a glass of corn— which is not much.

One trouble from the beginning was that while the product was sold as a cheap substitute for milk, it was unfortunately an expensive substitute for corn *atole*—costing nearly four times more.

Any new product has difficulty finding its consumer market and Incaparina was no exception. Its early concessionaires, after trying for several years, failed and gave up. Today the concession in Guatemala is held by a brewery. I talked with Eduardo A. Castillo who is in charge of its Incaparina operation and asked why he thought they could do a better job of selling Incaparina than the previous concessionaires. Castillo said marketing it like beer, with salesmen visiting their outlets almost every day, was part of the reason. Also the brewery was willing to take on the product "as social work" and as a means of helping the good name and image of the brewery. "Of course," he added, "we hoped to make some money, but we were doubtful when we started." After years of losses, the brewery made a small profit on Incaparina in 1968, and, in fact, sold 900 tons. Since then sales (promoted by TV ads and roadside signs) have been growing steadily.

When I asked Moisés Behar, director of INCAP, how he would describe the impact of Incaparina since its introduction, he said, "Perhaps everyone overestimated its acceptance and this, I suppose, was due to our own enthusiasm. We should have realized that Guatemala's nutritional problem will never be solved by any one project, but by a combination of several: education, better agriculture, transportation, medicine. Incaparina is only one of several aids in attacking the nutritional problem. We have learned to accept this view as a result of our experience through the years."

In surveying Incaparina's influence on the nutrition of Guatemala, I asked a number of small store owners who their customers were. This not-so-very-in-depth study turned up only a few answers, but it did show that most mothers were buying it for their children solely on the recommendation of their doctors. In fact, doctors would write it out as a prescription.

Dr. Erich Knoetzsch, who has a clinic in a low income suburb of Guatemala City and who prescribes Incaparina for children, told me the real problem is to get the children to continue to use it. "Once they are given a chance to stop, they do," he said.

In other words, the children for whom Incaparina was designed also regard it essentially as a medicine.

I repeated to Castillo what a former Salvadoran manufacturer of Incaparina had told me, "Incaparina is a failure here and I can find no evidence that it has been a success anyplace else. It has so little flavor or palatability that people will not use it."

Castillo agreed. "This is true," he said. "It just does not taste good. I don't like the stuff myself. But INCAP keeps telling us the taste is an acquired one and once children learn to like it, they will always like it. We probably will never reach adults with it because their tastes are already developed."

One AID official summarized it, "What INCAP does not realize is that animal feed does not appeal to people."

Unfortunately INCAP apparently has ignored, or at least not learned how to correct, the unpleasant, or bland, taste of Incaparina. Instead of using the expert talents of its staff to develop a better tasting, more acceptable product, the organization seems to have stubbornly continued promoting Incaparina along the same lines as when it was first introduced—a procedure that has already given disappointing results. Thus science has failed so far to make an impact on malnutrition through Incaparina. "The development of low-cost, high-protein foods is of little use if people don't eat them . . ."[4]

In 1967 AID started a program of contracting with fourteen U.S. commercial manufacturers to develop and test-market in various parts of the world a new generation of fortified foods. The U.S. government committed $750,000, but it was estimated "that some $1 billion worth of accumulated research and development expertise has been made available for these new food developments."[5] By enlisting the skills of private industry it was hoped science would be given a chance to find an alternative to the agricultural limitations of the hungry nations. Monsanto was awarded an AID contract to develop a soya beverage called "Puma" for Brazil and Guyana; Swift, a soya beverage for Brazil; Krauss Milling, a fortified corn product for Brazil; International Milling, a fortified wheat product for Tunisia, etc.

Pillsbury was awarded the first of the fourteen contracts. (The two Minnesotans who proudly officiated when this Minneapolis company signed the contract were Vice-President Hubert Humphrey and Secretary of Agriculture Orville Freeman.) Pillsbury made a drink called "Frescavida" and overcame the lack of palatability of Incaparina by making it fruit flavored. The AID contract paid for further development of Frescavida and for test-marketing it in El Salvador.

Children in two selected schools were tested to see which drink they would choose when offered Frescavida or milk. El Salvador turned out to be less than an ideal spot for testing. No sooner had the study begun than the teachers went on strike (the strike was unrelated to the test). Dr. Lloyd Holmes of the U.S. Department of Agriculture, stationed in El Salvador, told me the two schools also happened to be in an area where milk is seldom available; in any case milk there is usually shunned because its quality is low, due to poor sanitation and lack of storage facilities. Thus when the tests were eventually run, it was perhaps not surprising the children showed a preference for Frescavida.

What happened next, however, is not too clear. AID's new food approach was based on the desire to see Frescavida become a commercial success with wide consumer acceptance. That is why, presumably, the contract money had been given in the first place.

"At this point," Holmes told me, "the project got muddy." Strings were pulled to get the next phase under way. Someone came up with the idea that AID and the Salvadorans should now, without further testing, jointly pay the cost of Pillsbury's commercial introduction of Frescavida. To get it started, it was planned to have the U.S. Department of Agriculture give $100,000 of wheat (one of the ingredients) free to Pillsbury and the Salvadoran sugar mills were to contribute (free) 650 tons of sugar, another ingredient. The project was moving along well enough on paper, but then a rumor circulated that the Salvadoran government might buy the sugar needed for the project. This killed any chance of the sugar mills giving their sugar free. Then, out of the blue, it was discovered that no one had communicated with the U.S. Department of Agriculture about its supplying $100,000 of wheat.

As of this writing no one knows what Pillsbury or El Salvador or AID is doing with Frescavida. The project which received so much favorable attention when the contract was signed still remains in limbo.

Thus Frescavida, carefully designed for its palatability and nutritious qualities, and apparently successful in achieving those targets, remains an idea still knocking at the door.

Laboratories are filled with other test-tube possibilities: CSM (gelatinized corn plus soya and milk); WSB (fortified precooked wheat); Duryea (fortified degermed corn); and Vitasoy, Coca-Cola's Saci, and Monsanto's Puma (fortified soft drinks). All these are being test-marketed or commercial sales are being attempted in various parts of the world's malnutrition belt.

Michigan State University's Georg Borgstrom says, "Despite the euphoria over various new high-protein foods now emerging from laboratories . . . their impact on human nutrition has been insignificant."[6]

I asked Aaron N. Altschul, then special assistant for nutrition improvement to the secretary of agriculture, "Are any fortified food products a commercial success today?"

"As far as I know, only one—Vitasoy."

The history of Vitasoy contains a lesson for those who become prematurely enthusiastic about the future impact of Incaparina, Frescavida, or any of their brothers and sisters now gestating.

Long before the worldwide concern about malnutrition developed, an obscure American doctor, Harry Miller, was at work in China where for generations several processes for making soya milk have been used. Soya milk, in its simplest form, is dehulled soybeans ground up with water and perhaps a sweetener added. With this product in mind, Miller approached C. S. Lo, a Hong Kong businessman and owner of the local Pepsi-Cola franchise, and together they worked out a method of sterilizing soya milk for the first time. Lo merchandized this as a milk substitute. It was a new product to the Chinese only because it did not spoil.

This was before World War II. With the Japanese invasion, Lo was out of business.

During the war he had time to give thought on how he could improve his soya milk. When the war ended he went back into business, but this time he marketed it as a competitor for soft drinks, not as a milk substitute. He was also interested in how to get some protein into the diet of the Chinese refugees flooding into Hong Kong. The easiest way, he decided, was to get them to buy Vitasoy. It was, after all, a pleasant, tasty soft drink, not a strange substitute food or a medicinal product; also he could sell it more cheaply than the consumer could make it at home.

The Vitasoy story tells us something about mobilizing science to solve development problems.

Note that Vitasoy was not the result of research by nutritionists, nor was it an idea put forward by development officials or foundations, nor was it financed by government or semiofficial agencies. It was simply the end result of private initiative, developed within the traditional framework of private industry. Today Vitasoy is a success. But note also that Vitasoy began before World War II. It took a long time for this new food product, even though pleasant and tasty, to find a profitable commercial market—in other words, to achieve consumer acceptance.

In contrast, after fifteen years' work INCAP has yet to discover how to get people to eat its nutritious but unpalatable Incaparina. Frescavida, after hopes were fanned, is dead—though perhaps not yet buried.

Conclusions:
A Paradoxical Panacea

PRESIDENT TRUMAN said in his inaugural address in 1949, "For the first time in history, humanity possesses the knowledge and the skill to relieve the suffering of [the hungry nations] . . . We should make available to peace-loving peoples the benefits of our store of technical knowledge in order to help them realize their aspirations for a better life."

Since then every president has been saying we have the capacity to solve the world's development problems through the use of science and technology. And, in fact, nearly all the people of the world have come to place unquestioning faith in technology's capacity to resolve their problems.

One could list a dozen explanations for the ineffectiveness of foreign aid. I wonder if the basic reason is not our almost religious fascination with science and technology combined with our blindness to their limitations: for instance, the limitation that science and technology cannot compensate for the paucity of resources of a hungry nation; for instance, the ecology of most of the underdeveloped world can be as disastrously damaged by the technology of development as is already apparent in the industrialized nations.

"Our society is trained to accept all new technology as progress or to look upon it as an aspect of fate," said George Wald, Harvard's Nobel laureate biologist. "Should one do everything one can? The usual answer is 'Oh, of course,' but the right answer is 'Of course not.' "[1]

As we get deeper into the 1970s we may well regret many of the fine gifts technology has given us as we are forced to cope with their consequences—consequences not anticipated in the original planning or, worse, callously ignored.

The Aswan Dam, when completed, will increase Egypt's irrigated land by 1.3 million acres. The per capita income in Egypt is projected to increase by 10 percent,[2] although this sort of hoped for percentage statistic is mostly a figure of speech.

I visited the dam site during its construction. The temperature that day was 123 degrees Fahrenheit. Russian trucks were breaking down—dying like flies—in the heat and under the wear and tear of the abrasive granite base on which the dam was being built. Here was evidence how difficult it is for man to increase the amount of land he farms.

Construction of dams and the related irrigation works are enormously costly. In the long run, however, most of them do return a profit to the nation because irrigated fields are the most productive of all agricultural land and because the electricity generated can be a valid resource.

Nevertheless land reclaimed for irrigation often turns out to be a catastrophe. Due to faulty planning, more of such land is presently being lost from salting (making it unsuitable for farming) than is being put into production through new irrigation projects. One is reminded of the Sahara Desert which is steadily expanding because of man's misuse (abusive agriculture, overgrazing)—it is growing in size each year by 40,000 acres.

Since the earliest pharaohs, Egypt's narrow strip of agricultural land along the Nile has been remarkably resistant to abuse. This irrigated land still requires less fertilizer than that of most countries. Mother Nile carries the eroded soils from central Africa and the highlands of Ethiopia and thus replenishes each year the nutrients of Egypt's soils. Now, however, with the new high Aswan Dam, a very real fear exists that needed silt will settle in the dammed-up lake and the irrigation canals will no longer rejuvenate Egypt's land.

In fact, evidence already shows that a lack of silt carried by the Nile into the Mediterranean has reduced biological activity there, cutting off the food used by plankton which feed the fish that in turn support the fishing industry—an ecological consequence no one considered before undertaking to build the dam. And the latest report is that the Egyptian shoreline is rapidly eroding because of the change in the Nile flow.

But this is only part of the problem. Schistosomiasis, an internal infection often fatal in man, is another threatening result of the dam. The disease is transmitted by snails. When irrigation is seasonal, that is, dependent upon flooding or rainfall rather than controlled by dams, the snail population is generally short-lived. However when irrigation water comes from a permanent, steady source like a dam, "the incidence of this disease increases tremendously, usually from just a few per cent to well over one-half of the population, sometimes even approaching 100 per cent."[3] Schistosomiasis is one response by nature to man's disruptive use of the land. In 1952 the Sennar Dam, which converted 900,000 acres of savannah in the Sudan into irrigated lands, was reported to have brought about an explosion in the incidence of schistosomiasis within three years.[4]

The story of malaria control by DDT is well known. It was once widely taken for granted, not merely hoped, this terrible disease would be wiped off the earth. Instead, on the one hand DDT-resistant malarial mosquitoes evolved and, on the other, the pesticide is now recognized both to dangerously upset nature's ecological balance and to have injurious effects on humans. DDT is a classical example of a technological boomerang. Today governments ban its use but in 1948 Paul Müller received the Nobel Prize for its discovery!

Few diseases can revive as fast as malaria. Ceylon thought its malaria control campaign had licked the disease. A few years ago, health officials there found only seventeen cases of malaria; in the last two years an estimated 4 million cases have been found on the island.[5]

Maybe the use of science to fight the problems of development is like that ancient fable of the dragon's teeth. As the benefits of technology are strewn throughout the undeveloped world, the crop that rises is not the beautiful flowers of progress but a host of evil soldiers more threatening than any previous problem.

Perhaps the best illustration of this is the Green Revolution.

IN THE mid-1960s any agricultural scientist worth his salt was warning of impending famine in Asia, Latin America, and certain areas of Africa. The less-developed world was losing the capacity to feed itself. Yet most of these nations had been consistent and often major exporters of grain in the 1920s and 1930s. The reason for the change was, of course, the population growth.

But by 1970 the warnings were of a wholly different sort. The world had an overabundance of grain. If anything, the danger immediately ahead seemed to be oversupply and glut.

A startling turnabout had taken place in the agricultural output of several parts of the developing world. In 1970 the Philippines reported achieving self-sufficiency in rice for the first time in history. Malaysia, South Vietnam, and Indonesia predicted the same. Pakistan says it will shortly be self-sufficient in all cereals, and India expresses a similar hope. Optimism rides tall in the saddle even though there are indications that some of this self-sufficiency will be shortlived (the Philippines had to import 460,000 tons of rice in 1971, with still larger imports scheduled for 1972).

The increases are credited to a "green revolution" which is based on the introduction and the rapidly spreading use of new "miracle grains" in the rice paddies and wheat stands of South Asia.

The Green Revolution, it is said, is the result of a scientific breakthrough, the result of the marriage of scientist and development administrator.

Among many agriculturalists euphoria has blossomed that man's potential for feeding himself is now solved, at least for decades to come, and that it is now "possible for the developing countries to break away from hunger and poverty."[6] To many, the Green Revolution is a turning point in man's long war against the biological limitations of the earth.

On examination, however, "skirmish" seems a more accurate description.

Bert Tollefson gave the 1970 "official" U.S. AID story of the agricultural revolution in South Asia:

What has happened in less than three years is revealed in a few statistics . . . Overall food production has risen 14 percent in the period 1967–69. And, in South Asia alone—the crucial countries of India and Pakistan—the increase has been 27 percent. AID worked with foundations, universities and others in developing new farming methods, including the most efficient use of "miracle" wheat and rice seeds that have brought about the Green Revolution.[7]

The statement is misleading because it gives all the credit for this sudden, new Green Revolution to the contribution of science. Consider the following four items:

1. WEATHER

In South Asia 1965 and 1966 were poor weather years for the farmer, but the succeeding years have been good. From 1967 through 1970, the same years of the Green Revolution in rice and wheat, India increased production of barley, chickpeas, tea, jute, cotton, and tobacco by 20 to 30 percent, and did so with no new high-yielding varieties. A drought followed by rain will cause a spurt in production with or without new technology.

This improvement in weather is far and away the most important factor for increased production. But weather seldom gets the credit it deserves. When crops are poor, governments blame it on the weather. When crops are good, governments take the credit for their foresight and wisdom in providing fertilizer and loans to the farmer and for their clairvoyance in having conducted the scientific research needed to develop improved crop varieties.

Thus AID, when asking Congress for its 1970 money, said, "India's current successes in agriculture are largely due to a reappraisal of its agricultural strategy. . . . With the help of the United States, the World Bank and other interested agencies and countries, India developed a new strategy which placed top priority on investment in agriculture . . ."[8]

2. LIMITATIONS OF THE HIGH-YIELDING VARIETIES

Since the early 1950s, most of the developing world has been increasing its total agricultural production and its average yields per acre. This has been possible through greater use of fertilizer and irrigation, and also the opening up of new agricultural land.

India, from 1951 to 1961 (before the Green Revolution), increased agricultural production by 46 percent. This was done partially with new technology but primarily by putting new land into production. As new land became scarce, the increase tapered off. Simply to maintain current per capita consumption levels, India must now increase cereal production by 3 million tons each year.[9]

If the Green Revolution is to be a reality, production must increase faster than it has in the past. Bernard Nossiter, whose book on India examines that country's grain production figures, says, "In sum, over five years, and not counting the rainless period, food production had increased little more than 2 percent annually. This was less than the gain in population. It meant, 'Green Revolution' to the contrary, that the average Indian was eating less from his own resources than he had in the mid-sixties."[10]

This does not imply the new high-yielding wheats in India and Pakistan have not increased production spectacularly. Where irrigated and fertilized, crops have flourished. The same has been true with rice in Southeast Asia. But while other crops give a promise on which to base a Green Revolution, to date there are only two: wheat and rice.

The development of the new wheat and rice varieties having high fertilizer response without lodging resulted from imaginative research that indeed merits recognition. However, the press agent's "miracle" and "wonder" appellation given these cereals distorted out of proportion their influence on the world.

In India, where one-third of Asia's population lives, only the new wheats have made an impact. This is unfortunate since in India wheat is a far less important crop than is rice (the production of which is three times that of wheat). Actually, according to a recent study by economic forecaster Louis Bean, the trend in increased rice yields, which began in the early 1960s as a result of new technology, has leveled off and stagnated at the 1964–65 level. Thus the "miracle" rice has produced no miracle in India or in Bangladesh—a traditional rice-growing area—although it has done extremely well in Pakistan, normally not recognized as a major rice producer.

In discussing the new rice varieties for India, a U.S. Department of Agriculture report says, "For the immediate future, modest increases in yield from local (i.e., not the 'miracle' rice) varieties through improved fertilizer use offer the most promise."[11]

Bean calls it the "Brown and Green Revolution" to underscore its sporadic influence. In India, for instance, a third of the wheat land has been affected, but only 3 percent of the rice production has been touched, with the rest of the crops escaping its influence.

3. DEPENDENCE ON IRRIGATION

Irrigation is the lifeblood of the new cereals. Virtually all the new wheats in Mexico, India, Pakistan, and Turkey—the areas where they have made an impact—are grown under artificial irrigation. The new rice varieties also require carefully controlled irrigation. In the Philippines, where the new rice is grown under irrigation, harvests are reported as two to three times that of traditional local varieties. However on nonirrigated land the new varieties do no better than the standard ones.

This is important to understand. Ford Foundation's Lowell S. Hardin says that if one looks at a map "the land where this new technology, this Green Revolution, applies is a postage stamp on the face of the earth."[12]

The major reason is, unfortunately, that very little land is under irrigation. Where either irrigation or fertilizer is absent, there is no revolution.

4. DEPENDENCE ON SUBSIDIES

Green Revolution publicists ignore the financial cost at which wheat and rice production has been achieved in some countries.

To understand the role of subsidies, the Department of Agriculture's director of economics Don Paarlberg says,

This is the inescapable fact that a price artificially held above the competitive level will stimulate production, retard consumption and create a surplus. This will be true even if the commodity was originally in deficit supply. Thus a surplus is the result of deliberate intervention in the market. It is the product of human institutions, not simply a consequence of rapid, technological advance. It may or may not be accompanied by a scientific revolution. We could create a surplus of diamonds or uranium or of avocadoes or rutabagas simply by setting the price above where the market would have it and foregoing cost production control. A surplus is not so much a result of technology as it is a result of intervention in the market.[13]

The much-heralded Philippine rice self-sufficiency is a classic example of how Paarlberg's statement applies to the developing world. In 1966 the Philippine Rice and Corn Administration initiated a self-sufficiency program. Within a year it increased the price support paid for rice by 50 percent. In the words of James Keefer of the U.S. Department of Agriculture, the Philippines have "administered self-sufficiency" because they have artificially defined the level of consumption in the country. The people could consume more rice, but they cannot afford more at the price the government sells it.

Many of the Green Revolution countries subsidize in part the price of fertilizer, pesticides, and irrigation water; they all subsidize the production of the new cereals. Thus Turkey supports her wheat at 63 percent above the world's market price for quality grain, India and Pakistan at 100 percent. But since the quality of the grain from the new miracle cereals is low and they are sold at a discount, the subsidies are, in real terms, significantly higher.

The recent fear of a glut in world cereal markets was "largely attributable to expansion of production in the developed world,"[14] rather than to any Green Revolution within the hungry nations. The glut was related to the support policies which all grain-producing nations follow (wheat supports range from $1.40 a bushel in the United States to $4.29 a bushel in Switzerland), policies which are often used as justification for similar subsidies in Asia, Africa, and Latin America. It should be obvious, however, that what a developed nation may do with ease an undeveloped nation might find disastrous to try.

The United States has been subsidizing farmers with a sum annually approaching $4 billion, but this is in a nation where agriculture generates only 3 percent of the gross national product.

India's agriculture accounts for 49 percent of the GNP; Pakistan's, 47 percent; and the Philippines', 33 percent. In these countries, there are not enough other sources of income to generate for long the money needed to subsidize the large agricultural segment of the economy. Yet the new varieties require irrigation water, fertilizer, and additional labor. All are expensive. For the farmer, this means financial risk. For him, risk is justified because of the support price. But take that crutch away and fewer would take the risk.

With these high support prices, one of two things becomes obvious. Either the farmers are getting rich on the government subsidies or else the new technology which science has provided them is much more costly to use. There are reports of land prices skyrocketing in the area of the Green Revolution, of incipient social revolution with formerly absentee landlords returning to farm their land and evicting their tenants. All this may be true, but to what extent?

My guess is that the best farmers on the best land are profiting substantially from the Green Revolution. But the report that "hundreds of millions of rural people" are benefiting must be open to question.[15] Dana Dalrymple of the U.S. Department of Agriculture says, "It has been widely assumed that the increased returns from growing the new variety have exceeded the cost. Incomes have probably generally been increased in the short run. Yet there is little solid evidence on this point."[16]

In his book, *Seeds of Change,* Lester Brown has projected a highly hopeful agricultural future because of the Green Revolution. He reflects the opinions of many who feel that "thanks to the breakthrough in the cereal production, the problems of the seventies will be much more political and less technological than were those of the sixties. Their solutions lie more in the hands of politicians, less in the hands of scientists and farmers."[17]

But to overcome the biological limitations imposed by the land on agricultural production will require greater technological breakthroughs in the 1970s than anything we have ever seen. "What we have accomplished so far in the Green Revolution is the easiest part," says Will Meyers, vice-president of the Rockefeller Foundation.[18]

The new wheat varieties are essentially a transfer of temperate zone technology to temperate zone areas in Mexico, India, Pakistan, and Turkey. Tropical rice has so far had only limited success. Corn is going to be a more difficult crop with which to work because of the inability to move it successfully from latitude to latitude.

The "wonder" wheats and "miracle" rice varieties have been

quickly accepted in Asia, partly because governments encouraged their acceptance. Farmers who grew them found that loans for fertilizer and pesticides were made available to them. Governments were encouraged to do this partially out of fright stemming from the crop failures of 1965 and 1966 and partially from the pressure and salesmanship of foreign scientists and aid givers. Already many fear the consequences of this action.

The U.N.'s Food and Agriculture Organization recently held a round table discussion on the "genetic dangers in the Green Revolution" and concluded that progress in one direction "represents a calamitous loss in the other." Plant breeders unanimously agree it is dangerous to produce varieties with similar disease-resistant characteristics within an area. By eliminating the great number of genetically different types of wheat and rice and replacing them with substantially the same variety, there is a loss of variability from which to select resistance to new and still unknown diseases. Speaking of this, Dr. Jack R. Harlan, professor of plant genetics at the University of Illinois, says, "The food supply for the human race is seriously threatened by any loss of variability."[19]

The danger of a disastrous attack by either insect or disease is greatly enhanced when a region is planted to genetically similar varieties. "All across southern Asia (not just India) there has been a rush toward one dominant family of wheats prized for its yielding ability. . . . All of this wheat carries the same kind of rust resistance, which means that if a new race of rust to which it would be especially susceptible were suddenly to appear, much of the wheat crop of that whole vast stretch of the world could be devastated almost overnight."[20]

This is not without precedent. In 1946 30 million acres of U.S. land were planted to a new group of oats (two-thirds of the oat crop), all having what was called "Victoria type" resistance to rust. Within two years these oats had virtually disappeared because of the emergence of a new disease which had been unknown only four years earlier.[21]

In 1950 probably no single phase of the plant sciences was more highly developed than that related to the control of a disease on wheat known as "stem rust." A strain of that rust called 15B had been known and watched in the United States for ten years. Nevertheless 15B was able suddenly to build up to epidemic levels and in 1953 and 1954 it caused the almost total destruction of our durum wheat crop. Should this happen in India today, the results would be tragic.

Yet a country like India is particularly vulnerable. It has too few technicians to keep track of what is going on in its wheat and rice fields and too few scientists to develop new disease-resistant varieties and have them ready when needed. Furthermore its seed industry cannot quickly multiply a new variety and get it into the hands of the farmer if a crisis arises.

The recent epiphytotics (plant disease epidemics) of the developed world involved highly selected crop varieties derived from a narrow genetic base. The hungry world has had a degree of protection against this because of the multiplicity of types found within its unselected crops.

MANY BELIEVE the Green Revolution has bought time to solve the world's population problem.

To me this belief is thoroughly premature.

The potential of the current Green Revolution is too limited to expect it to provide anywhere near adequate time in which to find a solution to the population problem. Speaking of this, Bert Tollefson, AID assistant administrator, told a campus group that "AID hopes to see a breakthrough similar to the Green Revolution in individual country efforts to control population growth."[22]

Despite the active work in many laboratories, no such breakthrough is on the horizon. Although eventually more effective birth control procedures will no doubt be discovered, even to talk hopefully of one today is dangerously misleading.

The 1969 study of India's population by Emerson Foote puts the hungry world's population growth in true perspective. When India began her population control program seventeen years ago, her population was growing at the rate of 6 million a year; today it grows at an annual rate of 15 million. If things continue this way, Foote says, the population of India will be 1 billion in 2000. He continues:

Long before the one billion figure would be reached, the break point would occur . . . It is entirely possible that in India and in other parts of the world for the next three years, five years or even a bit longer, the "Green Revolution" will increase food production faster than population grows. But if this is the case, it will be a very temporary and misleading solace—only postponing the day of reckoning . . . The growth will be slowed either by rational means or by indescribable castastrophe.[23]

Premature hope stemming from the Green Revolution contains two dangers. They are: (1) The governments of the hungry nations will once again turn their thoughts away from the major problem of solving the agricultural and rural problems of their countries and resume their emphasis on pacifying the cities and worshipping before the idol of industrialization. (2) Of greater danger, however, is the likelihood of lessening concern over the exploding population.

In 1968, at the Second International Conference on the War on Hunger, held in Washington, D.C., the Philippine great "success" with the new rice was a major topic. (This was even before the term, "The Green Revolution," had been coined.) The Philippine undersecretary for agriculture, Dr. Dioscoro López Umali, brought with him a Philippine farmer who had markedly increased his production through the use of the new "miracle" rice. Before the distinguished audience, Umali translated the farmer's story as he spoke. The farmer in his closing statements referred to his ten children and said that because of the new high-yielding variety, he and his neighbors would now have enough food for all, and they could enjoy seeing their women in the condition in which they were the most beautiful—pregnant.

As the rigid limitation to the Green Revolution became apparent, the optimists who had at first gladly claimed the world food problem had been solved began to scale down their forecasts of "freedom from hunger."

Rockefeller Foundation's Norman Borlaug, the breeder of the new dwarf wheat, said in 1965, "It seems likely that through a combination of improvements in conventional and non-conventional food production methods, man can feed the world's mushrooming human population for the next 100–200 years."[24]

In 1969 he shortened this to "two or three decades."[25] (Writing of Dr. Borlaug's Nobel Peace Prize award in *Science* [October 30, 1970], Lester R. Brown shortened the time to "perhaps an additional 10 or 15 years.")

This apparently had been adopted as that year's official Green Revolution forecast because Robert MacNamara, president of the World Bank, repeated it. "I am confident that application of new technology will dramatically expand the rates of agricultural growth and will buy decades of time—admittedly the barest minimum of time—required to cope with the population explosion, and reduce it to manageable proportions."[26]

Unfortunately, no one tells the world what can be done with the "decades of time" which the Green Revolution has supposedly bought mankind.

Recently the head of the family planning program of a small country which provides contraceptive information and devices in its national health clinics said he was expanding his program as fast as he could. He had recently received considerable money from AID and two U.S. foundations in order to establish additional clinics for research on new approaches for disseminating birth control information. I asked him, "Today the population of your country is 3.5 million. What will it be in the year 2000?"

ANSWER: 9 to 10 million.

PADDOCK: If your president would, tomorrow, do everything you advocate and had the power to put into practice all your recommendations, what would the population be in 2000?

ANSWER: Don't quote me *(which is why I do not identify the speaker)* but it would probably be 9 or 10 million.

PADDOCK: If you just closed down this program and moved to Australia to get away from it all, what would the population be in the year 2000?

ANSWER: 9 or 10 million.

Whether the Green Revolution is fact or myth, the consequences of an agricultural breakthrough without an accompanying breakthrough in population control are ominous.

To feed today's world population requires the use of agricultural chemicals, the pollutants of which will have a deleterious effect on our children and on their children. By 1985 the demand for food in the hungry world will more than double. If it is then to feed itself by present methods, it must increase its use of fertilizers by 100 percent and pesticides by 600 percent.[27] Such an increase in the use of chemicals (at least of the types now known) to feed the projected populations must surely wreck the environment.

AGRICULTURALISTS (and I am one) too glibly damn modern medicine for trying to reduce mortality while striving to do exactly the same thing through improved agricultural technology. More food will certainly mean that more people will live, but this will accelerate the population explosion still more. Without effective population control, an agricultural breakthrough resulting in increased yields can lead only to catastrophe.

Should we then be disappointed that the Green Revolution is neither very green nor very revolutionary? Indeed, is the world ready for a Green Revolution?

Malthus' "Dismal Theorem" said essentially that if the only

check on the growth of population is starvation and misery, then no matter how favorable the environment or how advanced the technology, the population will grow until it is miserable and starves. Kenneth Boulding has, however, what he calls the "Utterly Dismal Theorem." This is the proposition "that if the only check on growth of population is starvation and misery, then any technological improvements will have the ultimate effect of increasing the sum of human misery as it permits a larger proportion to live in precisely the same state of misery and starvation as before the change."[28]

Boulding uses Ireland as an example of his Utterly Dismal Theorem. In the seventeenth century the population of Ireland had come into balance with the carrying capacity of her land. Two million Irish lived there destitute. Then came the Eighteenth Century's Green Revolution. The potato was introduced to the Emerald Isle from the Western Hemisphere. Agricultural production shot up. The carrying capacity of the land increased. The Irish multiplied accordingly. By 1835 8 million Irish lived where only 2 million had lived in the previous century and most were destitute. Then arrived a totally new plant disease called "late blight" and the potato crop was destroyed. In the resulting Irish famine of the 1840s, 2 million Irish starved to death, 2 million emigrated, and 4 million were left on the land in poverty.

When such a thing as a Green Revolution occurs, its name will be Disaster if it arrives ahead of a Population Control Revolution.

A WASHINGTON, D.C., minister once said from the pulpit, "We have now squarely to face this paradox . . . We have increased human hunger by feeding the hungry. We have increased human suffering by healing the sick. We have increased human want by giving to the needy. It is almost impossible for us to face the fact that this is so. The truth comes as a shocking discovery for we have all been brought up in the Christian tradition in which caring for the least of our brethren has been counted the highest virtue."[29]

Changing Over to
the International Route

====================================

"It's the peculiar nature of the animal: we pro-
vide the money and they control the bank."

—SENATOR FRANK CHURCH,
speaking of the
Inter-American Development Bank

A Full Closet

To KEEP LIFE *stimulating we eagerly grasp at the beginning of each new year for a "new look." The new dress style in 1970 was the midi. The new slogan in domestic politics was "law and order." The new fashion in foreign aid was the international approach.*

Thus President Nixon in a message to Congress called for a "new partnership among nations in pursuit of a truly international effort based on a strengthened leadership role for multilateral development institutions."[1] He said he would propose legislation to create a U.S. International Development Corporation, a U.S. International Development Institute, and a . . . but who knew what additional bureaucracies would be included by the time the legislation was enacted.

The womenfolk at my house, to cope with the midi look, rummaged through their closets for a few old outfits that could have the hem dropped. This put me to wondering if a few old international organizations might not be hanging around in the foreign aid closets. Perhaps they could be gussied up a bit to cope with the glittering new 1970 fashion of the "international approach."

I took a look. The closet was full!
*A partial list of the private and government in-
ternational organizations involved with economic
development in Latin America is provided in an
agency directory.[2] Space prevents including a similar list of those assisting Asia and Africa.*

Agribusiness Council
AID's Regional Office for Central America and Panama
(ROCAP)
American Cocoa Research Institute (ACR)
American Institute for Free Labor Development (AIFLD)
American International Association for Economic and Social
Development
Business Advisory Council of the General Secretariat of the
OAS
Catholic Relief Services
Center for the Economic and Social Development of Latin
America
Center for Inter-American Relations
Center for Latin American Monetary Studies
Central American Bank for Economic Integration (CABEI)
Central American Institute for Business Administration
Central American Institute of Public Administration
Central American Research Institute for Industry
Coffee Federation of America
Cooperative League of the U.S.A.
The Council for Latin America, Inc.
Cultural Action Committee (CAC)
Development Assistance Committee of the OECD
Export-Import Bank of Washington (EXIMBANK)
Federation of Industrialists Association of Central America
The Ford Foundation
Fundamental Education Center for Community Development
Futures for Children
Institute for Human Progress
Institute for Human Resources Development
Institute of International Education
Institute for Latin American Integration
Institute of Nutrition of Central America and Panama
(INCAP)
Inter-American Center for the Integral Development of
Water and Land Resources
Inter-American Center for Integrated Social Development
Inter-American Center for Research and Documentation on
Professional Training
Inter-American Center for Rural Development and Agrarian
Reform

Inter-American Center for Rural Education
Inter-American Center of Tax Administrators
Inter-American Children's Institute
Inter-American Commission of Women
Inter-American Commission on Human Rights
Inter-American Committee on the Alliance for Progress (CIAP)
Inter-American Cooperative Bank Development Program
Inter-American Council of Commerce and Production
Inter-American Council of Jurists
Inter-American Cultural Council
Inter-American Development Bank (IDB)
Inter-American Economic and Social Council (IA-ECOSOC)
Inter-American Export Promotion Center
Inter-American Housing and Planning Center
Inter-American Indian Institute
Inter-American Institute of Agricultural Sciences
Inter-American Institute of International Legal Studies
Inter-American Investment Development Center
Inter-American Juridical Committee
Inter-American Program for the Formulation and Execution of Development Projects
Inter-American Program for the Improvement of Science Teaching
Inter-American Program for Urban and Regional Planning
Inter-American Regional Labor Organization
Inter-American Rural Youth Program
Inter-American Statistical Institute (IASI)
Inter-American Statistical Training Center
Inter-American Training Center in Public Administration
International Bank for Reconstruction and Development, World Bank (IBRD)
International Center of Advanced Studies of Journalism for Latin America
International Coffee Organization (ICO)
International Development Association (IDA)
International Development Foundation (IDF)
International Executive Service Corps
International Finance Corporation (IFC)
International Monetary Fund (IMF)
International Regional Plant and Animal Health Organization
IRI Research Institute
Joint Tax Program OAS/IDB
W. K. Kellogg Foundation
Latin American Center on Demography
Latin American Development Administration Committee
Latin American Federation of Christian Trade Unionists
Latin American Free Trade Association (LAFTA)
Latin American Institute for Agricultural Marketing
Latin American Institute for Economic and Social Planning
Latin American Parliament

Latin American Population Center
National 4-H Club Foundation
Operation Niños
Organization for Economic Cooperation and Development
Organization of American States (OAS)
Organization of Central American States (ODECA)
Organization of the Cooperatives of America (OCA)
Overseas Education Fund of the League of Women Voters
Pan American Development Foundation (PADF)
Pan American Foot and Mouth Disease Center
Pan American Health Organization (PAHO)
Pan American Institute of Geography and History (PAIGH)
Pan American Railway Congress Association (PARCA)
Pan American Union (PAU)
Partners of the Alliance
Peace Corps
Permanent Secretariat of the General Treaty for Central American Economic Integration
Permanent Technical Committee on Labor Matters
Population Reference Bureau (PRB)
Regional Center for School Construction in Latin America
Rockefeller Foundation
Secretariat for Central American Tourism Integration
Superior Council for Central American Universities
Trade Union Technical Advisory Committee
United Nations Children's Fund (UNICEF)
United Nations Conference on Trade and Development (UNCTAD)
United Nations Development Programme (UNDP)
United Nations Economic Commission for Latin America (UN-ECLA)
United Nations Educational, Scientific and Cultural Organization (UNESCO)
United Nations Food and Agricultural Organization (FAO)
United Nations Industrial Development Organization (UNIDO)
Volunteers for International Technical Assistance, Inc. (VITA)

As the "international look" sweeps over the foreign aid fashion scene, a logical question arises: Is it also to be just another fad that will end up as successless as the preceding philosophies which have in their time excited the development bureaucracies?

Tithing by Faith

THE TENDENCY to have the United States turn its foreign aid money over to the international agencies to spend seems to be swelling like an irresistible tide. David M. Kennedy, then secretary of the treasury, speaking officially as a representative of the United States at an international conference, said, "Multilateral institutions will undoubtedly assume a greater role in providing financial and technical assistance."[1] The trend is well under way towards having most U.S. aid money spent this way.

The multilateral route has a big appeal to American officials because when a program fails Uncle Sam escapes the blame.

But some altruistic reasons are advanced, too, in favor of channeling more development funds through the international agencies. One is that it may give the developing nations themselves a greater voice in the allocation of the available money and, thereby, perhaps help them to build up a needed cadre of technical experts. Another is that it may help share the burden of funding development costs more equitably among the world's aid givers. In fact, a substantial consensus indicates the international route is a "more enlightened" way to develop the hungry nations than the "narrow" bilateral route of the past.

That it is a vastly different route should be noted, and the signs marking the way are few.

Consider, for example, the contrasting philanthropies of two men, both equally anxious to help the poor and needy.

Man One, with his own hands and his own money, works alongside a family to help rebuild its burned out ghetto home. When the job is finished, he knows how his money was spent and how well the work was done. Think of Man One as a bilateral foreign aid program. The United States sends its tax money directly to the hungry nation, where it is spent by a national under the eyes of a U.S. government employee.

Man Two sends a tithe to his church to support its plan to rebuild a burned-out ghetto. He has faith that his church can do the job and that his money will be well spent. He himself will not check on the project or even visit it. Man Two is the multi-lateral approach in foreign aid. The United States gives tax money earmarked for foreign aid to the United Nations or the Inter-American Development Bank or similar organizations. The United States accepts on faith that the international agency will spend the money wisely and honestly. If the money is misused, the fault lies with the international agency. No onus redounds to the United States.

Through the years the international development agencies have become such a permanent fixture on our landscape, we have forgotten that most of the larger agencies were created for the same reason as our own foreign aid program—as an active force to counter Communist expansion. We have forgotten that the "World Bank" is only a nickname, that its real name today is still the "International Bank for Reconstruction and Development." This grandfather of today's international banks was set up in 1946 specifically to reconstruct war-torn western Europe as a protection against Russian inroads. No sooner was it started than the new Marshall Plan took over this job and the bank went into the business of developing the undeveloped countries. One should remember that Russia and its subject states have never participated in the World Bank, nor do they support its activities.

The World Bank soon began spawning affiliates, as have many other international finance agencies that have been created since. The World Bank group now includes the International Finance Corporation (IFC) which promotes private-sector activities in developing nations and the International Development Association (IDA) which provides development financing on very easy terms to the growing number of countries which have exhausted all conventional sources of credit.

Under Eugene Black, its president for thirteen years, the World Bank developed an enviable reputation for investing in safe revenue earners. Being the first and only bank in this type of business, it had the pick of good loans it could make throughout the world. It made money. Thus its prestige was built on conservative banking. It became universally respected.

Because of this reputation it became the model for other international development banks.

The first area where this movement blossomed was Latin

America with the formation of the Inter-American Development
Bank (IDB). To understand the political implications involved,
some background data are necessary.

Latin Americans felt neglected when the United States spent
so much money rebuilding Europe through the Marshall Plan.
Of course, for 150 years they have felt neglected, and usually rightly so. Now, however, they had cause to feel shunted aside as the
United States handed out all this aid money to Europe. Communist Yugoslavia, for instance, with 20 million people, received
more aid from U.S. government sources from 1949 to 1959 than
did all Latin America with a population of 175 million.[2] Parallel
with this neglect, our political judgment in Latin America throughout the 1950s was indeed odd.

When Washington crowned its aid with bestowal of specific awards of
merit upon dictators Manuel Odria of Peru and Marcos Pérez Jimenez of
Venezuela, democratic elements [in Latin America] commenced seriously
to fear that the United States positively favored military dictatorships
because they might manage strictly to preserve law and order while keeping the country on a steadily anti-communistic course, whatever the cost
of personal freedoms to its citizens and in life and property to its victims.[3]

The ill-fated "goodwill" visit of Vice-President Richard Nixon
to South America in 1958 made the U.S. public aware of the intensity of the always latent anti-American feelings. Nixon ran into
a volatile, hostile reaction in several countries. He and Mrs. Nixon
were stoned and spat on and nearly killed on the streets of Caracas,
Venezuela, a shocking sight to Americans viewing it on their TV .
screens.

As a result President Eisenhower was finally stirred to action
and he sent his brother Milton to Latin America to study what
might be done to counteract the accumulated ill feeling. In January 1959, as Fidel Castro was victoriously marching into Havana,
Milton Eisenhower made his report, saying as if it were a great
discovery (as it apparently was to him), "Latin America is a continent in ferment." Indeed, throughout Latin America there was
an almost frenzied support for Castro. Washington was at last
willing to listen to any recommendation that might curtail Communist influence in the area.

Brazil's President Juscelino Kubitschek wrote to Eisenhower
in the wake of the Nixon visit to suggest that a crash development program was needed. The Brazilian leader's plan became
the basis for U.S. discussions with several Latin American leaders.

During the winter of 1958–59 representatives of the Organization of American States held a series of meetings to plan a development bank. In April 1959 the United States agreed to contribute $350 million and in December 1959 the Inter-American Development Bank (IDB) opened its doors.

Castro had been in power eleven months.

The need for a new policy had been given urgency by the Castro victory in Cuba. As his government and the Cuban press became increasingly anti-American and pro-Communist in tone during 1959 and 1960, U.S. policy shifted from a position of patience and tolerance. In March 1960 President Eisenhower approved initial work on a contingency plan [the Bay of Pigs] to overthrow the Castro regime. Four months later . . . President Eisenhower said the United States would support sweeping reforms in Latin America with financial assistance.[4]

And so the United States was off on a new wave of foreign aid which, hopefully, would be as successful as the Marshall Plan.

The establishment of the Inter-American Development Bank let loose a proliferation of regional banks around the globe. Asian and African development banks were set up. The movement has not stopped with regional banks. Soon regions within regions were petitioning for equal treatment. In Central America, for example, the United States lent money to support a new Central American Bank for Economic Integration. In 1968 six South American nations, with assurances of financial support from U.S. officials, set up the Andean Development Corporation. The Caribbean Development Bank was established in 1969; and on and on, not only in this hemisphere, but around the hungry globe.

Since IDB was organized, the World Bank—active throughout Asia and Africa—has played a relatively minor role in Latin America, so in this book I concentrate attention on IDB.

The Inter-American Development Bank has a membership of twenty-three nations, but it is U.S. money that enables it to function. Of IDB's three sources of funds, the United States contributes 77.3 percent to one ($1.8 billion up to 1970 to the Fund for Special Operations), 100 percent to another ($525 million to the Social Progress Trust Fund), and 42.4 percent to the third ($1.17 billion for paid-in and callable capital).[5]

The bank is able to sell its bonds in Europe and Japan because of the guarantee the United States gives them. At this writing, Congress is considering President Nixon's request for another $1.8 billion commitment to IDB.

The historical origins of the Inter-American Development

Bank should be remembered today as the United States yearns to follow the international route with ever more of her foreign aid money. While the many international development banks exude confidence in their ability to improve the economic level of the countries they serve, remember their origins were political, not economic. IDB remains a political entity today. Its loans are controlled first by political motives and only secondly by the logic of whatever development programs they support.

When I interviewed IDB's president, Felipe Herrera, I asked him, as I had other aid officials, to recommend some specific projects funded by his organization that I should visit. He suggested several.[6]

From those he recommended, I chose one which would be small enough to evaluate easily: the 13-megawatt hydroelectric plant at Los Esclavos, fifty miles southeast of Guatemala City, for which a $3.15 million loan had been made in 1964.

An indication of the home office acceptance of Los Esclavos' success was its choice as one of the few Central American programs for illustration in the bank's 1969 annual report.

Increasing the power capacity of Latin America was one of the earliest goals of the Alliance for Progress. In explaining the Los Esclavos project, Herrera referred me to an IDB document which states it is "generally recognized that the highest priority to further the economic development of Guatemala consisted in the expansion of electric power generating capacity." The bank's studies showed that by 1966 there would be a deficit of 17.4 megawatts of electricity in the Guatemala City area, which "obviously, would cause a serious obstacle to economic growth."[7]

The Los Esclavos plant was designed to supply power to "Guatemala City and vicinity. This area is the country's major industrial center."[8] The plant, it was said, "would also exert a favorable effect on the balance of payments, as compared to alternative thermo solutions, as a thermo plant of equal capacity would have required the importation of bunker C oil at a total annual cost of $230,000."[9]

Before going out to the power plant, I talked with Rudolfo Carrandi, the bank's representative in Guatemala City. Carrandi, a pleasant young Cuban, was trained as a public accountant and had spent several years in Central America.

I asked him about development priorities in Guatemala and whether he felt electrification should have "the highest priority."

"Yes," he said. "Guatemala needs cheap electricity to industrialize and we are emphasizing help to industry."

I told him Herrera had recommended I visit Los Esclavos as an example of this emphasis. At this, Carrandi seemed startled and asked, "Why that plant?"

"Because Herrera thinks it is one of the best examples in Central America and Mexico of a good loan made by the bank," I answered.

Carrandi replied that he really did not know what their most effective program was. "I have only been in Guatemala one and a half years," he said. He went on to say that in another year the bank would have more pride in its Guatemalan loans.

"It is too bad, but that is the truth," he said. The bank has had projects in Guatemala for many years, with the first loan given in 1961. In the beginning the bank's work went very slowly here, due largely to political instability and, Carrandi added in a confiding tone, because "Guatemala does not write loan requests very well."

Carrandi himself wanted to talk about future loans rather than the effectiveness of past ones. In this he was quite in character with all other development officials. And like them he, too, implied he knew very little about the programs started before his arrival.

But on one point Carrandi was certain: I was studying the wrong project. Once again it was brought home to me that actual progress in the field is seldom as the home office believes it to be.

Nevertheless I went to Los Esclavos in order to follow through with Herrera's advice.

As Carrandi had warned, there is not much to report. The plant is there. Of the total cost of $5.1 million, the Guatemalan Electrification Institute provided $2 million. This typifies most of the bank's loans because, quite rightly, it tries to get the borrower to pay as much of the total cost as possible.

I noted that all the visible equipment at Los Esclavos—the generators, etc.—was made in Germany. In this case, at least, the familiar Latin American complaint that U.S. money must be used to buy U.S. equipment is not valid.

It was the dry season and the power plant was operating at half capacity. It is able to run at full capacity only during the rainy season when the river has enough water to turn all the turbines.

The Washington IDB office had told me the power was to be used for industry in Guatemala City. Thus I was surprised to see power lines also branching off from the plant in the direction away from the capital. When I asked about this the plant superintendent said, "About one-half of the power goes to Guatemala City, the rest goes to Jutiapa, a nearby village. Eventually all the power will be used for villages around Los Esclavos."[10]

There are two reasons why my visit to Los Esclavos disturbed me.

First, neither sign of industry nor reason for it was evident in the villages around Los Esclavos. Therefore I can only assume the power will be used for such amenities as house lights and appliances. Thus this plant, which can function at full capacity during only a part of the year, was not built for the reasons announced publicly by the bank, namely, to further the industrialization of Guatemala City.

Second, as the reader must now realize, I question that electrification should be assigned "the highest priority" for a nation almost wholly dependent on agriculture for its economic development.

IN THE EAGERNESS to pursue the multilateral route with U.S. aid money, a basic question has never been answered: Can the international agencies do a better job than our own U.S. Agency for International Development?

"Who knows?" a House Foreign Affairs Committee aide told me. "Our committee has seen no evidence of it."

Over the decade of the 1960s the Inter-American Development Bank loaned a total of $3.4 billion. According to IDB's own immodest words, "the results of this lending are even more significant than the statistics. During the decade of the 1960's the Bank directly contributed to the welfare of one out of every four Latin Americans and indirectly benefitted far more."[11]

How does one reduce to facts such a grandiose, vague claim?

How does one find out how the bank really operates?

None of its member nations has inquired in any depth into the bank's operations. In the case of the borrowing nations, there obviously would not be any desire "to make waves"; to the contrary, they curry favor with its officials because the bank represents an easy source of investment funds for themselves.

For its part, the United States, being but one of more than a score of nations belonging to the bank, takes the position that it does not have the right unilaterally to question the bank's wisdom. That being so, the Inter-American Development Bank, like its sister international finance agencies, continues to operate entirely on its own, above all restraints, with no one to question its decisions or to assess and evaluate the effectiveness of the projects it underwrites.

Senator Frank Church of Idaho, speaking of IDB said, "It's the peculiar nature of the animal: we provide the money and they [the Latin American nations] control the Bank . . . I have wanted to give the Bank the benefit of the doubt. . . . If [it fails], the whole movement toward multilateral aid will be endangered."[12]

My own observation at Los Esclavos and the other bank-financed projects in Central America and Mexico which I visited is that IDB has no more foresight when it comes to supporting successful programs than do present or past U.S. foreign aid agencies, nor does it show any more originality in generating imaginative programs from the applicant governments. For one thing, it has followed the stale policy of putting more funds into the combination of industrialization and electrical power than it has allocated to the agricultural sector. Moreover the bank remains totally dedicated to the economic integration of the area and continues to use loans at every opportunity to push this dubious concept.

But the clearest example of the blinders the bank wears has been its bias against population control programs. The reasons may be many—from a fear of the political power of the Catholic Church to a lack of imagination on how to do anything about population growth. But the most likely reason, held by many within the bank, is that its first president, Felipe Herrera, simply did not believe in the need. Thus while the United States fed it money to spearhead a social and economic revolution, the bank during Herrera's ten-year reign watched indifferently as Latin America's population increased by 33 percent—the highest rate for any area of the world—a rate which is guaranteed to defeat any possible social or economic revolution.

A rare insight into why the bank has shown no more foresight in how it uses its money than have other development organizations is given by John P. Powelson, professor of economics at the University of Colorado, who was hired by IDB to make a private, in-house study.[13]

Powelson said that while it is a *development* bank, "the professional personnel of the Bank is not agreed on what a development bank is . . . The actual operating results of the Bank re-

flect all different concepts [of how it should function], weighed
according to the numbers and positional influence of their ad-
herents."

It is certainly difficult to zero in on the development target
when those doing the shooting are aiming in different directions!
Because of this confusion in finding a target, Powelson's study
stated, there is "a certain 'whitewashing' in which loan documents
appear to report the results of exhaustive economic studies which
on examination often prove superficial, and which rarely admit
that *anything* is wrong with a project. When they do, they usually argue that deficiencies are quickly resolved, often with the
simple application of a not-precisely-defined technical assistance."

The Inter-American Development Bank does, of course, issue
reports on its activities. In 1970 its report typically praised its
work with impressive, but vague, statistics: "Bank loans have
benefitted an estimated 6.7 million persons in the agricultural
sector, 26 million in the electric power sector, 49 million in the
water supply and sanitation sector, 2.2 million in the housing
sector and 600,000 in the education sector."[14]

Perhaps, but who really knows? The bank's reports need to
be read as one reads the Bible—with unquestioning faith.

But one should remember that IDB was established for political reasons. Because political goals are nebulous, a high degree of
faith again is needed for judging to what extent they have been
attained. Therefore I suppose it is unfair to judge IDB by such
things as the number of light bulbs actually installed, textbooks
actually bought, or water pipes actually laid.

The bank during its first ten years loaned Chileans two and
one-half times more money than it loaned, per capita, the rest of
Latin America. I have heard many say the bank's Chilean president, Felipe Herrera, was using these loans to build a political
base back home. United States officials, expressing confidence in
the bank's wisdom and direction, reminded skeptics that Chile
had a strong Communist party which needed neutralizing.

In September 1970, Dr. Salvador Allende, an avowed Marxist
and an outspoken admirer of Fidel Castro, was elected president
of Chile. Felipe Herrera radioed the newly elected president,
"Cordial congratulations on this most important moment of your
impeccable and significant career. . . . You can count on me personally as your life-long friend in confronting the difficulties and
hard task that lies ahead of you."

And Herrera meant it! He immediately wrote out his resignation from IDB, saying, "I would not want to be separated from my country in the new stage of its historic evolution which is beginning."

Yet it was this bank, under Herrera's firm control, to which Congress had committed $3.5 billion, to be used as he should direct in the (it was assumed) fight against Castro's active efforts to subvert and revolutionize Latin America. It is natural now, with Herrera back in Chile supporting Allende enthusiastically, to wonder how objective his actions were during all those years he controlled the bank's U.S. money.

In any case, $3.5 billion is a lot of aid money to be tithing by faith.

The Central American Common Market and Deficit Financing

The Inter-American Development Bank "has become a leading propagator of new ideas and concepts . . ."

The Inter-American Development Bank is "the Bank of Economic Integration."[1]

AMONG the more pleasant moments of preparing for my research field trip were my calls on the Washington ambassadors of the five Central American countries. I would usually begin the interview with an explanation that my projected book would be an analysis of the most effective development programs in this region because Central America had an outstanding growth record and was regarded as the most clear-cut success region in the developing world. In each case the ambassador's jaw would drop, so to speak, his eyes would pop, and he would say something like: "You mean there are people who consider Central America a success!" After this first startled reaction, his diplomatic poise would return and we would discuss the development projects in his country. An amused glint would remain in his eyes, as though he were wondering how naive I could be to regard his country as a "success" in development.

It is all relative. Central America is, for sure, distressingly poor and it is being overwhelmed with a mushrooming population. No one had implied that Central America had reached, or will reach soon, an acceptable plateau of overall prosperity. Yet the area was changing dramatically. The capital cities abounded with new bank buildings, new suburbs, new streets, and new industries; the provincial cities were reflecting the same changes. Statistics published throughout the 1960s depicted a booming economy which reports indicated was steadily moving forward along the road of progress.

Up to the time of my research, Central America had achieved an average annual economic growth rate of 6 percent. All publications I saw specifically attributed this remarkable growth to "regional integration," in other words, the Central American Common Market.[2]

Trade among the five countries (Costa Rica, Nicaragua, Honduras, El Salvador, Guatemala) grew remarkably after their Common Market was established in 1961:[3]

1960	$ 32.7 million
1964	106.2
1966	173.1
1968	213.6
1969	263.0

The U.S. State Department reported that in the first seven years of the Common Market interregional trade there had increased "nearly 700 percent, and trade with the rest of the world is up 60 percent."[4]

What better proof could there be of development progress?

Thomas Mann, former assistant secretary of state for Latin American Affairs, told me that the market "is a shot in the arm. It is exciting to see the results."

A New York City Bar Association report said, "The lusty young" market has accomplished a "practical, economical operation which has astonished even many of its ardent advocates and [created] machinery for resolving disputes which contains the seed of a regional system of law and judiciary."[5]

Felipe Herrera, president of the Inter-American Development Bank, told me, "Because of its Common Market, Central America has a future for the first time in its history."

Only five years after the birth of the market, President Johnson said, "The Central American Republics are already giving to their neighbors and to the world in general what is in my opinion an exciting example of what can be done, with good judgment and decisiveness, by free men of broad vision . . . They have, in a series of acts of the highest statesmanship, embarked upon a process of integrating their economies, which is one of the really most exciting undertakings of our world today . . . And the results are already apparent and already gratifying."[6]

Recently Juan de Onis, respected Latin American correspondent for the *New York Times,* wrote, "During the last decade this market has been the most successful regional effort in economic integration among the developing countries . . ."[7]

Clearly, this Common Market was something I should study as an effective development force. It was itself a valid development project to add to my list for inspection during my research in Central America. Here five small nations, which in the past were forever squabbling, had finally banded together and put themselves on the road to collective salvation. What a fine lesson for other bitterly divided areas of the developing world, said the development planners. They continued, if Central America can do it, then maybe South America can also, and indeed all of Latin America, and the regions of Africa and Asia.

The idea integral to any common market is to pool the purchasing power of several heretofore divergent peoples and thus gather into one economic unit enough customers to justify setting up industries.

Raúl Prebisch, an Argentine economist, is generally credited with having been the chief architect of the Common Market. At the time the market was in its embryo discussion stages in the 1950s, Prebisch was in charge of the United Nations Economic Commission for Latin America (ECLA), organized to be a sort of hemispheric development think tank. He was thus provided with a podium from which to expound his views. In the post-World War II period, while attention was focused on rebuilding war-torn Europe, Prebisch hammered away, anywhere and anytime he had the chance, on the need for worrying also about the developing nations.

In essence, Prebisch's thesis was that Latin America had been condemned by a cruel fate to produce food and raw materials that were processed elsewhere, that is, in industrialized nations. To make matters worse, Latin America was forced to buy back at inflated prices its own raw materials as manufactured goods.

Prebisch repeated this message again and again wherever he could find an audience. I once asked a journalist friend if he were going to cover a Prebisch speech before an important inter-American group in Washington. He said it was not necessary, he could easily write the story from having heard previous Prebisch speeches.

One of Prebisch's favorite illustrations was that the value of Latin America's commodities, when compared to that of imported manufactured goods, had fallen through the years. For example, a specific quantity of cotton which could be exchanged for a dollar's worth of nails in 1880 would buy only 69¢ worth of nails in 1947.[8]

Prebisch proposed that Latin America reverse this evolutionary trend by processing as much of its raw products at home as possible. He urged that the region convert its raw materials into finished or semimanufactured goods to sell both at home and abroad. INDUSTRIALIZE! he proclaimed.

Prebisch's emphasis on the need for more home-grown industry made him suspect among business and government circles in the United States. Economists in other quarters picked large holes in his theories and in his interpretation of statistics. But to Latin Americans, looking abroad for a scapegoat for their economic woes, Prebisch's words were intoxicating.

Whatever the merits or demerits of his case, Prebisch himself and his theories were to become extremely influential among opinion makers and program managers in the developing world. At the time he was propounding his theories he was one of the few prominent people anywhere wholly concerned with development problems. His dedication was acknowledged even by those who violently disagreed with his views.

At Prebisch's prodding, the cumbersome international and national bureaucracies were goaded into beginning to think about the advantages of integrating their economies. He eventually struck sparks in the five Central American countries. As the dominating spirit of ECLA, Prebisch made that organization serve as the focal point for the pre-1960 negotiations which eventually created the Central American Common Market. The meetings were countless and seemingly endless.

After nearly a decade of such buttocks-wearying conclaves, the Common Market was agreed to in 1958. But three years more of long and sometimes acrimonious debates remained before the formal agreement establishing the market was signed and ratified.

In theory, the market gathered into one economic unit 12 million consumers, a figure which the exploding population had increased to 15 million by 1970.

A basic trouble, not admitted by the planners, was that while the area contained 12 million *people,* all 12 million were not *consumers.* First, the average per capita income hovered just under $300 per year; second, two-thirds of the population lived from subsistence farming and did not participate as effective consumers in the national economies; third, the urban shanty dwellers did not muster much purchasing power. At the time the Common Market was formed this left as the *actual consumer market* approximately

2 million persons. In U.S. terms, the Common Market had about as many genuine consumers as did Mississippi. The difficulty of introducing one unified range of industries to serve a market of this size in Central America was compounded further by the fact that these consumers lived under five different governments, having five different bureaucracies, trade laws, enforcement agencies, and so on.

As for the new industries to be built, the Prebisch plan was based on allocating them fairly among the five countries, and on permitting them to be located in the Central American area only if what they were to produce was needed, taking into account overall market requirements.

The problem, as it turned out, was the vacuum arising because no strong regional organization existed between the time when the market was agreed to in 1958 and the time when it was formally established as an operating organization in 1961; only then did it receive the authority to enforce the ground rules that had been set up three years earlier.

In 1958, however, cupidity overwhelmed honor. A mad scramble—a chaotic rush—broke loose to establish as many industries as possible before the treaty-signing deadline. Industrialists, would-be industrialists, and carpetbaggers, aided and abetted by local governments, jockeyed for position before the Common Market rules would take force. Each government lavished tax concessions on entrepreneurs willing to rush to completion makeshift "factories" within its own boundary in order to provide "proof" of an already established industrial operation. Each delayed Common Market negotiations with its fellow republics to allow its entrepreneurs the maximum time to get things set up. Nationalism, never far below the surface in Central American affairs, ran wild. It became a matter of national honor to outfox one's neighbor in this business of preempting manufacturing rights.

Thus the Central American countries did not move ahead on a wave of brotherly love. Although they shared the hope for increased earnings from a common market, they did not share the common bonds of honorable colleagues when it came to sticking to the rules.

Foreign investors also paid not the slightest attention to such scruples; both public and private capital flowed into the area. The various international development agencies vied to outdo each other in priming the pumps. Funds from all sorts of places became plentiful for more factories, more power plants, more roads, as "everyone" reassured "everyone else" that the Common Market was going to reduce the risks of doing business in Central America.

The U.S. government was initially against this integrated industrialization. After it was apparent, however, that the initiative for the market had had its origins in Latin America the idea became more attractive because the market offered Washington the opportunity to project a positive image by supporting an indigenous effort.

Soon some U.S. officials were advocating an even larger common market, embracing all Latin America, to be built upon the structure of the tiny Central American market and incorporating some other fragmentary regional trading associations. In its eagerness, Washington overreacted and began to suffocate the very regionalism it wished to nourish.

Then, under the infectious verve of the Alliance for Progress—begun in 1961—the United States rushed to be in the vanguard of the market's enthusiasts. While maintaining its five existing missions in the area, AID soon established a regional office (ROCAP) to assist the integration of Central America financially. This new office became a major wellspring of cheerful progress bulletins, which further stimulated both the Central Americans and the officials back in the United States. The fever of excitement spread to all U.S. missions in Latin America. In Washington it took on epidemic proportions. There, the new machinery of the Alliance for Progress turned out ream upon ream of optimistic copy as each minor, but favorable, statistic came in, which in turn, produced its own disease of confidence.

International loaning agencies soon joined in, contributing to the brouhaha with such a tumble of competition that their loans were not even coordinated. The building of the highway to the Costa Rican town of Limón is an example. The World Bank first agreed to lend the money, but with some conditions attached. The Central American Bank for Economic Integration (which had been set up with the help of the Inter-American Development Bank) then offered to make the loan without conditions and committed $5 million for it from its Fund for Economic Integration. Next came U.S. AID with an additional $3 million. But not to be outdone, the World Bank came back and agreed to build the road,[9] taking on faith that its previous conditions would be met. Throughout this period of the formation of the Common Market, the Inter-American Development Bank was its most ardent backer.

The investments derived from all sources, both government and private, brought on ever more investments and the beautiful statistics became even more beautiful. The entire sum of international moneys put into the area by the U.S. government, World Bank, Inter-American Development Bank, etc., over the period of 1961–68, amounted to $877.5 million.[10]

In the midst of this boom euphoria officials of the lending banks and U.S. agencies, it is today obvious, became overfevered. For example, ROCAP originated a number of high-cost projects for which, as it happened, no local organization had enough money to continue. As a result, according to a responsible, highly placed official, none of these projects "were ever really brought to a successful conclusion."[11]

One illustration of this excess of excitement: The head of U.S. AID in El Salvador in a conversation with me railed against that nation for not using its credit fully to borrow all the money which the international lending agencies were begging it to take. He said El Salvador was failing to take advantage of the opportunities open to it for accelerating its development. "Last year the government here had a surplus at the end of the fiscal year and didn't spend it. Ridiculous," he declared, "for a developing country to act this way."

A Guatemalan businessman whom I have known for fifteen years and whose judgment I respect told me his country had been quite conservative in its handling of money until about 1966. Guatemala then began to borrow "a tremendous amount of money, by our standards, from the United States. Nearly all of this will have to be paid back in dollars when the grace periods of the loans are over. The government," he said, "will have to cut down on all but essential imports to conserve the dollars necessary just to pay back those loans. It is going to wreck a lot of businesses."

Unfortunately, no Jeremiah was around to warn that activity based on deficit financing and loans and aid grants does not ensure sound economic growth. Instead, everyone was accepting at face value the ever-rising development indices caused by the creation of all the new (and artificial) industries.

Washington took the lead in disregarding the results of deficit financing. Balance-of-payment problems were shunted aside in the rush to encourage new factories. Not content to rely on existing financing institutions to handle the flow of money, the United States aided and abetted the setting up of a host of new agencies and the strengthening of others which had previously existed mainly on paper. Some of these were:

ODECA—Organization of Central American States (newly chartered in 1962)
CTPS—Council of Labor and Social Welfare (1964)
MCP—Central American Joint Planning Mission (1962)
CCMEP—Coordinating Commission for Marketing and Price Stabilization in Central America and Panama (1964)
CCT—Central American Telecommunications Commission (1963)
CEC—Central American Economic Council (1960)
CETG—The Executive Council of the General Treaty (1960)
SIECA—The Permanent Secretariat of the General Treaty of Central American Economic Integration (coordinating responsibility assumed 1965)
BCIE—Central American Bank for Economic Integration (1964)
UMCA—The Central American Monetary Union (1964)
CCC—The Central American Clearing House (1961)
COCESNA—Central American Air Navigation Service Corp. (1960)
ESAPAC—Central American School of Public Administration (organized in 1954 but in 1961 began to concentrate on courses related to integration)
CSSP—The Superior Council of Public Health (1964)
INCAE—Central American Institute of Business Management (1963)
SITCA—Secretariat for Central American Tourism Integration (1963)
FCCC—Federation of Central American Chambers of Commerce (1961)
FECAICA—Federation of Central American Associations and Chambers of Industry (1959)[12]

Quite an impressive new regional bureaucracy to match the new regional Common Market! Or perhaps we should say an immense pandemic had sprouted from Prebisch's germ of an idea.

Many observers had pointed to the basic differences between the Central American Common Market, incorporating weak, undeveloped nations with little traditional trade between them, and the European Common Market, which had been established in 1957 among already industrialized and closely interrelated nations. But even these observers did not seem to understand the implications of the differences. And so support for the market did not just grow. It snowballed.

During the period of 1961–68, when the United States was priming the market pump with more than $600 million in loans, the public debts of the Central American governments rose from $350 million to $708 million.[13] The question that no one seemed to ask was how long could a common market be financed on a deficit?

THE ANSWER came in 1968 (after I had finished my interviewing in Washington and was about to leave for Mexico and Central

America) and the troubles all seemed to rise to the surface at once. The Central American nations suddenly seemed to owe everybody and there was little in the till. The situation in Costa Rica was so critical many Washington observers privately wondered if the country would topple into bankruptcy.

To stop the sudden drain of foreign currency the five republics agreed to impose a 30 percent surtax on luxury items. They had agreed to the legitimacy of such a move when setting up the first rules for the Common Market. However, in the absence of a clear-cut authority to operate the market, some of the nations willfully delayed signing the agreement that would have put the surtax measure into force because they hoped to gain some advantage by waiting.

By 1968 Nicaragua had had a disastrous cotton crop and had run up a deficit of $57 million. It now began enforcing its own surtax. When the other nations did not follow suit, President Somoza was furious. He charged that the rice which El Salvador was selling to his country had been produced in Mexico. He accused other countries of importing Hong Kong shirts, putting Common Market labels on them, and selling them as products originating within the market. Somoza then sealed off Nicaragua's border to "Salvadoran" rice and threatened to leave the Common Market. Similar incidents occurred and charges were made involving products carrying the Central American label. For example, truckloads of cigarettes manufactured by subsidiaries of U.S. firms in Central America were stopped at the border and, in some cases, confiscated.

The bloom was off integration and the Common Market!

The easy things that could be done to foster industrialization through incentives had already been done. Possible new foreign investors quickly retreated. The Common Market entered into what Kennedy Crockett, U.S. ambassador to Nicaragua, told me was a "shakedown period with an unpredictable future."

With the disintegration of the Common Market a threat, President Johnson flew to San Salvador to confer with the chief executives of the five Central American countries and to try thereby to revive enthusiasm and to bring back the original idealism.

Symbolically, as the six presidents met in the fine old residence which serves as a Secretariat for the Organization of Central American States, the lights went out due to a power failure caused by overloading the circuits with the press's equipment. In the darkness, the secret service guards of President Johnson were nervous. But, as credibly reported, it was President Somoza of Nicaragua who was the most fearful for his life because his imposition of the unpopular surtax had raised widespread resentment.

President Johnson flattered and cajoled and "pressed the flesh." In the end, the Central American leaders agreed to sign the 30 percent surtax provision. Johnson then extended an extra $65 million in loans and grants for the five republics. The group present was too polite to call it a bribe. The Common Market was saved, at least for the moment.

President Johnson, accompanied each of his fellow chief executives back to his own nation on U.S. Air Force Number One, a gesture accepted as *muy simpático* throughout Central America.

Obviously, however, there were problems within the Common Market which a plane ride could not cure.

The Central American Common Market
Puts the Cart before the Horse

WITH THE ADVANTAGE of hindsight one wonders how the United States came to give its support so fulsomely to the Common Market.

One reason was, of course, that the Common Market did indeed make sense—up to a point.

Suppose, for example, a bottle cap company in Central America must make 5 million caps per year to cover its production costs, including the importation of steel and cork. Say the total market for caps in the area is 10 million, enough to fill the orders of all beer and soft drink producers. If one company has this total market, it can obviously be a profitable operation. In fact, two companies can coexist and provide each other some competition, which will help keep prices down. But three or four companies? They will all go broke.

In the Dominican Republic I shared a taxi to the airport with a prosperous and aggressive Central American businessman. I asked him about the Common Market and whether it was helping his textile industry.

"No," he replied flatly, "because there is no discipline among the Central American countries. In the case of my business, the market has brought thirteen new companies into direct competition with me. Though the market has brought a larger number of customers under one roof, it has also created a lot more competitors. Few could survive if they were to lose their special tax concessions."

"What do you see as the future of your own business?"

"I plan to sell out within five years at whatever price I can get and move to Canada or the United States."

A deputy chief of mission in a U.S. embassy in Central America

277

confirmed what the businessman had said, adding wistfully, "The new enlarged market might have accommodated one or two major companies in each field, but not a dozen or more. If it had been left to normal business competition, this situation would have quickly worked itself out, and the efficient companies would have come out on top. Instead, each country continues to shelter its own little group of industries by giving them more and more tax breaks and other concessions. It has become a very nationalistic thing," he lamented. "Feelings run high."

The manager of a hotel where I stayed in Costa Rica offered yet another viewpoint on the market. "The products we now must buy are no good," he said. "I have to buy tires from a company in Guatemala, and they are pretty bad. I lose two ways, first because I must buy new tires more often than before. I also lose because eventually I'll have to pay more taxes to my government inasmuch as it no longer collects the tariff fees on the tires that previously were imported from abroad."

The ultimate absurdity is the practice of repackaging. In describing how this works, a businessman from León, Nicaragua, told me, "Guatemala buys pills in big bottles from the United States or West Germany, puts them in little bottles, and ships them here, where I must buy them. What has been accomplished?" he asked. "Guatemala may have made a profit on the deal, though probably not much of one, but Nicaragua has lost the tariff revenues it previously received on the pills I used to buy. One thing is certain: I do not make anything on the deal because the price of the pills to me is at least as high as it was before, and in some cases even higher."

I asked the U.S. AID mission director in one capital, "What has been the cost of repackaged pills to the local people in economic terms?"

"Tremendous!" he said. "This area really does not need six drug firms. Now that they are all in existence, they are a great drain on national treasuries, robbing them of the money formerly taken in from taxes on drug imports. What to do about it? I don't know. But the governments are keeping all these drug firms breathing by pumping them up with tax and other concessions which no one can rationally justify."

The optimistic statistics of intraregional trade, praised by President Johnson and everyone else, did not show such details as repackaging, that is, an aspirin imported into Guatemala, repackaged and shipped to Nicaragua. Yet the amount of aspirin consumed in Central America is the same as before. It is now apparent the regional trade statistics give a misleading picture of the increase in Central American industrialization.

Another prime source of false optimism is related to a misreading of statistical indicators. For example, if only one small cement factory was in operation prior to the market, the addition of another small plant automatically boosted cement production 100 percent, an impressive statistic. In the hands of publicists, this kind of figure could be used to show that the region had made the greatest gain in cement production in the world!

What about foreign businesses? In Managua I had a talk, over a lukewarm beer, with a salesman from a New York City specialty house handling sweaters, neckties, toys, religious pictures, and the like. I asked him, "How's the Common Market as far as you're concerned?"

"It's really no good for anyone," he said. "It's a peculiar setup. I sell things that would be considered bargain basement stuff in the United States. Here, however, so much duty is placed on them they become luxury items. And, of course, they are of better quality than comparable items made here. That's the only reason I can sell them."

"But if your items are so expensive and the quality so poor, who buys them?" I asked.

"Well, everyone seems to be broke here, but the population of the Common Market is big enough that I guess the law of averages works out, at least in the sense that some people have enough money to buy. As a matter of fact, I have a pretty fair business here."

The Central American side of this same story came from an industrialist, the only one in the market area producing certain chemicals used in both agriculture and heavy construction. "I can't get my manufacturing costs down to those of a U.S. factory," he told me. "The main reason is that my market is just not big enough. This means I cannot compete with U.S. prices or quality. Whatever success I have, and, fortunately, I am still in business, is due to two factors: first, I don't pay the transportation costs a U.S. company must pay to get its products here, and, second, I have a protective tariff going for me. But take away the tariff and the U.S. manufacturer could overcome the transportation handicap and put me out of business. Why? In a nutshell, the U.S. manufacturer is producing for a market of 200 million people. I am producing for an effective market of only half a million *real* buyers."

Another leading long-time Central American industrialist who has had broad experience with many facets of doing business in the area cited some of the damage caused by the rush to industrialize. "A bad feature of these new, artificial, competing industries is the drain on our foreign exchange that results from setting them up. All the machinery—even small tools—must be imported. Then, since our local production cannot compete on the world market (because of poorer quality and higher price), all of the output must be sold within the Common Market. Thus there is no way an industry can repay the original loss of foreign exchange (lost when it set up its own installation) by later generating new foreign exchange. The cost of these new industries must be borne entirely by our own local economy. This would be all right if a new industry could earn normal profits. But usually this is not the case; the 'profits' are derived out of tax concessions."

Like many other people with whom I talked, including the highest U.S. officials, this industrialist said, "Everyone is now talking about doing away with these tax concessions or at least equalizing them among the five republics. Unfortunately, no matter what mistakes have been made in the past, it's too late to turn back the clock. These new hothouse industries are already entrenched politically and they will continue to receive special protection."

The director of agricultural research in one of the countries said to me, "The Common Market's effort to achieve economic integration has been a series of awful errors, not errors of judgment necessarily, but of selfishness arising from each country's push to gain some temporary advantage over the others. The consumers are paying for these errors. The only profits anyone is getting from the Common Market are going to the successful industrialists— what few there are. Yet if the Common Market falls apart, I don't know what will happen here. There is nothing to take its place. Each country will have to struggle along again all by itself. We know from past experience this would mean more of the same old poverty and sadness."

What is revealing about this statement is its emphasis on the industrialist as the only one who has profited from the market. More and more, today's frustrations over the failings of the market take the form of polemics against business, both local and foreign owned. Criticism is especially bitter from the younger generation of technicians and officials in Central America, though similar comments are now being made by the older, higher officials trying to explain away the errors of the past.

In a conversation the vice-president of one Central American republic expressed views which I heard reiterated throughout all of Central America. He said, "I am an enemy of the Common Market. It is not a market for Central American business, but a market for U.S. business. The Common Market is no good because the Central American countries all produce the same things and they all end up competing with themselves for the same markets. Then, too, each country has a different currency, which means that each country pays a different price for the same things and different salaries for the same job. The Common Market makes it convenient for U.S. businessmen to come in here and invest, but it does not help to solve our problems. I look upon the Common Market as a tool of the United States."

I could plainly see an increasingly widespread belief in Central America that U.S. business takes out from the Common Market, in the form of profits and interest payments, more than it puts in, thus enriching itself at the expense of the local people.

By now a backlash against industrialization has become widespread. In my interview with Carlos Castillo, secretary general of the Secretariat for Central American Economic Integration (SIECA), he said a definite "antiindustrialization feeling is spreading in Central America because of all those special concessions which industry has received."

Another factor is even more germane to an analysis of what went wrong with the market. When I asked Castillo what sort of attention had been paid to agriculture in setting up the market, he said, "In the debates in the various republics leading up to the formation of the Common Market, the justification for the market was always the possibility of increased industrialization. No one ever said anything about agriculture."

One U.S. ambassador said, "The small farmers of Central America have been totally neglected by the people running the Common Market."

This was confirmed by other American officials on the scene. An AID mission director said it simply, "The Common Market has helped industry. Agriculture remains untouched." A U.S. technical advisor said, "The only thing the Common Market has going in agriculture is the basic grains protocol. However, this has never been put into effect, and only the Lord knows when it will be made operational."

I met with a group of old friends at the Coffee Association offices in Guatemala City. Their spirits were low. The crop had been poor and prices depressed for the past five years. All of them were short of money; some were heavily mortgaged. When I asked, "What is the Common Market doing for you?" they gave me an answer, but it is unprintable.

What most irritated these coffee growers in Guatemala was the realization that they, the agriculturalists whose coffee is Guatemala's number one export earner, were being forced to subsidize the growth of the artificial industries.

I found the same awareness among large farmers in all five countries. They know that tax concessions granted to the new industries and losses thereby accruing to the tariff revenues must be made up somewhere. They also know that they, and their exports, are the only source of taxes to make up these losses.

A U.S. AID mission director told me that agriculture is forced to pay full fare in the Common Market, while industry rides along as a "deadhead passenger." The same thing, he said, "happened in Argentina and Chile, and you can see what a mess their economies are in today as a result. Perón squeezed the cost of industrialization out of Argentina's farm community and wrecked the country and it has yet to recover."

When I commented to Carlos Castillo that Central American farmers felt they were bearing the cost of industrialization, he said, "That's an interesting new idea. No one here has discussed this point." He thought to himself for a moment, then added, "In a sense, one can say that agriculture is indeed paying for industrial growth . . . I suppose it's true that in order to make up for the loss of revenues, tax structures have to be revamped, and in this case it's the farmers who are hit with higher taxes."

The countries' allocation of development funds reflects this fact and is detailed in a monograph of the Bank of London and Montreal: "The main weight [of the Common Market] is concentrated on developing a road network and modernizing port facilities . . . The second major item of expenditures is . . . almost exclusively devoted to electricity production . . . The third . . . is an up-to-date system of telecommunications."[1] Meanwhile the desperate plight of agriculture is overlooked, left by the wayside.

As one authority has written, "After twenty years the task of transforming Central American agriculture has hardly begun, and the programs started do not have sufficient national support to be expanded without continued encouragement from development assistance."[2]

How COULD the U.S. government become so enthusiastic and give so much money to a program like the Common Market which completely ignored the basic economy of the region?

In the beginning the United States was, in fact, against the whole idea. Even when the Central American governments in 1958 agreed to go ahead on their own, the United States looked upon the concept of integration of industries with "cold indifference."[3] For in Washington, Prebisch's one-note development symphony glorifying the industrial development of Latin America had been listened to most skeptically.

But the next year, 1959, President José Maria Lemus of El Salvador called on President Eisenhower. Lemus, who had been "elected" (after all political parties either had been barred or had withdrawn their candidates), needed a plum to take home. He argued persuasively for support for the Common Market because it would benefit El Salvador the most as the only country in Central America which could be called (somewhat) industrialized. When Lemus left Washington, Eisenhower had blessed the Common Market.

The United States accordingly plunged into one more development exercise which put the cart before the horse—industry before agriculture.

This incident illustrates the casual, haphazard, almost indifferent way in which the United States frequently handles its development resources—which could well be one reason why we fail to learn how to use these resources effectively.

As for Lemus, he was thrown out of office eighteen months after obtaining the U.S. blessing—a fate most any Latin American specialist could have predicted.

As for the Common Market—a real cart-before-the-horse contraption—its fate could also have been predicted if the economists and officials had taken the time to sit back and examine it.

The Central American Common Market and a Demographic War

ON JULY 14 (Bastille Day), 1969, war broke out in Central America and the Common Market cracked wide open.

At six o'clock in the evening, units of the Salvadoran Army and National Guard advanced into Honduran territory all along the frontier. The proclaimed objective of the invasion was the protection of the rights of some 200,000 to 300,000 Salvadorans who had settled in Honduras over a period of several generations.

To the outside world, the short war, which lasted only 100 hours and cost about a thousand military and civilian casualties on both sides, seemed at first a comic opera. The press tagged it "The Soccer War" because it was precipitated by a series of hotly contested soccer games between teams from the two nations. Rioting followed those matches in both capital cities and fanned such intense hatred (soccer is the big emotion in Central America) that a play-off match had to be held on neutral ground in Mexico.

Amusing as the miniwar may have seemed elsewhere, it was pitifully serious to those involved, pitiful because it was fought so viciously and with such a miscellany of outdated, rather ridiculous equipment. United States Army P-51 Mustangs (World War II vintage) from the Salvadoran air force tangled with archaic U.S. Marine Corps gull-winged Honduran Corsairs over the rugged frontier. The ragtag Honduran army, which was mustered hastily to face the Salvadoran invasion, was largely composed of short-term conscript soldiers who had never fired the arms they were carrying into battle.

Especially pitiful were the thousands of Salvadoran migrants living in Honduras in whose behalf the Salvadoran invasion was ostensibly launched and whose lives were now suddenly jeopardized. Also to be pitied were the thousands of people all along the border who suffered the horrors of warfare; their cows were killed, personal possessions carried off, villages sacked by the invaders. Yet most of these isolated folk had not the faintest inkling of what the war was all about.

By 1962 the population of El Salvador had grown to the point where there were 40 percent more people per acre of cropland than in India.

As an agriculturalist I view this with horror.

A recent study by Howard E. Daugherty shows the rate at which the Salvadoran population is doubling.[1]

Year	Population	Years to Double
1850	400,000	
1900	800,000	50
1937	1,600,000	37
1968	3,300,000	28
1987	6,600,000 estimated	19

One draws back in consternation, wondering how a nation, any nation, can keep from sinking into complete anarchy when, *just to stand still,* it must double all its facilities—power supply, housing, potable water, schools, medical facilities—in the next nineteen years. The evidence is obvious: El Salvador is not succeeding in this; hence the spiraling tensions.

As its population swelled, El Salvador was only too happy to export, over the years, some of its surplus citizens to Honduras, a feat accomplished without any formalities. In the great majority of cases the transfer from one country to the other was a matter of moving one's feet. *Campesino* families merely walked across the border which was marked and systematically controlled at only two main highway crossings. Along the rest of the frontier, which is hilly and rugged, they could pass over easily without benefit of official clearance. In fact, many of the *campesinos* who crossed the border were unaware they had settled in a foreign country. For many years Honduras had quietly ignored this migration in exchange for El Salvador's support in Common Market (and other) negotiations.

Those U.S. officials who thought about this problem, considered it a good thing. Two U.S. ambassadors and two assistant secretaries of state for Inter-American Affairs justified it to me on the basis that Honduras has such a lot of empty space in which to absorb the Salvadorans. They pointed out that in El Salvador there is only one acre per person, while in Honduras there are five. To these officials, land is land; they do not recognize that much of the five acres per capita in Honduras is worthless. Thus the only thing Honduras had to offer the Salvadoran migrants was physical space, not useful tillable land. (A sizable percentage of the Salvadorans did have money with which to buy land; also a considerable number of white-collar persons obtained jobs with such companies as United Fruit.)

This relaxed state of affairs might have continued indefinitely if the pressures of the population explosion in both El Salvador and Honduras had not intervened, pressures which finally forced into the open the enormous social tensions that had been building up in both countries.

The fuse that detonated the bomb was lit when the Honduran president began to enforce an agrarian reform law which made it difficult for nonnationals to own land. This suddenly put many of the emigrated Salvadorans in a bind. Next came the soccer riots. El Salvador invaded Honduras ostensibly to "protect" its nationals. A demographic war had started. Throughout Central America "everyone" believed the real intent was to seize a piece of Honduras. Public opinion in the hemisphere rather quickly mobilized against El Salvador and a ceasefire was arranged.

THOSE WHO EXPECTED the Common Market to calm this kind of problem had not reckoned with the surge in population growth, the skyrocketing numbers of young people entering the labor market, or the antagonisms, not only among the nations but also within the confines of the individual countries.

At the same time, the Common Market carefully avoided facilitating any free movement of laborers among the five countries. This has created in each Central American country, right up to the present, a problem caused by the illegal entry of laborers from one country to another.

A story is commonly told of a Guatemalan businessman who, after a trip through Central America during which a great deal of time was spent passing in and out of customs at each border, finally arrives at the home of a Costa Rican friend.

"My, what fine clothes you are wearing," says the Costa Rican. The Guatemalan, flattered, explains, "My shoes come from El Salvador, my shirt from Honduras; my suit was made in Nicaragua, my hat in Costa Rica; the tie is a product of my native Guatemala. All these items circulate freely among the Common Market nations; the only thing that can't is me, the person inside."

Unhappily, the troubles stirred up by the war between El Salvador and Honduras are a long way from over. Some 30,000 to 50,000 war refugees still remain in the border area, mostly Salvadorans who have chosen or been forced to leave the hostile atmosphere of their adopted country and to cross back into El Salvador. Border incidents are a frequent occurrence, including brigandage of the kind associated everywhere with groups of desperate, homeless people.

Honduras still keeps its roads closed to Salvadoran commerce, thereby cutting that country off completely from land transport to Nicaragua and Costa Rica. Equally important, El Salvador is cut off from its cheapest route for commerce with the United States and Europe, through the Honduran port of Puerto Cortés.

About the only thing the two nations have agreed on is the setting up on a permanent basis of a three-mile-wide no man's land along their common border. This strip is patrolled by some thirty military observers drawn from some of the member nations of the Organization of American States. There was a note of poignancy in the two countries' insistence that the military observers should come from non-Central American nations.

That war should break out in 1969 was a surprise. But the greatest shock was the intensity of the frenzied hatred which erupted between the citizens of El Salvador and Honduras. It was fanatic, demented. Why?

In my own opinion it was caused by the accelerating distrusts and animosities that had exacerbated everyone's nerves as the countries and individuals had jockeyed during the period of the Common Market negotiations and cheated and pushed and shoved to win this or that advantage over the others. In addition to all the previous frictions that had existed since independence in 1821, now, for the first time, the new problem of intense economic competition had been added. The Central American countries had always produced more or less the same things: sugar, cotton, coffee, and, with the exception of El Salvador, bananas. All were equally deficient in the resources that could create industrialization. The Common Market competition now fanned into a new type of hatred the animosities which had always simmered below the surface.

During the formative years of the Common Market, El Salvador had developed a reputation among the other four republics as being the most aggressive, the most devious and, therefore, the most successful member nation. All Central America resented the success of its entrepreneurs.

No country felt its economy had been more usurped by El Salvador's economic "imperialism" than Honduras, the poorest of the five. Honduras was forced to watch its neighboring countries, especially El Salvador, build the industries from which the Common Market now forced it to buy. To add extra insult, Honduras was even expected to provide a home for the excess people from El Salvador.

These heretofore rather equal neighbors had become unequal "partners" within the Common Market.

Optimistic observers say the Soccer War has set back the Common Market only a few years. People like myself feel the war has blown the market apart for the foreseeable future because it brought into the open the false premises on which it had been based.

No program which had so heavily committed five small nations to creating an uneconomic structure of make-believe industry could really have survived anyway. The market intensified, not minimized, the area's problems. In the long run, it may be found that perhaps the most tragic result growing out of the Common Market is that it distracted economic planners and foreign aid donors from paying attention to the onrushing demographic catastrophe.

Central America is poor not because it has too few industries, and not because it is being victimized by foreign capitalists. It is poor because it has too few resources for its population. And now the overwhelming population pressures have indeed reached the crisis point.

In 1968, speaking to the Central American presidents gathered in El Salvador, President Johnson praised effusively the unifying results of the Common Market, saying that no U.S. investment "could have been better spent than it has been here" in Central America. He finished his speech eloquently, "The single strand is weak; the woven strands will endure and clothe the coming generations. Your example has given hope and guidance to a movement that now reaches every continent."[2]

What beautiful, tauntingly ironic words in today's divided Central America.

CIRCULATION DEPARTMENT - STROZIER LIBRARY-BOOK REQUEST CARD

Today's Date ___/__/8   Not needed after (Date) ___/__/8

Call No. _____

Author _____

Title _____

Your social security number _____

Your bar code number 2 1254 _____

Your name and address _____

- -

CLSI

___ Checked out   ___ Missing/Lost   ___ Not in stacks
___ In LVR   ___ Subbasement   ___ Item

___ On Shelf   ___ Printout/IBM
___ No Item   ___ TITLE KEY
___ Not on File   ___ In Shelf list
                         ___ This vol. not   ___ Hold Placed
                             in shelf list.

CIRCULATION DEPARTMENT – STROZIER LIBRARY–BOOK REQUEST CARD

Today's Date ___/_/8___   Not needed after (Date) ___/_/8___

Call No. _____

Author _____

Title _____

Your social security number _____

Your bar code number 2 1254 _____

Your name and address _____

- -

CLSI

___ Checked out   ___ Missing/Lost   ___ Not in stacks
___ In LVR   ___ Subbasement   ___ Item

___ On Shelf   ___ Printout/IBM
___ No Item   ___ TITLE KEY
___ Not on File   ___ In Shelf list
                         ___ This vol. not   ___ Hold Placed
                             in shelf list.

CIRCULATION DEPARTMENT - STROZIER LIBRARY-BOOK REQUEST CARD

Today's Date _/ /8_   Not needed after (Date) _/ /8_

Call No. _____

Author _____

Title _____

Your social security number _____

Your bar code number 2 1254 _____

Your name and address _____

- -

CLSI

___ Checked out	___ Missing/Lost	___ Not in stacks
___ In LVR	___ Subbasement	___ Item
___ On Shelf	___ Printout/IBM	
___ No Item	___ In Shelf list	___ TITLE KEY
___ Not on File	___ This vol. not	
	in shelf list.	___ Hold Placed

Conclusions:
Broadcasting the Combination
of the Vault

THE CONCEPT of channeling aid funds through the international organizations is not uniquely President Nixon's. It is a philosophy that has long been advocated in many quarters. Economist Barbara Ward has claimed these organizations are the "first instruments of planetary justice," and she makes an appealing case for using them to build a society "in which men can live without destroying each other."[1]

Furthermore a popularly held belief is that the hungry nations find it more honorable to do business with the international agencies than with individual donor countries or private organizations. I suspect this belief has little basis in fact. The respected Roberto Campos, former head of Brazil's development plan, has said, "Only the person who has never entered into an international negotiation can think that General Motors limits economic liberty more than the World Bank, Inter-American Development Bank, or U.S. AID."[2]

Those who advocate channeling more U.S. aid money through the international agencies tend to ignore three problems:

1. There is no evidence that these agencies can be depended on to administer the additional money any more effectively than in the past.

2. Once U.S. money is given to the international agencies, Congress has neither control over it nor knowledge of what happens to it. Thus the United States cannot correct problem number one.

3. Nothing indicates that the U.S. government cares enough about the money it gives the international agencies to solve problem number one even if it could.

The U.N. development agencies are a good example of this first problem.

> . . . The U.N. development system, through rapid growth and adminis-
> trative neglect, has become a tangled, monstrous nonsystem. It groups 30
> politically competitive governing boards which lack any effective coordina-
> tion, agreed priorities or sound evaluation procedures, and 90 client states
> scrambling to commandeer easy credit for often imprudent prestige proj-
> ects. The U.S. and other donor nations simply will not be willing to
> channel more funds through the U.N. until this snakepit of a development
> system is cleaned out.[3]

So editorialized *Life*—incorrectly. For the United States is going ahead with channeling more and more funds through this "snake-pit of a development system." Yet it is difficult to see how the United Nations' snakepit can ever be cleaned up without a thorough overhauling—and that is surely a remote, never-never bemusement.

A diplomat once compared reform of the United Nations Development Programme (UNDP) to the mating of elephants. "It is on a high level, there is a lot of trumpeting and stirring of dust, but any further development is at least 23 months away." Certainly a vast amount of change would be necessary to carry out effectively what Lester Pearson's widely acclaimed report of the Commission on International Development advocated: doubling the activities of the U.N. organizations and "perhaps quadrupling them if at the same time the total volume of official aid should" achieve its target.[4] A doubling or quadrupling on top of the present confusion does indeed boggle the mind.

Note that in 1968 there were fifty-seven members who were each assessed only 0.04 percent of the U.N. budget, yet each of these countries had the same voting strength as the United States which was assessed 31.57 percent,[5] a major factor why the United States has little power to insist on changes.

The many ministates lack the personnel to participate effective-ly, thus befuddling the U.N.'s administration. In 1970, out of 126 members, 16 had a population of less than 1 million. Even a nation with the personnel resources of the United States can barely keep up with today's United Nations which, in 1968, held 6,717 com-mittee meetings and produced 739,507,676 printed pages of docu-ments and speeches! Canada's External Affairs minister, Mitchell Sharpe, said the United Nations is "drowning in a sea of words."[6]

TESTIFYING RECENTLY before the House subcommittee on International Organizations, Elmer Staats, comptroller general of the United States, said the member governments of the United Nations cannot tell how proposed programs are carried out, nor are there "means of effectively assessing the overall development program. . . . Other than using the same financial year, not one aspect of budget presentation was uniform throughout the budgets of all U.N. agencies[7] . . . They don't even know what it is they are spending . . ."[8]

A better glimpse into the workings of the United Nations and its subsidiary organizations (to which, through 1970, the United States has contributed $3.9 billion)[9] can be seen in a series of recent reports to the Congress by Staats.

Concerning UNDP, designed to assist the hungry nations in their technical, economic and social development and to which the United States during the 1960s gave $550 million, Staats said, "Year after year the State Department has requested the Congress to appropriate increasing funds to be contributed to the program despite the fact that it is not, and has not been, in a position to give the Congress basic assurance that such funds have been used satisfactorily to accomplish intended objectives." Assistance in the amount of $100 million was granted to countries which were either "relatively developed or seemingly in a position to pay for such assistance . . ."[10] "There has been considerable evidence," Staats says, "that some of the United Nations agencies no longer have the capacity to administer effectively the ever-increasing number of United Nations Development Program projects being assigned to them."[11] Nevertheless President Nixon in 1970 requested that another $100 million again be given to this program.

In looking at the Food and Agriculture Organization (FAO), perhaps the most prestigious of the U.N. agencies, the comptroller general told Congress that while the U.S. contribution (of $219 million) pays 40 percent of FAO's budget, the United States has "no firm basis for making informed judgments, except in very broad terms, as to just what FAO is doing or plans to do with the contributions it has received. . . . It is therefore difficult, if not impossible, to determine the extent to which FAO activities are consistent with U.S. interest."[12]

Although our continuing contributions to the United Nations Children's Fund (UNICEF) total $260 million, U.S. officials have simply stopped analyzing the fund because they are not supplied with adequate information. "Current evaluations are insufficient in scope and coverage for officials to make informed, independent judgments relative to the efficiency and effectiveness of UNICEF . . ."[13]

At the hearing Congressman Dante B. Fascell asked, "What do we have to do . . . about clear and firm direction?"

STAATS: We don't think there is any doubt that the Secretary of State has this responsibility.

FASCELL: I think we have an absolute right to know whether we have accomplished what we have set out to do in those international organizations. . . . We certainly have the right to examine the results.

STAATS: Otherwise, you are simply going along for the sake of participating in an international body . . .

FASCELL: I am sure in many cases we are just doing that because it is politically necessary, but if we are to identify it as a political necessity, we ought to write it off as a political necessity. . . . Tell me this. Since the responsibility of the Secretary of State is so clearly defined, and he has the authority, what is wrong?

STAATS: I think, to be very honest about it, there is some feeling that some of the other agencies have more power.

FASCELL: You mean political power?

STAATS: More political power . . .[15]

This puts our contributions to the international agencies in their correct perspective. The money is given to gain political objectives, not to achieve development in the hungry world.

As with the U.N. agencies, we also do not have the authority to audit the activities of any of the international banks, such as the Inter-American Development Bank to which (up to 1970) we have subscribed $14.8 billion and have paid $8.1 billion.[16]

When the comptroller general's office insisted that it be given certain information, the Inter-American Development Bank, responding to this outside "pressure," did order an operational audit. A consultant who had been hired by the bank, John P. Powelson, whom I quoted in a preceding chapter, reported, "There is no integrated set of files by which a professional analyst can study a project as a whole. . . . It is to be predicted that these auditors will discover that the Bank files do not contain all the information they need to do their work properly."

It would appear that Powelson was correct. In 1970 Staats

testified that the Inter-American Development Bank is ". . . still in the process of making their first country review [audit]. . . . It has been three years now . . . It is an incredible situation . . . We have not been able to comment on draft audit reports, as the Congress contemplated that we would, because there have been no reports."

Fascell stated, "This problem exists all across the board in international agencies in which the United States is represented."[17]

The comptroller general emphasized that the United States was not getting the information from the Inter-American Development Bank to which it was already entitled.

STAATS: We would like to make a similar review to that which we made at these U.N. bodies, of the Inter-American Bank, but they will not give us the information.

FASCELL: Well, I really can't understand that attitude; . . . What is so sensitive about having the opportunity to examine facts and figures, policies and programs, which relate to the way in which U.S. contributions are spent?

STAATS: They act almost as if it was improper that we would even ask them a question.[18]

When money is appropriated for a program within the United States, Congress has a dozen direct and indirect ways to learn how well the money is spent, such as from constituents and the press. Even so, Congress does not spend taxpayers' money on a program at home without first providing that the expenditures be audited. Congress does, however, give billions of dollars to the international development agencies even though it does not have the power to order an audit of how they are used.

Obviously not all in Congress are willing to accept such an arrangement. The late Congressman James Fulton, Congressman Edward Roybal, and others included the following amendment to the 1971 foreign aid bill: "None of the funds herein appropriated for 'International Financial Institutions' shall be available to assist in the financing of any project or activity the expenditures for which are not subject to audit by the Comptroller General of the United States." When Congressman Fascell asked for comment, assistant secretary of the Treasury for International Affairs, John R. Petty, said the Nixon administration opposed the amendment because it would "seriously impair the [U.S.] ability to participate in the Asian Development Bank, the International Development Association, part of the World Bank family . . . It would be legally impossible for these institutions to accept the United States contributions with new conditions [without changing the ground rules] . . .'' The amendment was defeated.

Petty put the problem in perspective, saying, "It is basic to their character that no individual member can impose its own auditing requirements on the Bank as a condition of the use of its funds.''[19]

The charters of the international agencies place them beyond the purview of the men who provide the financing (the legislatures of the member states). Although agencies' decisions on development assistance are theoretically reviewed by boards of governors, or directors, or political councils, the actual situation is that the staffs are immune to the sort of thorough probings which U.S. government officials expect from Congress as a matter of course. For example, the presidents of both the World Bank and the Inter-American Development Bank would refuse to appear before a congressional committee even if asked to do so. They are not exactly above investigation; they are simply not affected by it.

Even if the United States *could* improve the efficiency of these agencies, no evidence is at hand to indicate that the United States cares enough to do so.

Frustrated at trying to get information out of the United Nations, the State Department asked its embassies throughout the world in 1967, 1968, and 1969 to evaluate how well the U.N. development agencies were conducting their assistance programs. "The nature of the responses did not present a convincing case that U.S. officials in the field were much aware of U.N. programs . . . or whether the projects were efficiently and effectively administered."[20] Billions are given to the international agencies and then American officials forget all about them.

Because President Nixon desires what he calls a "low international profile" and Congress desires to avoid the responsibility for making American foreign aid effective, we can expect that a greater and greater percentage of the U.S. foreign assistance budget will be turned over to the international agencies. The trend has been going on for years. From 1963 to 1970 U.S. contributions to the U.N. organizations increased by 59 percent while during the same period Congress appropriated 55 percent less for bilateral economic aid.[21]

Because it is apparently politically advantageous—not because it is an effective use of development funds—we now stand ready to give the international agencies still more money. And we stand ready—nay, we are eager—to do this without the audits and safeguards that prudence dictates.

"The new multilateral emphasis could be tantamount to broadcasting the combination of a vault."[22]

EACH YEAR the world spends the incredible sum of $200 billion on armaments and defense. The poverty-stricken, discouraged hungry nations themselves spend $26 billion of that sum. Typically, India spends about four and one-half times more money on defense than on education. Similar outlays are made by most of the struggling nations of Asia, Africa, and Latin America.[23]

Of such are created the ashes of the great hopes for peace expressed at the San Francisco conference in 1945 that gave birth to the United Nations. At the time, I remember, it was called the most important human gathering since the Last Supper. The specific purpose of the conference was to establish a method for maintaining international peace and security. The preamble of the U.N. Charter declares that its goal is "to save succeeding generations from the scourge of war."

Unhappily for everyone the United Nations has failed to accomplish this. Instead, its energies go into proliferating a multitude of agencies in all sorts of fields: children's welfare, prospecting for mineral resources, preinvestment studies, science "years," and so on. The United States itself is forced to allocate from its own tight budget ever-increasing funds because it pays roughly 31 percent of the expenses of these U.N. programs, organizations, and agencies.

The United Nations could obviously contribute most toward the economic development of the hungry nations by fulfilling the role designated for it: preserving law and order throughout the world. For if the United Nations were to succeed in its major responsibility of peace keeping, then the developing world could take the money it now buries in armament and put it into development. Lester B. Pearson, winner of the 1957 Nobel Peace Prize and chairman of the World Bank's Commission on International Development, doubts the United Nations will be around for its fiftieth anniversary unless it becomes more effective in dealing with the problem of peace.[24]

As we move into the 1970s, the world faces the specters of overpopulation, famine, and worsening poverty. Maybe it is not yet too late to make one more try to find a new approach for maintaining peace through the channel of the United Nations.

Resourceful and rich though this nation is, it has not found a way to make its aid effective. Nor do I think the international agencies are doing, or will do, any better with aid money than has my own government. Today the average American citizen is disappointed with foreign aid. Although some are still beset with feelings of guilt about their privileged affluence in a largely hungry world (and therefore urge Congress to pass foreign aid appropriations) all should be concerned that U.S. aid money remains so ineffective.

Despite my original intention to write an optimistic book describing effective development projects in Mexico and Central America that could be used as models elsewhere (remember my rather forlorn opening statements in the Prologue?), I have ended up by presenting a thoroughly unhappy account of the present status of all forms of foreign aid. I feel I must conclude this section with an effort to make these criticisms constructive. Thus I here propose a new approach for foreign aid action by the United States and by the United Nations. (At least I have not come across this proposal elsewhere.)

I present a one-two-three alternative to the armament drain, an alternative for which the United States itself can take the initiative.

1. Let the United States, unilaterally, make an annual contribution to the formation of a U.N. peace-keeping force. The amount would be whatever sum Congress would otherwise be willing to contribute to the development of foreign countries via all channels (AID, U.N. agencies, international banks, and the like), for the purpose of argument, say 2 billion dollars. This would be placed in escrow while the details of how to organize and regulate the peace-keeping force are worked out by the more than six score members of the United Nations. As they undoubtedly would haggle about this in their usual fashion for several years, the building up of this kitty each year might cause the United Nations to come forward with a firm set of controls for the peace-keeping force. The money accumulating in escrow would remove the problem of how to finance such a force, always until now the great handicap.

2. Hopefully the small, undeveloped nations would now accept this force as a realistic deterrent to the threat of invasion from across their borders. Thus they should feel adequately safe

and be willing to reassess the need to spend money for defense from their limited resources, and instead, spend that money for their own development. To aid and abet this reassessment, the United Nations would:

a. Contribute from its own development funds money to the small nations in proportion to the extent they cut their military budgets.

b. Extract from its industrialized member nations a pledge to offer special trade concessions to any hungry nation that does away entirely with its military budget and turns the maintenance of its security over to the U.N. peace-keeping force. Such trade concessions could be a vigorous step toward the much-advocated goal of "trade, not aid."

Experience has shown that those who talk about world peace plans seem to be impractical idealists, far removed from reality. But the ever-accelerating pell-mell race toward death in these last years of the twentieth century may provide the right climate for another try, at least in this specific area of the developing world. Certainly it is ridiculous for those nations hungrily to suck in aid at one end while at the other they flush it down the armament drain.

How can the United Nations be made effective?

Not through revamping all those nearly innumerable special agencies (International Refugee Organization, Children's Fund, Food and Agriculture Organization, Expanded Program of Technical Assistance, Commission on Narcotic Drugs, World Health Organization, etc., etc., etc.). Worthy though these organizations may be in concept, they are secondary to the United Nations' assigned function of protecting the world's peace. The effect which these agencies are having today is miniscule when compared to the exciting impact that could occur if the hungry nations would divert the $26 billion they now spend annually on armament to their own development.

Let Us First Learn How

"The admission of ignorance is the beginning of knowledge."

—ANON.

ASTOUNDING SURGES FORWARD have been made in the economic well-being of some of the areas I studied, such as Monterrey, San Pedro Sula, and Ciudad Obregon. In addition, I found the capital cities of the area bristling with new buildings and in most cases one can now safely drink the water and find an acceptable hotel room. The suburbs have inflated. The roads are better. The universities are bigger. Television aerials are most everywhere. Cars and their fumes bedevil the cities.

But these changes were due to the natural continuation of previous historical development, to the modern centralization of the regions's economy into a few major cities, and to the countries' own normal growth under the influence of the post-World War II boom—growth accelerated by bigger populations and huge debts. The changes are not, so far as I can see, the result of any catalytic stimulus brought about by external foreign assistance.

In my research I learned two things:

First, development professionals do not know how to carry out an effective economic development program, either a big one or a small one. *No one knows how*—not

the U.S. government, not the Rockefeller Foundation,
not the international banks and agencies, not the missionaries. I don't know how. You don't know how. No one
knows how.

Second, we don't know that we don't know how.
Those who give the money are thousands of miles removed
from where it is spent. No channel is provided whereby
they can get unbiased opinions about their projects in the
field in place of the usual fulsome reports of "great success." One barrier to this is that those who exercise their
profession in the field, who "work among the natives,"
soon acquire a Messiah complex. To wit: a corn breeder
in Iowa does not talk about his program SAVING Iowa.
But a corn breeder from Iowa who goes to Guatemala does
talk of his program as saving not only Guatemala but all
Central America and maybe even all the tropics. Such men
are biased sources of information about how well they are
spending the money given them. Yet they are the only
usual sources of information available to the journalist,
the congressman, or their own officials back home. Add to
this the fact that our aid programs maintain no memory
banks. Both the files and the personnel are ignorant of
previous programs, ignorant as to the reasons why they
were started, ignorant as to what the prevailing conditions
were then, ignorant as to why they failed and were
abandoned.

The result: We do not know that we do not know
how. We have no knowledge of our own ignorance.

I WRITE THIS on the 26th anniversary of Nazi Germany's
surrender to American forces under Eisenhower and remember my own confidence in the future, even though I
cheered the victory from a bed in a Marine field hospital
in the Pacific. Eisenhower's "Crusade in Europe" had indeed been a crusade. We had fought for a good cause and

we had won. Soon Japan would also surrender. We had saved the world through dint of our arms. Perforce, we had also become a supremely confident nation. Part of this confidence was later transplanted into massive foreign aid efforts to "develop" the world we had saved.

I was as certain as anyone in the postwar days that we could do the job. In making a plea that the American agricultural scientist should turn his talents to increasing the crop yields in the hungry nations, I wrote: "For, like the 'Triton among the minnows,' the [scientist's] power to increase agricultural production in an underdeveloped area might dwarf the increases he could perform in our own highly technological agriculture . . . One cannot minimize the importance of a science which seeks to destroy that on which communism feeds—hunger."[1]

We all thought then that science and technology, combined with our national energy and ability, had the answer for everything. All of us—certainly all of us in the development profession—passionately justified and tried to implement throughout the developing world great new programs which had barely been tested elsewhere, if at all. To us in the various branches of foreign aid, the glamour of a problem 10,000 miles across an ocean and down a winding jungle trail proved more compelling and exciting than the mundane problems at home. We were so sure of ourselves we did not even bother to set development priorities. To have done so would have been to acknowledge we had limitations.

When in 1949 President Truman asked that we share our technical skills (which he called "inexhaustible") with the developing world we had only 660,000 men under arms (today we have 1.3 million), our population was 25 percent smaller, we had $25 billion in gold and owed less than $4 billion (today we have $11 billion and owe more than $15 billion), our campuses were tranquil ("Black Power" was unborn). In 1949 only a few knew the word "ecology" and still fewer were aware of our accelerating environmental degradation.

Nevertheless today we continue our foreign aid as though it should have the same priority, the same urgency, and the same goals it had in 1949. Those who today are dedicating their lives to helping the hungry world still speak with the same passion and with the same phrases they used in the 1950s. Note that the following statements were all made in 1970:

"We must continue our assistance to the developing nations because the very survival of our civilization is at stake."[2] (Averell Harriman)

Foreign aid is man's "rendezvous with destiny"; if he cannot continue it "then possibly we are destined not to see but to foresee a planet empty—still spinning but no longer carrying the human race."[3] (Barbara Ward)

"A planet cannot survive half slave, half free, half engulfed in misery, half careening along toward the supposed joys of almost unlimited consumption."[4] (Lester Pearson)

Reduction in aid will mean world "disaster."[5] (Jan Tinbergen, Nobel Laureate)

Now, looking back from the vantage point of the early 1970s, we realize that appalling changes have been rising to the fore at home, although few saw the handwriting on the wall. Even now much of the development profession has yet to recognize the effect these changes must inevitably have on the future course of foreign aid. They do not recognize that crusades which once were given such high priority must now be superseded.

A bipartisan group of U.S. senators can accurately say, "Today . . . citizens bludgeon each other in the streets of New York, students die in a campus eruption. Buildings explode. Banks burn. The nation's colleges are shut down. The population is polarized, and there are parades of protest everywhere. Not since the

days of the Civil War have Americans treated each
other like this."[6]

Those who have so long advocated the need for
America to use its energies and talents in helping the
hungry nations can no longer ignore these frightening
changes at home. To paraphrase Senator Philip A.
Hart, "It's exciting to build a power plant in Brazil, but
it's important, also, to go shopping around the corner
without a police escort."[7]

No one, including myself, would question the
wisdom of the U.S. government having spent, since 1946,
$100 billion (plus the monies of foundations, missions,
individuals, etc.) in foreign assistance *if* its primary
objective had been achieved, namely, world stability
(or a semblance of it) through a greater well-being
for mankind. Indeed, no one would object to committing
another $100 billion—and another and another—*if* it
would buy us that dream.

The advocates of foreign aid condemn those who
would now curtail it by labeling them "isolationists." But
he who is against foreign aid is not automatically an
isolationist, just as an internationalist is not automatically
in favor of foreign aid. As for myself, I do not say to
withdraw from the United Nations, or to stop paying
our political assessments due the United Nations
development agencies, or to alter our military posture
throughout the world, or to modify our "4,500 treaties
and agreements"[8] which bind us to the community
of nations.

Yet I can no longer advocate foreign aid until we
first learn how to make it achieve its goals. Hence I
urge that we first use our own country as a laboratory:

To make hillside farming in Honduras profitable,
let us first learn how to solve the problems of subsistance
farming in Appalachia.

To motivate Catholic Colombians to limit their

family size, let us first learn how to motivate Puerto Ricans to cut their population growth.

To provide housing in restless Bombay, let us first learn how to rebuild our own ghettos.

To serve the medical needs of Ecuadorian Indians, let us first learn how to provide medical care to the Indians in Arizona.

To advise how to improve governmental procedures in Nicaragua, let us first learn how to modernize our own government, ranging from the problem of eliminating the stultifying seniority system in Congress to the problem of bringing the parasite suburbs into their proper municipal system.

To eradicate malaria in Ceylon let us first learn how to eliminate gonorrhea in Los Angeles.

To advise how to prevent Uruguay's socialism from destroying the nation's stability, let us first learn how to make Medicare pay as it goes.

To make the wheat farmers of India competitive with the world, let our cotton growers first learn how to farm without subsidies.

To eliminate the electrical power shortage in Rio de Janeiro, let us first learn how to do this in northeast United States.

To induce Pakistan to cut spending on armaments, let us first learn how to curtail our own $80 billion military budget.

To advise how to prevent political activists from disrupting the University of Caracas, let us first learn how to do this at the University of Wisconsin.

To help control the inflation which hobbles development in Indonesia, let us first learn how to control it at home.

To stop the disruptive migration to the cities in Peru, let us first learn how to slow the migration to our own suburbs.

To lower the sewage content of the Ganges, let us first learn how to clean up the Hudson and the Missouri.

To make literacy a development resource in Costa Rica, let us first learn how to profitably employ the unskilled among our own population.

To eliminate hunger in the world, let us first learn how to improve the diets of the 5 million malnourished Americans who cannot afford the food they need.

To advise how to stop kidnappings and terrorist bombings in Guatemala, let us first learn how to do this in New York City and San Francisco.

The list can be as long as the problems found throughout the hungry nations.

List of Personal Interviews

THE FOLLOWING is a list of persons interviewed during the course of our research on this book as well as those consulted (for a few by letter or telephone) for supporting information. Not included here is a variety of villagers, farmers, cooperators, volunteers, hospital patients, tourists, taxi drivers, pedestrians, *ejidatarios,* shopkeepers, and tax collectors:

Angel Aguilar C., Campbell's de México, S. A. de C. V., Mexico; Oscar Alfaro, head of Social and Population Study Center, Costa Rica; Armando Alfonzo A., Productivity Center, Mexico; Aaron Altschul, special assistant to the secretary of agriculture, Washington, D.C.; Fernando Alvarez, secretary of agriculture, Dominican Republic; Severiano Arias, farmer, Mexico; Robert Armour, director, Panamerican School of Agriculture (EAP), Honduras; Ragnar Arnesen, director, AID, Nicaragua; Dario Arrieta M., director general of horticulture, Mexico; César Artega G., agricultural scientist, El Salvador; Edwin Astle, AID, Honduras; Antonio Aycinena, businessman, banker, farmer, Guatemala.

Alicia Baca G., primary school principal, Mexico; Jasper Baker, assistant vice-president, United Fruit Co., Washington, D.C.; John Barber, commercial attaché, U.S. Consulate, Mexico; Lloyd Barber, ROCAP/AID, Washington, D.C.; Marcial Barrios, experiment station director, Guatemala; Mario Barrios, businessman, cabinet maker, Guatemala; Edwin M. Barton, Columbia University School of Medicine, New York City; Linn Bates, graduate student, Purdue University; Moisés Béhar, director, INCAP, Guatemala; Carroll Behrhorst, medical doctor, Guatemala; Andrew B. Bellingham, agricultural officer, U.S. Embassy, Mexico; Frank Bendaña, agricultural consultant, Nicaragua; Oscar Beneke, director, Demographic Association, El Salvador; Edgar F. Berman, medical doctor, Baltimore, Md.; Antonio Berrios M., minister of agriculture, El Salvador; Benjamin Birdsall (retired), AID, Washington, D.C.; Alfonso Blandón, economist, Banco Nacional, Nicaragua; Isaias Bolio B., government official, Mexico; Clarence Boonstra, U.S. ambassador, Costa Rica; Norman Borlaug, Rockefeller Foundation, Mexico; Brian R. Bosworth, ROCAP/AID, Guatemala; William G. Bowdler, U.S. ambassador, El Salvador; Damon

Boynton, U.S.D.A., El Salvador; Oscar Brauer, director of graduate studies, Escuela Nacional de Agricultura, Mexico; Robert Bravo, AID, Dominican Republic; Augustín Brenes B., medical doctor, Nicaragua; Dwight S. Brothers, Harvard University; Aaron Brown, former U.S. ambassador to Nicaragua, interviewed in New York City; Harold Brown, College of Physicians and Surgeons, Columbia University, New York City; Lester Brown, senior fellow, Overseas Development Council, Washington, D.C.; William Brown, vice-president, Pioneer Hybrid Corn Co., Des Moines, Iowa; Almyr Bump, businessman, Guatemala; Victor R. Burgos, World Tapes for Education, El Salvador.

Arturo Cabezas, Clinica Biblica, Costa Rica; Rudolfo Calles, farmer, Mexico; Gilberto R. Campos, University of San Carlos, Costa Rica; Carlos H. Canales, director general of public health, Nicaragua; José Antonio Cantón, director, PUMAR, Nicaragua; Antonio Carillo Flores, foreign minister, Mexico; James R. Carpenter, Peace Corps volunteer, El Salvador; Rudolfo Carrandi, Inter-American Development Bank, Guatemala; José Ramón Carvallo, medical doctor, Nicaragua; Carlos Castillo Q., deputy minister of public health, Nicaragua; Carlos Manuel Castillo, secretary general, SIECA, Guatemala; Eduardo Castillo C., assistant manager, Cerveceria Centro Americana, S.A., Guatemala; Luis Manlio Castillo, hybrid seed corn producer, Guatemala; Maria Victoria Castillo C., businesswoman, Guatemala; Ramiro Castillo, assistant manager, Castillo Hermanos, Guatemala; Yvonne Ortega de Castillo, nurse, Nicaragua; Juan José Castro, AID, Costa Rica; Alva la Cayo, Nicaragua; Gregoria Pérez v. de la Cayo, PUMAR committee member, Nicaragua; Alphonse Chable, AID, Guatemala; Jaime Chacón, manager, National Colonization Program, El Salvador; Carlos Chávez, Campbell's de México, S.A. de C.V., Mexico; Manuel Chávez, head of customs service, El Salvador; Milcíades Chávez, PUMAR supervisor, Nicaragua; Norman Christianson, businessman, Mexico; Heríberto Cisneros, president, Alliance, S.A., El Salvador; George R. Clark, Girard Trust Bank of Philadelphia; Philander P. Claxton, Jr., assistant to the secretary of state on population matters, Washington, D.C.; Darryl Cole, farmer, Costa Rica; Joseph S. Courand, AID, Guatemala; Rogelio Cova, American Friends Service Committee, Mexico; Milo Cox, head of rural development, Latin American Bureau, AID, Washington, D.C.; Kennedy M. Crockett, U.S. ambassador, Nicaragua; Harry Cromer, staff director, Foreign Affairs Committee, Washington, D.C.; Luis Crouch, director of agricultural school (ISA), Dominican Republic; Ernesto Cruz, head of business school (INCAE), Nicaragua; Robert E. Culbertson, deputy assistant secretary of state (AID), Washington, D.C.; John Curry, U.S. Embassy, Mexico.

Dana Dalrymple, U.S.D.A., Washington, D.C.; David S. Davies, program office, AID, Washington, D.C.; Nathaniel Davis, U.S. ambassador, Guatemala; Carrol Deyoe, AID, Honduras; Manuel Díaz P., manager, Textiles Hércules, S.A., Mexico; Nicholas Díaz, director, Del Monte, Mexico; Edward L. Doheny, Catholic agricultural missionary, Guatemala; Ricardo Dominguez, ministry of agriculture, El Salvador; William Drummond, Crop Quality Control (Minneapolis, Minn.), Mexico; Edwin Duckles, commissioner for Latin America, American Friends Service Committee, Mexico.

Miguel Elvir, Inter-American Institute of Agricultural Sciences, Guatemala; Lucila Esquivel A., government clerk, Mexico.

Arthur Faber, businessman, Mexico; Arturo Falla C., coffee farmer, Guatemala; Pedro Alfonso Fernández, PUMAR committee president, Nicaragua; Romeo Fernández, Ralston Purina agent, Guatemala; Paul Findley, member, House of Representatives, Washington, D.C.; William A. Flexner, population officer, AID, El Salvador; Victor Flores H., Banco Fomento, Guatemala; Victor C. Folsom, United Fruit Co., Boston, Mass.; Hernán Fonseca, University of San Carlos, Costa Rica; Luis Fonseca F., port authority, Honduras; Martin Forman, AID, Washington, D.C.; Aureliano Franco B., *ejidatario*, Mexico; Carlos Franco C., director, Plan Chontalpa, Mexico; Fulton Freeman, U.S. ambassador, Mexico; Richard Froberg, North Dakota State College study team, Mexico; Alejandro Fuentes, Ministry of Agriculture, Guatemala; Oscar Fuentes, Ministry of Agriculture, Guatemala.

William K. Gamble, Ford Foundation, Mexico; Pierre Ganthier, Cornell University population study team, Honduras; Mario García Salas, cotton farmer, Guatemala; Louis Gardella, AID, Nicaragua; Hanun B. Gardner, United Fruit Co., Boston, Mass.; Antonio Garza M., Campbell's de México, S.A. de C.V., Mexico; John Gibler, Rockefeller Foundation, Mexico; Juan Gil Preciado, secretary of agriculture, Mexico; Ana Gomez, U.S. Embassy, Mexico; Alberto González, businessman, El Salvador; Vance Goodfellow, Crop Quality Control (Minneapolis, Minn.), Mexico; George Goodrich, Campbell's de México, S.A. de C.V., Mexico; Thomas Gore, World Neighbors, Oklahoma City, Okla.; Eric S. Graber, Iowa State University study team, Guatemala; Victor E. Green, University of Florida/ AID, Costa Rica; Henry Greene, Panamerican Development Foundation, Washington, D.C.; Sam Greene, Penny Foundation, Guatemala; Allan Greenstreet, British MD volunteer, Guatemala; Wade F. Gregory, U.S.D.A., Washington, D.C.; José Guevara C., assistant head, INIA, Mexico; Robert Gussick, missionary, Guatemala; Gilberto Guttiérez, Ministry of Agriculture, Costa Rica; Rodrigo Guttiérez S., dean of medical school, Costa Rica.

Donald Halper, Harvard University professor, INCAE, Nicaragua; John Hannah, director, AID, Washington, D.C.; Lowell Hardin, program officer, Ford Foundation, New York City; Vernon Harness, U.S.D.A., Washington, D.C.; James Harrington, CIMMYT, Mexico; Lawrence Harrison, mission director, AID, Costa Rica; Nathan Haverstock, columnist on Latin America, Washington, D.C.; Arlon Hazen, director for research, North Dakota State College, Fargo, N.D.; Lewis M. Hellman, HEW, Washington, D.C.; Luciano Hernandez, American Friends Service Committee, Mexico; Felipe Herrera, president, Inter-American Development Bank, Washington, D.C.; Larry Herrmann, Pan-American Development Foundation, Washington, D.C.; Reed Hertford, U.S.D.A., Washington, D.C.; Dean R. Hinton, mission director, AID, Guatemala; Donald Hinz, missionary, Guatemala; Lloyd Holmes, U.S.D.A., El Salvador; Fred Holschuh, Public Health Service, Dept. of Indian Affairs, Keams Canyon, Ariz.; Claud L. Horn, U.S.D.A., El Salvador; Gerard F. Horne, AID, Guatemala; Eduardo P. Hovelman, executive secretary, Chamber of Commerce, Mexico;

Sylvia Hurtado, PUMAR nurse, Nicaragua; B. Hutchinson, Peace Corps director, El Salvador; Earl E. Huyck, population officer, AID, Costa Rica.

Ernest Imle, American Cocoa Research Institute, Washington, D.C.

Edward Jamison, U.S. consul, Mexico; Dorothy Jester, economist, U.S. Embassy, Mexico; Charles B. Johnson, AID, Nicaragua; Elmer C. Johnson, Rockefeller Foundation, Mexico; Harvey Johnson, United Fruit Company, Honduras; Joseph J. Jova, U.S. ambassador, Honduras.

Thomas Keane, businessman, Guatemala; John Keppel, Foreign Service Institute, Washington, D.C.; Miner Kielhauer, businessman, Guatemala; Thomas Killoran, AID, Washington, D.C.; James King, AID, Guatemala; Barry Klein, AID, Costa Rica; Erich Knoetzsch, medical doctor, Guatemala; Carl D. Koone, AID, Nicaragua; Uwe Kracht, Quaker Oats, Chicago, Ill.; Max Vance Krebs, U.S. Embassy, Guatemala; A. E. Kretschmer, University of Florida/AID, Costa Rica; Bernardo Kummerfeldt, businessman, Guatemala.

Carlos Lara, pediatrician, Guatemala; Marion Larson, U.S.D.A., Washington, D. C.; Milton Lau, AID, Guatemala; Juan J. Leiva, Ministry of Agriculture, Costa Rica; Humberto León, National Development Bank, Honduras; Francisco Linares-Aranda, Guatemalan ambassador to U.S., Washington, D.C.; Norman Lind, businessman, Guatemala; Francis A. Lineville, ROCAP/AID, Guatemala; Norman Lodato, AID, Washington, D.C.; George C. Lodge, Harvard University, Washington, D.C.; Clarence D. Long, member, House of Representatives, Washington, D.C.; Andrés F. Lopez, Chamber of Commerce, Honduras; Antonio H. Lopez V., Ministry of Natural Resources, Honduras; Alfonso Lovo C., Ministry of Agriculture, Nicaragua.

Robert McColaugh, AID contract, Guatemala; Paul and Mary McKay, World Neighbors, Guatemala; Vernon Madrigal, medical director, Demographic Association, El Salvador; José Romeo Maeda, Catholic priest organizing cooperatives, El Salvador; Thomas C. Mann, former assistant secretary of state, Washington, D.C.; Parker G. Marden, Cornell University population study team, Honduras; Hugo Margáin, Mexican ambassador to the U.S., Washington, D.C.; Clemente Marroquín Rojas, vice-president, Guatemala; Gregorio Martinez, CIMMYT, Mexico; Porfirio Masaya, Ministry of Agriculture, Guatemala; Mrs. N. K. Masten, granddaughter of Davis Richardson, early developer of Ciudad Obregón area, Mexico; Roberto Maurer, wheat farmer, Mexico; Gabriel Mejía, president, Financia Hondureña, S.A., Honduras; Emilio Mendizábal, department head, Public Health Service, Guatemala; Amador Mendoza N., Department of Water Resources, Mexico; Fernando Mendoza, executive secretary, mayor's office, Ciudad Obregón, Mexico; Pedro Mendoza G., executive secretary, Querétaro Chamber of Commerce; Mexico; Henry Alirio Menendez, extension agent, El Salvador; Ricardo Midence, Honduran ambassador to the U.S., Washington, D.C.; José Mirón M., ANACAFE, Guatemala; Paul A. Montavon, ROCAP/AID, Guatemala; Francisco Montenegro G., minister of agriculture, Guatemala; Abelardo Morales, American Friends Service

Committee, Mexico; Benedito Morán H., colonist, Guatemala; Alvaro Muñoz, Ministry of Agriculture, Costa Rica; Guillermo Muñoz, National Production Council, Costa Rica; Gabriel Murillo, Escuela de Agricultura "Antonio Narro," Mexico; Delbert Myren, CIMMYT, Mexico.

José Jesus Neve, Ministry of Agriculture, Mexico; Robert Newbegin, former U.S. ambassador to Honduras, Washington, D.C.; A. H. Newhall, Cornell University professor emeritus, Washington, D.C.; John S. Niederhauser, Rockefeller Foundation, Mexico; Jorge Nieto, INIA, Chapingo, Mexico; Don Novotny, U.S.D.A., Washington, D.C.

James J. O'Connor, St. Joseph College (Philadelphia, Pa.) study team, Guatemala; Paul L. Oechsli, mission director, AID, El Salvador; Covey T. Oliver, assistant secretary of state, Washington, D.C.; Enrique Ordoñez, farmer, Guatemala; Francisco Osegueda, director, National School of Agriculture, El Salvador; Robert D. Osler, Rockefeller Foundation, Mexico; Roberto Osoyo A., director general of agriculture, Mexico.

Bailey Pace, AID, Washington; Guillermo Padilla, director, Technical Institute, Guatemala; Raphael Pérez Palma, attorney, judge, Mexico; Mildred Palmer, businesswoman, Guatemala; Felipe Pasquara L., Campbell's de México, S.A. de C.V., Mexico; Henry Passmore, American Friends Service Committee, Mexico; Raúl Peimbert, Ralston Purina de México, S.A. de C.V., Mexico; J. Antonio Peraza, minister of public health, Honduras; Gregoria de Perea, PUMAR committee member, Nicaragua; José G. Pérez, director, Extension Service, El Salvador; John L. Peters, president, World Neighbors, Oklahoma City; Virgil Petersen, AID, El Salvador; George D. Peterson, U.S.D.A., Nicaragua; Ruben Pimental, U.S. Embassy, Mexico; Julio C. Pineda, minister of natural resources, Honduras; Galo Plaza, secretary general, O.A.S., Washington, D.C.; Joseph Polakoff, ROCAP, Guatemala; Fidencio Puente, experiment station director, Mexico; José de la Puente, director general, Forestry Service, Mexico.

Roberto Quesada, farm manager, Mexico.

Gustavo Reta P., director general of animal industry, Mexico; Padre Rentko, missionary, farm cooperative organizer, Mexico; Efraín Humberto Reyna, director of coffee research station, Guatemala; Julio Adalberto Rivera, El Salvador ambassador to the U.S., Washington, D.C.; William Roberts, Rockefeller Foundation, Mexico; Leonel Robles, director, Instituto Technológico, Mexico; Richard J. Roderick, general manager, Productos del Monte, S.A. de C.V., Mexico; William L. Rodman, U.S. Embassy, Mexico; Antonio L. Rodríguez, Impresora del Norte, Mexico; Edgardo D. Rodríguez, businessman, Honduras; José Rodríguez V., Coker of Mexico, S.A., Mexico; Juan Rodríguez, PUMAR committee member, Nicaragua; Bernardo Roehrs, farm manager, Guatemala; Juan Rohrmann L., vice-president, ANACAFE, Guatemala; Alvaro Rojas, Ministry of Agriculture, Costa Rica; John Rouleau, Department of State, Washington, D.C.; Armando Ruíz, PUMAR committee secretary, Nicargua; Hector Luis Ruíz, PUMAR committee member, Nicaragua; Roberto Ruíz, president, Embotelladora la Victoria, S.A., Mexico.

Andres M. Sada, businessman, Mexico; Carlos A. Salas, University of San Carlos, Costa Rica; Angel Salazar, DeKalb Seed Corn Co., Nicaragua; Jorge M. Salazar, Ministry of Agriculture, Costa Rica; Luis Salazar A., president, ANACAFE, Guatemala; José P. Saldaña, author, newspaperman, Mexico; Carlos Sánchez L., municipal treasurer, Mexico; Dolores Sánchez, farmer, Mexico; Nicolás Sánchez D., director of agricultural research, Mexico; Plutarco Sánchez G., Banco de Mexico, Mexico; Leopoldo Sandoval, O.A.S., Guatemala; Ruben Sarmiento O., Chamber of Commerce executive secretary, Mexico; William Schaeffer, AID, Costa Rica; Eugene Schieber, Ministry of Agriculture, Guatemala; Fred P. Sheehy, United Fruit Co., Honduras; Lyle Schertz, acting director, International Development Service, U.S.D.A., Washington, D.C.; Richard Smith, U.S. Embassy, Mexico; Francisco de Sola, businessman, El Salvador; Ramón Solano, AID, Honduras; Arturo Solórzano F., vice-president, ANACAFE, Guatemala; Oscar Nery Sosa, director of agricultural extension and research, Guatemala; William E. Spruce, U.S. Embassy, Mexico; Raymond Stadelman, AID, Guatemala; G. A. Stanford, U.S. Embassy, Mexico; James H. Starkey, III., U.S. Embassy, Mexico; James Stevenson, Ford Foundation, Mexico; John Strohm, publisher, Chicago; Phillip Stubblefield, Peace Corps, Washington, D.C.; J. Mayone Stycos, Cornell University study team, Honduras.

Alceo Tablada S., deputy minister of agriculture, Nicaragua; Guillermo Tamacas, Ministry of Agriculture, El Salvador; Philip B. Taylor, Johns Hopkins University, Washington, D.C.; Charles Teller, Cornell University study team, Honduras; Theodore Tenorio, AID, Mexico; Morris A. Thompson, director of operations for Mexico and Latin America, Del Monte, Mexico; Earl Threadgold, Peace Corps volunteer, El Salvador; Luis Demetrio Tinoco, Costa Rican ambassador to the U.S., Washington, D.C.; Luciano Tomassini, assistant to the president, Inter-American Development Bank, Washington, D.C.; Humberto Toval, Fertica, El Salvador; Walter Turnbull (retired), United Fruit Company, Mexico.

T. Graydon Upton, executive vice-president, Inter-American Development Bank, Washington, D.C.

Rodolfo Valdés M., Industria del Hierra, S.A., Mexico; Machado Valle, United Fruit Co., Honduras; H. Van Nes, manager, Del Monte plant, Mexico; Alberto Vargas, Compañia Agricola Nainari, L.C., Mexico; Siffrein Vass, managing director, Ford of Mexico, Mexico; Jack Vaughn, director, Peace Corps, Washington, D.C.; Emmy Velis, Peace Corps, El Salvador; Gustavo Víchy, department head, PROSA, Guatemala; Juan Villanueva, experiment station director, Mexico; Ismael Villasenos R., high school principal, Mexico; Ramón Villeda M., former president, Honduras; Frederick J. Vintinner, chief public health advisor, AID, Guatemala; William Vogt, conservationist, author, New York.

James Walker, AID, Guatemala; E. J. Wellhausen, Rockefeller Foundation, Mexico; Jorge Wellman P., Ministry of Agriculture, Guatemala; George Westcott, Robert Nathan Associates, El Salvador; Donald Winkelmann, Ford Foundation, Mexico; Sterling Wortman, Rockefeller Foundation, New York City.

Guillermo Yglesias P., minister of agriculture, Costa Rica; Stephen Youngberg, medical missionary, Honduras.

William Zaumeyer (retired), U.S.D.A., Beltsville, Md.; Jacobo Zelaya, Panamerican School of Agriculture (EAP), Honduras.

NOTES

===

PROLOGUE

1. The total U.S. government expenditure for foreign aid since 1946 is $149.5 billion which is broken down as follows: Agency for International Development and predecessor agencies $51.5 billion; military programs $42.0 billion; Export Import Bank $13.7 billion; Food for Peace $19.7 billion; other (such as contributions to international organizations) $22.6 billion. (U.S. Overseas Loans and Grants, preliminary FY 1971 and trend data, October 29, 1971, AID Office of Statistics and Reports, Washington, D.C.)

CAMEO (PART 1)

1. U.S. Overseas Loans and Grants, p. 46. AID special report prepared for the House Foreign Affairs Committee, April 24, 1970.

CHAPTER 1

1. *Maize Cultivation in Northwestern Guatemala,* Contributions to American Anthropology and History, no. 33 (Washington, D.C.: Carnegie Institution, 1940).
2. Max F. Millikan and David Hapgood, *No Easy Harvest* (Boston: Little, Brown, 1967).
3. Lehman B. Fletcher et al., *Agricultural Development and Policy in Guatemala* (Ames: Iowa State University Press, 1969).
4. Letter from Associate Director Richard E. Kaegi to William Paddock, April 17, 1970.

CHAPTER 2

1. Broadcast, Manion Forum, March 1, 1970.
2. A. T. Knoppers, Hearings before the Subcommittee on Foreign Economic Policy, May 19, 1970.

CHAPTER 3

1. Townsend Hoopes, *Limits of Intervention* (New York: McKay, 1969), p. 205.

2. *Asian Drama,* vol. 1 (Boston: Pantheon, 1968), p. 22.
3. July 9, 1970.
4. *Washington Post,* July 5, 1970.

CHAPTER 4

1. "A Mobile Rural Health Services Program in Central America and Panama," *American Journal of Public Health,* May 1968, pp. 907–14.
2. During my stay in Nicaragua, an assortment of complications arose in connection with research on other parts of this book. Time ran out for me to complete this particular study on my own. Accordingly, I relied on David Mangurian, an old friend and a free-lance journalist with three years' experience in Central America, to finish the research for me. Either he or I or both of us interviewed all higher-level Nicaraguan and U.S. government officials concerned with PUMAR and visited villages served by different mobile units. To be consistent, I continue to use the editorial "I."

CHAPTER 5

1. Figure covers expenditures from July 1945 to June 1970 and represents economic aid. Military aid has cost an additional $40 billion. Source: Office of Statistics and Reports, Agency for International Development, Washington, D.C.
2. *Dacor Bulletin,* June 1970. Published by Diplomatic and Consular Officers, Retired, Washington, D.C.
3. *Ceres,* March–April 1970, p. 15.
4. *New York Times,* November 19, 1969.
5. Message from the president to Congress, transmitting proposals to redirect our efforts in foreign aid, May 28, 1969.
6. U.S., Congress, Senate, *Congressional Record,* 91st Cong., 2nd sess., March 26, 1970, p. S4594.
7. "The Challenge of Development," AID Publicity Release, August 1969.
8. Felix Belair, *New York Times,* July 10, 1970.
9. March 17, 1970.
10. U.S., Congress, Senate, Committee on Foreign Relations, *Hearing on S. 2347,* 91st Cong., 1st sess., July 14, 1969.
11. Figures obtained by telephone from Norman Lodato, manpower coordinator, Management Planning, AID, July 6, 1970.
12. *Washington Post,* March 29, 1970.
13. Donald S. Green, deputy executive director, Peterson Task Force, *War on Hunger,* May 1970.
14. *Front Lines,* September 24, 1969.
15. Lloyd A. Free, *Front Lines,* September 24, 1969.
16. Public and Parliamentary Opinion (internal document), AID, April 7, 1971.

CHAPTER 6

1. "The Road to Peace," in *The Peace Corps,* ed. Aaron J. Ezickson (New York: Hill & Wang, 1965), p. 2.
2. Ibid.
3. Ibid., pp. xi, xii.
4. Unpublished minutes of J. K. Rouleau, meeting of the Science for the

Alliance Committee of the Bureau of International Scientific and Technological Affairs, Department of State, February 21, 1963.

5. "The Road to Peace," pp. 52–56; Glenn D. Kittler, *The Peace Corps* (New York: Paperback Library, 1963), pp. 32, 60, 61, 96—100; "Peace Corpsman in Tonacatepeque," *St. Jude,* May 1963, pp. 29–33; Rebecca Allerding, "Variety Spices Peace Corps Life," *State Lantern* (Columbus, Ohio), March 12, 1964.

6. Letter from Richard H. Hancock to Dr. Maude A. Stewart, May 18, 1963.

CHAPTER 7

1. Interview with Edwin Duckles, November 13, 1968.
2. "'Friends' for Rural Mexico," *Mexican-American Review,* June 1969.
3. Latin American Program Report of Agricultural Experiment, Cuauhtenco, Tlaxcala, Mexico, 1967–1968. American Friends Service Committee, Inc., August 1968. (Mimeographed)
4. "'Friends' for Rural Mexico."

CHAPTER 8

1. Earlier talks with a former head of the Lutheran missionaries in Central America have convinced me that while they are interested in "saving souls," they also have as sincere, as deep-rooted, and as active a desire to alleviate the poverty and sickness found in the Guatemalan Indian community as does any group working in the area.
2. *Cross and Caduceus,* November–December 1966.
3. Edwin Barton, *Physician to the Mayas, The Story of Dr. Carroll Behrhorst* (Philadelphia: Fortress Press, 1970).
4. *Cross and Caduceus.*
5. On the NBC Today Show (October 7, 1970) Dr. Behrhorst said, "Where we work in the central highlands of Guatemala, we serve over 400,000 people."
6. Letter to William C. Paddock, July 24, 1970.
7. *Cross and Caduceus,* November–December 1966; *Roche Medical Image* (undated).
8. "Report on the effects of the Behrhorst program on the health, agriculture, and health care resources of the Department of Chimaltenango, Guatemala," p. 19. Undated, but covers a study made during March, April, and May 1968, Department of Community Medicine, College of Medicine, University of Kentucky.
9. Without knowing it was discrediting Dr. Behrhorst's number, World Neighbors gave me their figures which indicated the actual number of IUD's inserted was, at the time, less than 500.
10. John F. Kantner, in *Family Planning and Population Programs: A View of World Developments,* ed. Bernard R. Berelson et al. (Chicago: University of Chicago Press, 1966), p. 404.
11. Letter from William H. Kohn to William Paddock, June 11, 1969.
12. Letter from John L. Peters to Elizabeth Paddock, June 2, 1970.
13. Letter from Carroll Behrhorst to Elizabeth Paddock, June 3, 1970.
14. *Cross and Cauduceus,* November–December 1966. Other Lutheran publications discussing Dr. Behrhorst: *Cross and Caduceus,* January–February 1970; *The Badger Lutheran,* November 20, 1969; *Vanguard,* March 1970; *Torch,* April 24, 1970; *Bridge,* March 1970.
15. U.S., Congress, Senate, *Congressional Record,* 91st Cong., 2nd sess., July 1, 1970, 116, pt. 17:22436.

CHAPTER 9

1. William Vogt, "Comments on a brief reconnaissance of a resource use, progress and conservation needs in some Latin American countries." (Washington, D.C.: Conservation Foundation, 1963), p. 8.

2. "The Population Problem of El Salvador," *Proceedings of the Conference on the Population Explosion and the Developing Professional,* Warrenton, Va., 1969.

3. J. Mayone Stycos, *Human Fertility in Latin America* (Ithaca: Cornell University Press, 1968), p. 49.

CHAPTER 10

1. AID congressional presentation, June 1969, p. G-42.

2. The Ford Motor Company also does not know how. It designed an excellent tractor for peasant agriculture and market surveys showed its price was right. But to sell it Ford chose people who were totally unfamiliar with conditions outside of the United States and who had no experience negotiating with local governments for the needed import permits. With a former Philco Company (electronics) public relations man in charge, the sales group was ignorant of both the problems of the small tropical farmer and of credit sources available to him. Not surprisingly, they located few buyers. Thus rather than trying further and possibly getting another Edsel on its face, $2 million in development technology was scrapped.

3. William Schock, Voluntary Agencies, AID, Washington, D.C., by telephone, July 6, 1970.

4. *Britannica Book of the Year 1971* (Chicago: Encyclopaedia Britannica, Inc., 1971), pp. 520–521.

CHAPTER 11

1. José P. Saldaña, "Apuntes Históricos Sobre la Industrialización de Monterrey, Centro Patronal de Nuevo León, 1965; Secretaría de Industria y Comercio, Dirección General de Estadística, Anuario Estadístico de los Estados Unidos Mexicanos 1964–1965, Talleres Gráficos de la Nación, Mexico, 1967.

CHAPTER 12

1. Stacy May and Galo Plaza, *Case Study of the United Fruit Company in Latin America* (Washington, D.C.: National Planning Association, 1953), p. 20.

2. Letter from Hanun B. Gardner, United Fruit Co., Law Department, to William Paddock, June 30, 1969.

3. By telephone from Jasper Baker, United Fruit Co., Washington, D.C., July 7, 1970.

4. Calculated from data in the *Carta Informativa* no. 86, SIECA, Secretaría Permanente del Tratado, General de Integración Económica Centroamericana, December 1968; letter from Hanun B. Gardner with data obtained from the controller's office of the United Fruit Co., June 30, 1969.

CHAPTER 13

1. Charter of Punta del Este, section 6, title I.

2. Clyde Mitchell and Jacob Schantan, in *Agricultural Development in*

Latin America: The Next Decade (Washington, D.C.: Inter-American Development Bank, April 1967), pp. 79–80.

3. *Guatemala, World Development Program, Final Report, 1955–1956* (Washington, D.C.: International Development Services, Inc.), pp. 1–2.

4. Ibid., p. 10.

5. Ibid., p. 8.

6. Ross Pearson, "Zones of Agricultural Development in Guatemala: An Experiment in Land Reform," *Journal of Geography* (January 1963), pp. 11–22.

7. IDS report, p. 11.

8. Pearson, p. 22.

9. The name comes from the principal river in the region; the colonization program is part of the *Plan de la Chontalpa,* which is under the *Comisión del Grijalva.* I use "Grijalva" for the sake of simplicity, which is the same reason I refer to the *ejidatarios* as "colonists" in this chapter.

10. Thomas T. Poleman, *The Papaloapan Project, Agricultural Development in the Mexican Tropics* (Stanford, Calif.: Stanford University Press, 1964), pp. 139–40.

CHAPTER 15

1. If this is the first time the land has been planted for several years, the farmer will have a good "burn" as he touches the match to the brush. He will have relatively few weeds or insect problems that season. In successive seasons there will be less to burn, the heat of the flames will kill fewer weed seeds and insects, and the competition from weeds and the damage from insects will increase. After three or four years, it will be easier for the farmer to move on to a new piece of land than to stay and fight the rapidly proliferating weeds and insects.

2. An exception is areas of the tropics where rice is raised under irrigation—flooding acts as an easy means of weed control.

CAMEO (PART 4)

1. Population Crisis Committee, Washington, D.C. "Birth Control Expert Reports on Family Planning in India," news release, June 21, 1966.

2. *Planned Parenthood Monthly Bulletin* (Bombay: Family Planning Association of India), April 1970; Shri Govind Narain, "India, the Family Planning Program since 1965," *Studies in Family Planning* (published by the Population Council), November 1968.

CHAPTER 16

1. Dr. Benjamin J. Birdsall, now retired, was a most experienced foreign aid technician. From 1942 to 1946 he directed the U.S. program in Tingo María, Peru, which was, by my calculation, the first sustained foreign assistance program undertaken by the United States. In addition, he had headed agricultural programs in Panama, Indonesia, and El Salvador.

2. Undated memo received from Covey Oliver, September 4, 1968.

3. *Los Angeles Times,* March 7, 1968.

4. Report by Benjamin Birdsall, November 18, 1966. Yields have been converted here from quintales per manzana to bushels per acre.

5. Benjamin J. Birdsall, Report on the Mass Fertilizer Demonstration Program in El Salvador—1965–66–67 (mimeographed), AID, Washington, D.C., November 20, 1967.

6. George Westcott, Agricultural Education, Research, and Extension and Salvadoran Agricultural Development. (Unpublished report written for the Consejo Nacional de Planificación y Coordinación Económica, Casa Presidencial, San Salvador, October 1, 1968, pp. 12–13.)

7. Benjamin J. Birdsall and Carlos Quiteño, Report on the Mass Fertilizer Demonstration Program in El Salvador—1965–66–67 (mimeographed), AID, Washington, D.C., October 26, 1967, p. 4.

CHAPTER 17

1. Letter from Carl H. Krieger, president, Campbell Institute for Food Research, to William C. Paddock, October 2, 1968.

2. Letter from Robert S. FitzSimmonds to William Paddock, May 7, 1969.

CHAPTER 18

1. David C. Fulton, "The Ex-desert of Northwestern Mexico," *Financial Development*, no. 3, 1968, p. 4; statistics from Ana Gomez, Economic Office, U.S. Embassy, Mexico City.

2. Although I shall keep referring to the "foundation's" programs in Mexico, it does not have any of its own in the literal sense, and never has had. When it first began agricultural research in Mexico in 1943, the Office of Special Studies was set up as a semiautonomous agency of the Mexican Ministry of Agriculture and Animal Husbandry. Technically, this office has been in charge of all the foundation's research work, although both the funds used and the top personnel were primarily from the foundation. In 1963 a new organization, the International Maize and Wheat Improvement Center (CIMMYT), was established, which took over the research programs in corn and wheat on an international basis. CIMMYT is governed by a board of prominent persons from several countries, although its director is a Rockefeller Foundation employee. Other organizations can make contributions to its work, but the guiding force is clearly from the foundation. Although both the Office of Special Studies and CIMMYT have been consistently controlled and directed by foundation employees of American nationality, Mexicans have been trained to assume increasingly responsible positions in both institutions.

3. "The Green Revolution as an Historical Phenomenon." (Paper prepared for a hearing-symposium before the House Foreign Affairs Subcommittee on National Security Policy and Scientific Development, December 1, 1969.)

4. Lester R. Brown, "Planning for the Future of the Green Revolution." (Paper prepared for a hearing-symposium before the House Foreign Affairs Subcommittee on National Security Policy and Scientific Development, December 1, 1969.)

5. *Gross National Product*, Office of Statistics and Reports, Bureau for Program and Policy Coordination, AID, Washington, D.C., April 30, 1970.

6. Claudio Dabdoub, *Historia de el Valle del Yaqui* (Mexico, D.F., Mexico: Librería de Manuel Porrua, 1964), p. 374.

7. W. Whitney Hicks, "Agricultural Development in Northern Mexico 1940–1960," *Land Economics*, November 1967, p. 400.

8. Octavio Ortega Leite, "Datos de la Explotación Agrícola del Valle de Yaqui, Sonora," Uniones de Crédito Agrícola de El Valle y Cajeme, December 1946, p. 76.

9. Ibid.

10. E. C. Stakman, Richard Bradfield, and Paul C. Manglesdorf, *Campaigns against Hunger* (Cambridge: Harvard University Press, 1967).

11. Hicks, p. 402.

12. CIMMYT, *Report 1968–69 on Progress Toward Increasing Yields of Maize and Wheat*, 1970, p. 9.

13. Henry Hopp, "Mexico Joins Wheat-Exporting Nations of the World," *Foreign Agriculture*, June 18, 1964, p. 4.

14. Hicks, p. 397.

15. Hopp, p. 4.

16. Norman E. Borlaug, "The Impact of Agricultural Research on Mexican Wheat Production," *Transactions of the New York Academy of Sciences*, 20 (January 1958): 281.

17. Hicks, p. 397.

18. Reed Hertford, "The Development of Mexican Agriculture: A Skeleton Specification," *Journal of Farm Economics*, 49, no. 5 (December 1967): 1177.

19. Lehman B. Fletcher and Bernard L. Sanders, The Effects of Agricultural Pricing Policies in Mexico on Basic Subsistence Commodities. (Report submitted to the Economic Research Service, U.S. Department of Agriculture, from the Department of Economics, Iowa State University.) (undated) Received August 9, 1968.

20. Hertford, p. 1177.

21. Wade F. Gregory, Agricultural Development in Greece, Mexico and Taiwan. (Paper presented at the CENTO conference on Agricultural Development Policy, Istanbul, Turkey, September 11–16, 1967.)

22. CIMMYT Report, p. 9.

23. J. G. Harrar, Testimony before the House Ways and Means Committee, February 19, 1969.

24. Vernon L. Harness, "Mexican Cotton Production—A 1969 Close-up," *Foreign Agriculture*, July 28, 1969; and by telephone October 8, 1969.

25. J. George Harrar, testimony before the Subcommittee on Inter-American Affairs, House of Representatives, April 22, 1969, p. 255.

26. Letter from Thomas B. O'Connell, assistant agricultural attaché, to William Paddock, April 2, 1970.

27. Letter to William Paddock, June 17, 1967.

28. J. George Harrar, *Strategy toward the Conquest of Hunger* (New York: Rockefeller Foundation, 1967), p. 288.

29. Don Paarlberg, address before the Twelfth Annual Meeting of the Agricultural Research Institute, National Academy of Sciences, Washington, D.C., October 18, 1963.

30. Hopp, p. 3.

31. Calculated from data obtained from Donald J. Novotny, U.S.D.A., by telephone, October 8, 1969.

32. Clifton W. Wharton, ed., *Subsistence Agriculture and Economic Development* (Chicago: Aldine, 1969), p. 437.

CHAPTER 19

1. L. Frank Baum, *The New Wizard of Oz* (New York: Bobbs-Merrill, 1944), p. 156.

2. Raymond B. Fosdick, *The Story of the Rockefeller Foundation* (New York: Harper Brothers, 1952), p. 184.

3. Reed Hertford, "Sources of Change in Mexican Agricultural Production" (Ph.D. thesis, University of Chicago, March 1970). Data somewhat updated in unpublished revision for U.S. Department of Agriculture for internal use.

4. Hertford. Table 41 shows there was a negative rate of growth for beans of 4 percent from 1954 to 1962.

5. J. George Harrar, testimony before the House Subcommittee on Inter-American Affairs, House of Representatives, April 22, 1969, p. 255.

6. E. C. Stakman, Richard Bradfield, and Paul C. Mangelsdorf, *Campaigns against Hunger* (Cambridge: Harvard University Press, 1967), p. 58.

7. Ibid., p. 51.

8. Fosdick, p. 187.

9. Marion Clawson, *International Development Review,* June 1968, p. 28.

10. Stakman et al., p. 170.

11. Hertford.

12. Meeting of the American Association for the Advancement of Science, Rockefeller University, New York, December 28, 1967; letter from William Paddock to Revelle, January 5, 1968.

13. J. George Harrar, *Strategy toward the Conquest of Hunger* (New York: Rockefeller Foundation, 1967), p. 288. Quote comes from speech given in 1966 before the 33rd Annual Meeting of the National Agricultural Chemicals Association at White Sulphur Springs, West Virginia, September 8, 1966.

14. Data fom Master Card File, Mexican Ministry of Agriculture.

15. Hertford.

16. James W. O'Donnell, Population Reference Bureau, Washington, D.C., by telephone, October 22, 1970.

17. Reed Hertford, by telephone, December 1, 1969.

18. Calculated as follows: Average annual corn yields in Mexico from 1936 to 1940 were 565 kg per hectare (data from Mary Coyner, USDA); 1946–50, 735 kg; 1956–60, 890 kg; 1966–70, 1156 kg (data taken from Master Card File in the Mexican Ministry of Agriculture with the 1969 and 1970 yields estimated at 1200 kg).

19. Dana G. Dalrymple, "New Cereal Varieties: Wheat and Corn in Mexico," *AID Spring Review,* July 1969.

20. William Paddock, "Can We Make the World Feed Us All?" *Saturday Evening Post,* October 18, 1952.

21. U.S., Congress, House, Committee on Ways and Means, *Hearings on Tax Reform,* 91st Congress, 1st sess., February 19, 1969, p. 248.

22. Hertford, Table 40.

CHAPTER 20

1. *War on Hunger,* August 1969, p. 19.

2. Richard L. Shaw, "The Flour of San Vicente," *Americas,* February 1960.

3. John Balcomb, "Incaparina," *Journal of Home Economics,* January 1962, p. 36.

4. Marti Mueller, "Protein Supplements: AID Focuses on Background Problems," *Science,* August 9, 1968.

5. Edward H. Koenig and Aaron M. Altschul, "Proteins: Breaking the Poverty Cycle," *Journal of the Albert Einstein Medical Center,* Spring 1970, pp. 14–24.

6. "The Dual Challenge of Health and Hunger—A Global Crisis," *Population Reference Bureau Selection No. 31,* January 1970, p. 5.

CHAPTER 21

1. *Time,* December 19, 1969, p. 25.

2. Dael Wolfle, *Science,* June 20, 1969, p. 1345.

3. Henry van der Schalie, "Schistosomiasis, the Disease of Slowed-down Waters, in *The Unforeseen International Ecologic Boomerang. Natural History,*

special supplement, Conservation Foundation Report on Symposium held at Warrentown, Virginia, December, 9–11, 1968.

4. Ibid.

5. *Wall Street Journal,* April 14, 1970, p. 19.

6. Chairman of the Nobel Peace Prize Committee, on the occasion of the announcement that the 1970 Peace Prize was being awarded to Norman Borlaug as the "prime mover in the 'green revolution.'" *New York Times,* October 22, 1970.

7. Agency for International Development press release, February 24, 1970.

8. Agency for International Development congressional presentation, May 29, 1969, p. H-3.

9. Lyle P. Schertz, "The Green Revolution: Production and World Trade," *Columbia Journal of World Business,* vol. 5, no. 2 (March–April 1970), p. 58.

10. *Soft State* (New York: Harper & Row, 1970), p. 22.

11. Guy L. Haviland, "Rice in India, Promising New Varieties Will Face Problems," *Foreign Agriculture,* December 22, 1969, pp. 20–21.

12. Lowell S. Hardin. Symposium, Subcommittee on National Security Policy and Scientific Developments, House Committee on Foreign Affairs, December 5, 1969.

13. Address before the 12th Annual Meeting of the Agricultural Research Institute, National Academy of Sciences, Washington, D.C., October 18, 1963.

14. Schertz, p. 56.

15. Norman Borlaug et al., "A Green Revolution Yields a Golden Harvest," *Columbia Journal of World Business,* 4 (1969):1019.

16. *Technological Change in Agriculture, Effects and Implications for the Developing Nations,* Foreign Agriculture Service, U.S. Dept. of Agriculture, 1969, p. 41.

17. *Seeds of Change: The Green Revolution and Development in the 1970's* (New York: Praeger, 1970). (Published for the Overseas Development Council.)

18. A.D. Horne, *Washington Post,* December 6, 1969.

19. Anonymous, "Genetic Dangers in the Green Revolution," *Ceres,* September–October, 1969, pp. 35–37.

20. Carroll P. Streeter, *A Partnership to Improve Food Production in India.* A report from the Rockefeller Foundation, 1969.

21. William C. Paddock, "Histological Study of Suscept-Pathogen Relationships between *Helminthosporium victoriae* M. and M. and Seedling Oat Leaves," *Cornell University Memoir,* no. 315, March 1953, p. 3.

22. AID press release, February 24, 1970.

23. *Observations and Recommendations on Mass Communications in Family Planning* (New Delhi, India: Kapur Press, 1969), p. 23. (Published by the Central Family Planning Institute on behalf of the Department of Family Planning, and Works, Housing and Urban Development.)

24. Norman Borlaug, "Wheat, Rust and People," *Phytopathology,* 55 (1965): 1097.

25. Borlaug et al., p. 1019.

26. *Front Lines,* May 15, 1969.

27. President's Science Advisory Committee, *The World Food Problem,* vol. 1 (Washington, D.C.: U.S. Government Printing Office, 1967), p. 22.

28. Kenneth E. Boulding, "The Utterly Dismal Theorem," in *Population, Evolution and Birth Control,* ed. Garrett Hardin (San Francisco: W. H. Freeman, 1969), p. 81.

29. Duncan Howlett, All Souls Church, Washington, D.C., from sermon delivered on December 6, 1969.

CAMEO (PART 5)

1. "U.S. Foreign Assistance in the 1970's: A New Approach," September 15, 1970.

2. *Directory of Agencies Concerned with Latin American Development* (Washington, D.C.: Alliance for Progress Team, Organization of American States, 1968).

CHAPTER 22

1. Address at the Eleventh Meeting of the Board of Governors of the IDB, Punta del Este, Uruguay, April 1970.

2. Robert N. Burr, *Our Troubled Hemisphere* (Washington, D.C.: Brookings Institution, 1967), p. 22.

3. *Ibid.*, p. 24.

4. Harvey S. Perloff, *Alliance for Progress, a Social Invention in the Making* (Baltimore: Johns Hopkins Press, 1969), p. 16.

5. *1969 Inter-American Development Bank, Tenth Annual Report*, Washington, D.C., March 23, 1970.

6. I visited at least a dozen IDB-financed operations while researching this book: several university projects in Mexico, Nicaragua, and Costa Rica; a Mexican iron foundry; housing programs in Guatemala and El Salvador; the port development in Honduras; colonization and irrigation programs in Mexico; etc. In addition, I traveled on a number of the highways and access roads financed through IDB loans. The integrated colonization project at Grijalva, Mexico (discussed in Chapter 18), is 47.9 percent IDB financed.

7. Undated paper prepared at the request of Mr. Herrera by his assistant, Mr. Luciano Tomassini, received October 18, 1968.

8. *Activities 1961–1968, Inter-American Development Bank* (Washington, D.C.: Inter-American Development Bank, 1969), p. 61.

9. Tomassini paper.

10. Later an IDB official told me Los Esclavos was built as a part of an integrated national hydroelectric system with the power being channeled where needed and thus "it is difficult to determine for a given recipient of electrical power precisely where such power originated from, just as it is difficult to earmark, in a water system with several reservoirs, a specific gallon of water and trace it from source to destination . . . Guatemala City is receiving sufficient power today." (Memorandum from David B. Atkinson to T. Graydon Upton, November 4, 1970.)

11. *1969 Inter-American Development Bank, Tenth Annual Report*, March 23, 1970, p. 1.

12. A. D. Horne, *Washington Post,* December 14, 1969.

13. I quote from a copy which, I hasten to add in order not to compromise friends within the bank, was sent to me by someone whom I have yet to meet.

14. Press release covering the *Tenth Annual Report, Inter-American Development Bank,* April 10, 1970.

CHAPTER 23

1. Anonymous, *Ten Years of Work in Latin America* (Washington, D.C.: Inter-American Development Bank, n.d.), pp. 5, 48.

2. For example, undated mimeographed Facts on the Central American Common Market, U.S. AID ROCAP handout, 1968; *World Business, Central American Common Market,* January 1968, Chase Manhattan Bank publication.

3. Data from Lloyd Barber, ROCAP desk, AID, Washington, D.C., May 5, 1970. (Although Costa Rica did not come into the market as a full partner until 1963, 1961 is usually referred to as the year the market began to function.)

4. Introduction, "The Woven Strands: Cooperation in Central America," an account of President Lyndon B. Johnson's Central American trip July 6–8, 1968, U.S. State Department.

5. Report by the Committee on Foreign Law, June 1962.

6. June 4, 1966.

7. July 26, 1970.

8. John F. McCamant, *Development Assistance in Central America* (New York: Praeger, 1968), p. 247.

9. Unreleased report of a staff survey team of the Committee on Foreign Affairs, House of Representatives, relating to observations on AID programs in Central America during May 22–June 22, 1968, p. 4.

10. Data from Lloyd Barber, ROCAP desk, AID, Washington, D.C., July 30, 1970.

11. Committee on Foreign Affairs, staff survey report, p. 10.

12. McCamant, pp. xv, xvi.

13. Lloyd Barber.

CHAPTER 24

1. Anonymous, *The Central American Common Market* (published by the Bank of London and Montreal, Ltd., n.d.), p. 21.

2. John F. McCamant, *Development Assistance in Central America* (New York: Praeger, 1968), p. 351.

3. James D. Cochrane, "United States Attitudes toward Central American Economic Integration," *Inter-American Economic Affairs,* 18 (Autumn 1964): 75.

CHAPTER 25

1. "Population Problem in El Salvador," *Proceedings of the Conference on the Population Explosion and the Developing Professional,* Warrentown, Virginia, November 20–23, 1969.

2. July 6, 1968.

CHAPTER 26

1. *Front Lines,* January 30, 1969.

2. *Fortune,* October 1969, p. 208.

3. "How Relevant is the U.N.?" *Life* (editorial), May 8, 1970, p. 92.

4. H. W. Singer, *Financial Times,* March 17, 1970.

5. Elmer B. Staats (comptroller general of the United States), U.S., Congress, House, Subcommittee on International Organizations and Movements of the Committee on Foreign Affairs, *Hearings on the 25th Anniversary of the United Nations,* 91st Cong., 2nd sess., March 5, 1970, p. 316.

6. *Life,* p. 92.

7. Staats, p. 314.

8. Staats, p. 330.

9. Staats, p. 309.

10. Staats, p. 319.

11. Staats, p. 319.

12. Staats, p. 321.

13. Staats, p. 321.

14. Staats, p. 325.
15. Staats, pp. 328–29.
16. Staats, p. 318.
17. Staats, p. 340.
18. Staats, p. 341.
19. U.S. Congress, House, Subcommittee on Inter-American Affairs of the Committee on Foreign Affairs, *Foreign Policy Implications of U.S. Participation in the Inter-American Development Bank*, 91st Cong., 2nd sess., June 4, 1970, p. 74.
20. Staats, p. 315.
21. Calculated from Staats' testimony, March 5, 1970, pp. 307, 308.
22. Richard Alfred, *Quincy* (Mass.) *Patriot-Ledger*, April 23, 1970.
23. S. H. Zahar, "The Poor Man's Arms Race." (Paper delivered at the 19th Pugwash Conference Series, January–February 1970.)
24. *New York Times* (editorial), May 30, 1970.

EPILOGUE

1. William C. Paddock, "The New Frontier for Plant Pathology," *Plant Disease Reporter*, 36 (1952):370–72 .
2. *New York Times*, May 17, 1970.
3. *War on Hunger*, April 1970, p. 13.
4. *Ceres*, March–April 1970.
5. *New York Times*, January 16, 1970.
6. Senators McGovern, Hatfield, Goodell, Hughes, and Church, NBC television, May 12, 1970.
7. *Washington Post*, December 21, 1969.
8. Dean Rusk, as quoted in the *Jacksonville* (Fla.) *Journal*, October 6, 1970.

INDEX

AFSC, Cuauhtenco project, 79–81
Agency for International Development (AID)
  as agent of pacification, 21
  Behrhorst Clinic, 96, 97
  bureaucracy, 56
  costs, 56
  expenditures in U.S., 54, 55
  farm loans (Toluca, Mexico), 30–32
  Guatemala rice cooperative, 18–21
  India program, 58
  international police training academy, xii, xiii
  population problems, 101–2
  purpose, 55
Agricultural Development and Policy in Guatemala, Iowa State University, 16–17
AID programs
  crash programs, futility of, 194
  lack of continuity, 11
  staffing, 11
Alliance for Progress, 36
Ambassador, role of, 34–35
American Friends Service Committee. *See* AFSC
Aswan Dam, problems, 238–40

Bajío (Mexico), 196–99
Banana plantation, development, 137–38
Bárcenas Agricultural School, 12–13
Behrhorst, Dr. Carroll
  background, 87–88
  clinic, 88–89
    birth control program, 95–96
    conclusions, 98
    financial support, 96–98
    medical Indians, 92–94

Birth control need, economic terms, 101
Bojorge, Dr. Augustín Brenes, 41, 42, 43
Borlaug, Dr. Norman, 202, 203, 206–9
  personality, 208–9
  predictions about food production, 248
  Toluca research center, 206
  work with dwarf wheats, 207–8
Boulding, Kenneth, 250
Bush pilots, as observers of development, 117–19

Campbell Soup Company
  association with Rockefeller Foundation, 200
  effect on Mexican farmers, 195–200
Cárdenas experiment station (Mexico), 157
Center of International Studies (MIT), AID study, 14
Central America
  antiindustrialization attitude, 281
  debts (1961–68), 274
Central American Common Market, 268–76
  background, 268–70
  neglect of agriculture, 281–83
  surtax provision, 275–76
Chávez, Milcíades, 47
Chemicals, agricultural use, 249
Chimaltenango area (Guatemala), medical facilities, 91–92
Ciudad Obregón (Mexico), history of development, 204–5
Claxton, Philander P., 100, 101, 102
Community development projects, PUMAR, 39. *See also* PUMAR
Confiscation of land, Mexico, 160